Calling Down Fire

Charles Grandison Finney and Revivalism in Jefferson County, New York, 1800–1840

Marianne Perciaccante

State University of New York Press

Published by
State University of New York Press, Albany

Printed in the United States of America

For information, address State University of New York Press,
90 State Street, Suite 700, Albany, NY 12207

Production by Dana Foote
Marketing by Fran Keneston

Library of Congress Cataloging-in-Publication

Perciaccante, Marianne, 1964–
Calling down fire : Charles Grandison Finney and revivalism in Jefferson County, New York, 1800–1840 / Marianne Perciaccante.
p. cm.
Includes bibliographical references and index.
ISBN 0–7914–5639–0 (alk. paper) — ISBN 0–7914–5640–4 (pbk. : alk. paper)
1. Revivals—New York—Jefferson County—History—19th century. 2. Finney, Charles Grandison, 1792–1875. 3. Jefferson County (N.Y.)—Church history—19th century. I. Title.

BV3774.N7 P47 2003
269′.24′097475709034—dc21 2002036450

10 9 8 7 6 5 4 3 2 1

Calling Down Fire

Jefferson County
Alexandria Bay
ALEXANDRIA
THERESA
ANTWERP
Theresa
Clayton
ORLEANS
Philadelphia
CAPE VINCENT
CLAYTON
PHILADEL
Cape Vincent
LYME
Evans Mills
Chaumount
PAMELIA
BROWNVILLE
Brownville
Glen Park
Dexter
Black River
CHAMPION
Carthage
West Carthge
Sackets Harbor
City of Watertown
HOUNSFIELD
WATERTOWN
RUTLAND
ADAMS
HENDERSON
Adams
RODMAN
Key
TOWN
Village
ELLISBURG
LORRAINE
WORTH
Ellisburg
Mannsville

CONTENTS

For my nieces and nephews:

Eileen LePage
Emily LePage
Michael Keane
John O'Sullivan
Jessica Perciaccante
Matthew LePage
Margaret Keane
Andrew Perciaccante
and Laura O'Sullivan

ACKNOWLEDGMENTS

Numerous church members and pastors in Jefferson County were gracious enough to let me into their church safes to see if any relevant records existed. In some cases, churches brought in safe crackers. Where relevant records were extant, church members let me into their closed churches during the week so that I could read them over. Others let me into their homes to read records. I am grateful to all of them. There are so many of them, though, that I can't possibly name them all. I couldn't have written this book without them.

Early on in my research, the pastor of the First Presbyterian Church in Watertown, the Rev. Brent Eelman, suggested that I speak with John B. Johnson Sr., who was then the editor and publisher of the *Watertown Daily Times.* Mr. Johnson was a great source of ideas, as well as research help. More recently, his son, John Johnson Jr., the current editor and co-publisher of the newspaper, has assisted me as I made the final preparations to publish the book.

I was fortunate to have John Corrigan as my dissertation advisor. I remember my conversation with him when I thought I would never find sufficient research resources. He was right that I would eventually find the resources and, under difficult circumstances, he proved an exemplary advisor.

As I wrote this in its initial stage as a dissertation, almost daily I showed the newest pages to my father, who made helpful comments. In addition to this, in a number of significant ways, he and my mother made it possible for me to research and write the dissertation.

I am also grateful to Ron Helfrich for encouraging me to submit the manuscript to him at SUNY Press. Lately, as I have transformed the dissertation into a book, a number of people have helped out. Kristen Summers read over sections of the book and made perceptive criticisms. I bounced ideas off Ned Bachman and Patty Reilly. And Ken Moffett Jr. provided encouragement and amusement.

Finally, thanks to Whitney Cross, who died long before I started my research, for providing the title of the book. When I was researching the dissertation, I found correspondence between Cross and his dissertation advisor, Arthur Schlesinger Sr., in the Cross papers at Cornell. Cross proposed entitling his dissertation, "Calling Down Fire." Schlesinger opposed the idea, and suggested "The Burned-Over District."

I
Introduction

> The first shed we come to, the preacher was lining out a hymn. He lined out two lines, everybody sung it, and it was kind of grand to hear it, there was so many of them and they done it in such a rousing way. . . . The people woke up more and more, and sung louder and louder; and towards the end, some begun to groan, and some begun to shout. Then the preacher begun to preach; and begun in earnest, too; and went weaving first to one side of the platform and then the other, and then a leaning over the front of it, with his arms and body going all the time, and shouting his words out with all his might; and every now and then he would hold out his Bible and spread it open, and kind of pass it around this way and that, shouting, "It's the brazen serpent in the wilderness! Look upon it and live!" And people would shout out, "Glory!—A-a-*men!*". . .
>
> . . . You couldn't make out what the preacher said anymore, on account of the shouting and crying. Folks got up everywheres in the crowd, and worked their way, just by main strength to the mourner's bench, with the tears running down their faces; and when all the mourners had got up there to the front benches in a crowd, they sang and shouted, and flung themselves down on the straw, just crazy and wild.
>
> —Mark Twain, *The Adventures of Huckleberry Finn*

In both Charles Grandison Finney's rural New York and Huckleberry Finn's fictional Missouri, genuine,[1] popular revivals were characterized by disorder and a level of excitement occasionally verging on hysteria. Moreover, in both New York and Missouri, as Huck goes on to note, the reform interest that often followed from revivalism and acted as a counterpart to true revivalism usually functioned as a desire to expand the evangelical message of the revival rather than to improve the moral conduct of the local population:

> He ["the king"] told them he was a pirate—been a pirate for thirty years, out in the Indian Ocean, and his crew was thinned out considerable, last spring, in a fight, and he was home now, to take out some fresh men, and thanks to goodness he'd been robbed last night, and put ashore off a steamboat without a cent, and he was glad of it, it was the blessedest thing that ever happened to him, because he was a changed man now, and happy for the first time in his life; and poor as he was, he was going to start right off and begin his way back to the Indian Ocean and put in the rest of his life trying to turn the pirates into the true path. . . .[2]

Although the king was a con man falsely seeking financing for his mission to the pirates, and although Mark Twain intends the description as a satire of revivalism, the desire to extend the revival message rather than a moral message is a significant and now infrequently noted characteristic of antebellum revival and reform. When middle-class urban and semiurban populations began to participate in revivals in the northeast much of the disorder disappeared in favor of more seemly expressions of piety held in churches rather than sheds, and the reform interest shifted from nonmoralistic, evangelical missionary work to stridently moralistic and legalistic efforts to reform society. Charles Grandison Finney was the bridge from Huck's revivalism to middle-class revivalism.

Finney's earliest religious experience closely resembled Huckleberry Finn's. At the Baptist church Finney attended in Henderson, New York, the preacher commonly exploded in emotional preaching, and his congregation responded equally emotionally. This was not a reaction to social or economic changes; it was the normal state of affairs in Jefferson County, New York, in most Baptist and Methodist congregations. The congregations' emotional responses generally resulted less in opposition to "excessive use of ardent spirits," or in efforts to enforce doctrinal tests than with attempts to improve the condition of the oppressed and those "destitute of the gospel." As a rule the beneficiaries of the Baptist missionary work do not seem to have included pirates, but they did include Burmese, slaves, Native Americans, "victims" of Masonry, and occasionally women.

The New England-descended Presbyterian population surrounding Finney, many of whom Finney later revived, differed enormously from the Baptists and Methodists. They would have considered the excitement of Huck's camp meeting a sign of immorality, and they would probably have shown little interest in the king's story, as they would have been more concerned with fighting the extensive whiskey drinking and fighting that

Huck identified in a near-by town.[3] Although New York State's antebellum revival and reform impulse in many ways resembles Huck's depiction, as well as the understanding of most historians, in other ways it has been forced to fit the historiographical paradigm of the Burned-over District.

Thus, in researching the course of Finney's developing career as a revivalist in Jefferson County, New York, and the course and extent of revivalism in Jefferson County, I disregarded the most accepted interpretations of revivalism in the Burned-over District, beginning with the use of the term "Burned-over District."

The "district" is as fictional as both the camp meeting in Pokesville and the pirates in the Indian Ocean; its historiographical use resembles that of "Great Awakening," which Jon Butler has described as "interpretive fiction." Participants in the awakening did not refer to it as a "Great Awakening," and the event has defied precise definition. Nonetheless, "Great Awakening" serves historians as a means of describing a broad range of events.[4] Analogously, historians frequently use "Burned-over District" to describe the area of New York State west of the Adirondacks and Catskills and north of the Erie Canal, because, they have argued, the area was "burned" by the fires of revivalism. Through the unquestioned use of the term, which many erroneously believe to have originated in the nineteenth century,[5] historians have succeeded in furthering the interpretive fiction rather than in understanding the actual historical context. Historians have made a number of assumptions: the primacy of the Erie Canal in encouraging revival fervor; a connection between revivalism and reform; a tendency toward urban revivals in the district; Finney's exceptional popularity; an unusual proclivity among the population toward forming "experimental" new religions; and a virtually static expression of fervor from 1820 to 1840.

While "Burned-over District" has served as a useful shorthand for referring to revivalism in antebellum New York State, many of the assumptions behind the fiction cannot be applied to Jefferson County. In the early nineteenth century it was an isolated rural region far from the Erie Canal; of the religious "experiments" that have come to define the Burned-over District, only the Mormons established a significant presence; Finney's methods did not revolutionize revivals in Jefferson County; revivalism and reform were not necessarily connected with each other; and the most disastrous socioeconomic development in the county's history, the opening of the Erie Canal, did not drastically alter the course of religious history in the county.

Recognizing distinctions in Jefferson County's secular and religious history has led me to a new interpretive framework for religious fervor in the nineteenth century. Three different geographically defined socioeconomic regions of varying religious expression are apparent in the county. Each region understood orthodoxy and orthopraxis differently. And within each region two different denominational means of expression, with the Baptists and Methodists on one end and the Presbyterians on the other, are also apparent. For the Baptists and the Methodists, fervor constituted a normal expression of piety; and for the Presbyterians until 1830, fervor represented disorder and thus impiety. On the other hand, for Presbyterians moral stringency represented piety. By 1830, after years of mutual contact, these regions and denominations, while preserving their original characteristics, grew more similar. Among the denominations, Baptists and Methodists tempered their fervor and developed a greater interest in reform; and Presbyterians accepted the tempered fervor, translated for them largely through Finney's work, while they overlaid their moralistic interest onto their acceptance of revivalism. The interpretive fiction has emerged from a tendency to study the post-1830 expressions of fervor and reform.

Finney's earliest theology formed amid the earliest geographical and denominational distinctions. And just as these regional and denominational distinctions diminished after 1830, they melted together in Finney's theology after 1830 so that he became more acceptable to well-to-do urban congregations, while Methodistlike perfectionism nonetheless grew more predominant in his theology. By failing to acknowledge the distinctions underlying Finney's theology, historians have failed to notice that Finney's success, and the success of the Second Great Awakening in general along the northern frontier is not a Presbyterian success in the Second Great Awakening; it is a Baptist and Methodist success.

Finney brought the Baptist and Methodist revivals of rural New York State to the urban middle class, who nonetheless sought to distance their form of revivalism from both Finney's and Huck's. Finney accepted and fostered much of this re-creation, although he maintained an interest in evangelical reform movements, while the urban middle class adopted revivalism as a vehicle for societal moral reform. Both revivalism and Finney changed with contact with the middle class, but originally both resembled the revival and the preacher at Pokesville.

Thus, the history of revivalism in Jefferson County, New York, where Charles Grandison Finney had his conversion experience and where he first preached, does not suggest or support theories that rely on economic or cultural stressor arguments to explain the causes of Second Great Awakening revivalism. Strain and crisis cannot succeed as explanations of the background of revivalism in Jefferson County. Moreover, the history of revivalism in Jefferson County suggests that revivalism did not encourage reform. In fact prior to 1830, revivalism and reform were disjunctive.

The history of revivalism in Jefferson County does indicate that revivalism or fervid religion was a normal form of piety among loosely organized rural congregations before 1830; and that moral reform was the most esteemed form of piety among well-organized congregations. While the pre-1830 paradigm did continue to influence both fervid congregations and moralistic congregations, after 1830 these congregations grew alike.

Often, but not always, the less-organized congregations were Baptist; and the more-organized congregations were Presbyterian. Charles Finney grew up under the influence of a rural Baptist church in Jefferson County, where he learned the value of fervor as an expression of piety, and where he learned to place less value on efforts to reform society. As a Presbyterian minister in rural northern Jefferson County in 1824, he successfully adapted Baptist values for congregations of rural Presbyterians. His success in 1824 in rural northern New York, where social and economic conditions permitted diversity of expression among a normally rigid denomination such as the Presbyterians, allowed him to develop his revival methods six years before most Presbyterians became interested in expressions of fervor. His early experience in bringing Baptist values to Presbyterians made him unusually well adapted to succeed in the 1830s. The history of Jefferson County also provides a new perspective for examining Finney's career as a revivalist, as his years in Jefferson County have been largely overlooked.

The story of the success of revivalism in New York State suggests that cultural hegemony is not imposed by elites onto nonelite culture.[6] In *Bobos in Paradise,* David Brooks discusses a phenomenon that mirrors what happened in New York State almost 150 years earlier.[7] According to Brooks, young sixties radicals, outside the business world, rejected the order and morality of the fifties WASP elites. The radicals valued self-expression, human relationships, and social equality over the "arid self-control" of the elites.[8] Ultimately, according to Brooks, the sixties radicals became elites themselves, who created a new and revitalized bourgeois culture, and "at the moment it looks as if the bourgeoisie has, in fact, revived itself by absorbing (and being absorbed by) the energy of bohemianism."[9] Brooks sees order and structure among those working in commerce, and antinomianism among those initially outside that culture. Later, when, in effect, the commercial culture lost its vitality, and when the antinomian culture could no longer maintain its lack of order and structure, the two merged and shared values.[10] I contend that during the 1820s much the same thing happened. Nonelites, mostly in agricultural areas with relatively little commercial development favored highly emotional religious expression, while elites in commercial areas prized morality and order above all else, and rejected emotional religious expression as unseemly. Eventually, in 1830, the two merged so that moral reform became more connected to emotional religious expression.

This then is the story of the interplay between structure and anti-structure, Victor Turner's terms to describe respectively "the roles, norms, and institutions that constitute a given society," and "forces in a society that contradict or negate the structure."[11] It is the story of the effect of popular (or nonelite), religion on mainline (elite), religion.

In acccord with Turner's terminology, Peter Williams has described popular religion as a marginal movement:

> In the gaps and interstices that emerged among the various traditional religious communities, whether Catholic, Protestant, Jewish, or Native American, new movements began to form—sometimes fairly systemic and organized, more often inchoate and unformed—which at least temporarily helped to bridge the gap between the experience of chaos and its symbolic resolution into order. Some of these movements developed structures and formal organizations and endured, while others disappeared or continued to exist loosely at the fringes of the "official" churches and religious communities. . . . Many of them had little influence on anyone except a small band of dedicated followers, and thus slipped through the nets of historians concerned with the broadly representative and influential. Others eluded notice by students of religion because they did not seem religious in a strict or conventional sense of the term. What they all had in common was that they could not be easily classified according to traditional categories.[12]

This has meant that historians of popular religions have concentrated on officially unapproved, peripheral movements within denominations, or that they have been interested with cultural or civil religion.[13] Williams also includes in this classification "sectarian" and "cultic" movements, some of which he considers "voluntarily segregated," such as the Mormons, Hasidic Jews, the Amish, Mennonites, Hutterites, and the Doukhobors, as well as others that were short-lived, such as the Father Divine Peace Mission. As long as any of these movements has not attained status as an "established" church or sect he considers it "popular.[14] In effect, these movements were unofficial or "extraecclesiastical" organizations that gave evidence of "antistructure." This follows from his summarization of the factors that denote both popular religion and antistructure:

> The beliefs and lore of these movements are transmitted through channels other than official seminaries or oral traditions of established religious communities, whether tribal or modernized.
>
> Popular movements . . . generally look for intervention or manifestation in the realm of everyday experience. This may take the form of possession by the Holy Spirit: of the expectation of an imminent millennium; or miraculous healings or other providential intervention into the natural or social realm; of new revelation from on high; or, conversely, of the demonic disruption of everyday life in the form of witchcraft.[15]

In contrast to this, he indicates that "'official' religion tends to take on characteristics consonant with the broad sociological process called 'modernization.' It usually is routinized and bureaucratic."[16]

I contend, though, that the easily identifiable Baptists and Methodists within their "official" denominational structures constituted popular religions in the early-nineteenth-century North. Although neither would qualify under the imprecise terms "cult" or "sect," and although neither would qualify as "voluntarily segregated," neither was "routinized" or "bureaucratic" before 1830. Nor did their ministers generally attend seminaries, which could inculcate an official tradition. And each was intensely interested in the action of the Holy Spirit among its members in the form of fervor, or what has become known in its institutional form as revivalism. These denominations constituted antistructure in contrast to the structured and bureaucratic Presbyterians and Congregationalists.

As descendants of the Puritans, whom Williams recognizes as bureaucratic and routinized, the Congregationalists, and their counterparts on the northern frontier, the Presbyterians, imposed structure upon the frontier, and were the most apt to participate in the commercial and political affairs of the county.[17] Although in those areas of Jefferson County where Presbygationalist structure was not matched by a secular structure, Finney's revivals did best. Amid the chaos of frontier conditions, however, Baptists and Methodists expressed the chaos of their secular lives in the chaos of fervent worship. In further contrast to Williams's description, this fervent response did not serve "to bridge the gap between the experience of chaos and its symbolic resolution into order," it served as an expression of the experience of chaos.

Eventually, though, as Williams, using Turner, remarks, antistructural groups are bound either to disappear or bureaucratize and routinize, while structural groups continue to bureaucratize until they reach a crisis point that requires that they accept some antistructure.[18] This is what happened in northern frontier revivalism in the nineteenth century: the Presbygationalists became more like the Baptists and Methodists, while the Baptists and Methodists became more like the Presbygationalists.[19] Williams and I differ in our understanding of this process.

As we differ in the role of chaos in encouraging fervor, we differ in our explanations of the meaning of revivalism. Williams uses Turner's concept of *communitas* to explain a transitory expression of "spiritual equality" that occurred during a frontier revival, and

> provided an important counterpoint to the social distinctions that characterized the structure of the settled parts of the region as a whole. On the one hand, the social and moral chaos of frontier life was forever repudiated and left behind. On the other, a new life in a rigidly structured community, in terms of both moral self-discipline and acceptance of rigid social, sexual, and racial roles was made more palatable.

Turner makes distinctions between forms of *communitas* all of which allow it to function in the "interstices" of society as Williams describes it.[20] Williams's description relies on the assumption that popular religion in America functions in the interstices of accepted religions, or that antistructure is not a free-standing phenomenon but one that depends on its relationship to structure. However, in the case of Jefferson County, where popular religion does not fall into the interstices but is in fact a denomination unto itself, such a description is inadequate. Moreover, it is excessively functionalist; I am not seeking here to describe why fervor succeeded, but to point to where and how it did succeed.

Although fervent congregations did maintain a spiritual and a secular equality, *communitas* does not describe as well as Henri Bergson's concepts "closed religion" and "open religion" the distinctions between religious communities in Jefferson County.[21] Closed religion seeks to maintain the status quo and to prevent the intrusion of possibly destructive outside forces. This form of religion is dogmatic and legalistic. Open religion, according to John Macquarrie, is "free and spontaneous, and culminates in the mystical union of the soul with God."[22] Thus, while agreeing with Turner's use of structure and antistructure, I reject his depiction of it as an idiosyncratic counterpart to structure.[23] Instead of viewing antistructure as a temporary means of coming to terms with structure, I follow Durkheim in considering the form of the religion an expression of the form of the participants' secular lives. Hence, closed religion is an expression of structured, legalistic, and dogmatic lives outside of the churches, or an expression of commercially and politically oriented secular lives. Similarly open religion is an expression of less bureaucratically oriented lives, which one would expect to find in regions known more for their agriculture than business.[24] Open religion is just as susceptible to bureaucratization as closed religion is susceptible to an infusion of antistructural values.

George Thomas's *Revivalism and Cultural Change: Christianity, Nation Building, and the Market in the Nineteenth-Century United States* describes the congruity between daily life and institutional or religious life as isomorphism. I agree with his contention that strain and crisis theories do not satisfactorily explain the social mechanism behind nineteenth-century revivalism. Although he is concerned with describing the interplay between urban revivalism and the emerging market economy as a form of "practical rationality," his description of "substantive rationality" as a characteristic of isomorphism in the South does hold for the "open" or antistructural religion seen in the rural revivalism among Baptists and Methodists in the North. In the substantive revivalism of both the South and the rural North, "authority relations are not abstract and legal in the sense of being standardized and universalistic."

Within these communities, "there is no autonomous economic system because exchange relations are governed by moral rules and communal authority." However, practical rationalization applies to closed religion which entails a bureaucratic environment.[25]

In describing how this isomorphism functioned in the earliest revivals in Jefferson County, I use the terms "antiformalism" and "formalism." Antiformalists, who favored substantive rationality, were Baptists and Methodists who valued direct contact with God above all else. Fervor served as the means of expressing this contact. These communities in which all people had equal access to God's grace tended to be egalitarian and non-hierarchical. Additionally, they placed as low a value on an orderly society outside of church as they did on an orderly church. They often viewed orderly churches as unholy, since these churches did not seek contact with God; and they viewed attempts to bring moral order to the outside community as misdirected religion. After 1830 their piety routinized. Their fervor toned down, and they began to take an interest in moral reform. However, moral reform tended to center on issues of social inequality rather than on a lack of social order. These churches favored missionary work, antimasonry, abolitionism, and women's rights. In accord with Thomas's isomporphism, these churches tended to dominate rural, egalitarian communities. Hereafter, I will use antiformalist as a synonym for rural Methodist and Baptist piety. This form of piety resembles Victor Turner's antistructure and Henri Bergson's open religion. As discussed earlier, open religion will occasionally experience bureaucratization.

Formalists (who accepted practical rationality) were Presbyterians and Congregationalists who viewed order and morality as the two greatest values of religion and who placed emphasis on maintaining the ecclesiastical and social hierarchy. For these congregations among whom disorder and fervor represented unseemliness equal to sexual misconduct, morality and reform—notably concerns with temperance, sabbatarianism, and orthodoxy—consistently maintained positions of prominence. By 1830, though, their rigidity had developed to excess so that they needed an infusion of tempered fervor in order to remain viable. Nonetheless, their post-1830 fervor or institutionalized revivalism tended to be much more orderly than what the antiformalists had practiced. Additionally, they used revivalism as a vehicle to encourage their longstanding concern with order and moral reform. In accord with Thomas's conception of isomorphism, these hierarchical, orderly churches dominated commercial regions. Hereafter, "formalist" will denote Presbyterian. Although Congregationalists were also formalists, few Congregationalist churches survived in Jefferson County; almost all Presbyterian or Congregationalist churches in Jefferson County opted for Presbyterianism after the Plan of Union of 1801.[26] Formalists resemble Turner's structure and Bergson's closed religion. As open religions are susceptible to bureaucratization, closed religions are susceptible to infusions of antistructure or open religious values.

In the course of making this argument, I will frequently note the differences between Jefferson County and other regions of the state whose revivalism has been studied more thoroughly. Jefferson County, for example, depended on agriculture more than industry, even after the building of the canal. Thus nonelites, or those most likely to participate in an antistructural worship, made up the bulk of the population.

This difference does not mean, though, that the evolution of revivalism in Jefferson County necessarily differed greatly from that of other areas. It does mean that these conditions are more obvious in Jefferson County and that they have been overlooked in areas with more prominent "modern" commercial and industrial economies. Thus, more than have the histories of other areas, the history of Jefferson County makes evident the prominence of the Baptists and the Methodists in driving an acceptance of fervid worship.

The following chapter reviews the history of Jefferson County that provided the background for revival and reform. The county's unusual attraction for European nobility and its formation of three socio-economic regions in the south, midsection, and north provided distinct settings in which formalists and antiformalists expressed their religiosity. In the midst of these unusual circumstances, Finney was able to develop and express his new theology, and antiformalists and formalists were able to borrow from each other to create new values and practices.

Chapter 3 covers two aspects of revivalism in Jefferson County. First, it relates the backgrounds of Jefferson County's successful revivalists. By far, outside of Jefferson County, Finney was the most notable of this group, but significantly, within Jefferson County, Finney was not exceptional. Finney differed from them in his ability to translate revivalism in Jefferson County to revivalism in more populated areas, but he was not alone as a revivalist in Jefferson County. Still, he deserves prominence in this narrative, since one of the things that makes Jefferson County interesting is that it was where Finney first succeeded as a revivalist. Following the discussion of the revivalists, chapter 3 details the religious status quo in Jefferson County before 1830, as formalists attempted to maintain order through church trials and reform work, and antiformalists encouraged missionary work inside and outside their congregations chiefly through emotional preaching.

Chapter 4 develops on this theme. After 1830 formalists continued to seek to maintain order, while antiformalists encouraged missionary work. However, formalists after 1830 were more willing to employ revivalism to achieve order, and antiformalists were more willing to employ reform to missionize.

Chapter 5 indicates the ways in which reform was transformed in order to meet the changes within the ranks of the formalists and antiformalists after 1830. It is true that revivalism and reform often coexisted, but antiformalists forwarded missionary-oriented reform in addition to their revivalism, while formalists resorted to revivalism in order to further legalistic, orderly reform.

Map 1.1 indicates Jefferson County's separation from the rest of the

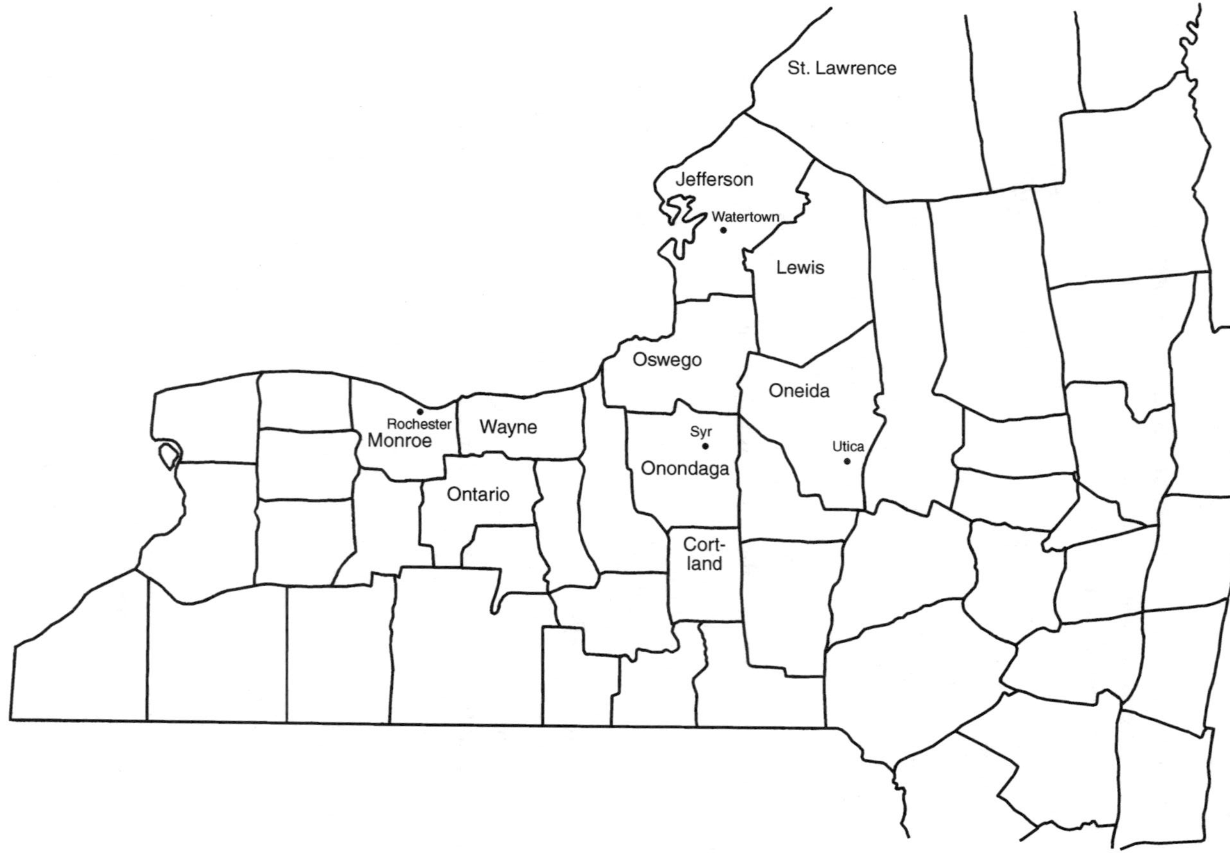

Map 1.1 Map of New York State. Adapted from a map that appears in the Whitney R. Cross Papers, 1941–1951, collection #1678. Division of Rare and Manuscript Collections, Cornell University Library.

state and its distance from the Erie Canal, which ran through central regions of the state such as Monroe County, Onondaga County, and Oneida County. This map without the inclusion of county names appears in the Whitney R. Cross Papers, 1941–1951, collection #1678. Division of Rare and Mancuscript Collections, Cornell University Library. Cross copied the map from the New York Mercantile Union, *Business Directory* (New York, 1850). See Cross, 358. Town and county names have been added to the map by the present author.

2
Jefferson County

Jefferson County's isolated location far from the Erie Canal as well as its Vermont immigrant population provide a valuable context in which to study revivalism; most obviously because revivalism was a national phenomenon in the nineteenth century, primarily centered in rural areas. And although revivals' characteristics differed significantly between regions and denominations, few regions or denominations remained unaffected. Urban areas, however, outside New England—where a different form of enthusiasm prevailed—were likely the least susceptible to early excitement.

Methodist camp meetings represent the paradigm of Second Great Awakening revivals, the spontaneity of which required economically and socially marginal communities. Communities and churches whose members did not apparently shape social mores and whose members had nothing to gain by the maintenance of the status quo most readily accepted and encouraged the excitement of the revivals. In effect, the success of revivalism along the northern frontier in the early nineteenth century represents the success of popular religion over elite religion. For example, the merchants and other paragons of Paul Johnson's Rochester would never have tolerated the pandemonium of the early rural revivals. But when the revivals were formalized in 1830, they became more acceptable to urban populations, and more like the New England urban revivals.[1]

Yet urban areas have dominated the literature on the Second Great Awakening, while their populations were not the chief participants, only the most in charge of the media, namely newspapers. Furthermore, studies of urban areas (especially those along the Erie Canal) have tended to conclude erroneously that it was the urbanization and commercialization coincident with the revivals that led to social dislocation and the promotion of the revivals.[2] Such a conclusion ignores Whitney Cross's assertion that "the phenomena of Burned-over District history belong to a stage of economy either of full or of closely approaching agrarian maturity"; and Cross's conclusion that "areas whose prosperity failed to approximate advance expectations, like the triangle between Lake Ontario, the Black River, and Oneida Lake [roughly and most notably the southern half of Jefferson County] . . . provided a fertile soil for isms."[3]

While the residents of Utica and Rochester were adjusting to a radically redefined lifestyle after the arrival of the canal, the residents of Jefferson County maintained to a large extent their former lifestyles. The population grew and the economy suffered when the Erie Canal redefined the major trade routes (the St. Lawrence River and Lake Ontario) and removed them from Jefferson County, but Jefferson County on the whole changed little. It was an agricultural county, largely isolated from other areas.

George M. Thomas's discussion of isomorphism in *Revivalism and Cultural Change: Christianity, Nation Building, and the Market in the Nineteenth-Century United States* provides the most helpful explanation of the social processes at work in Jefferson County. According to Thomas, religion reflects culture. Thomas disputes "crisis" and "strain" theories; as he asserts that religion and culture are isomorphic. Religions, rather than reacting against cultural change, make sense out of the culture by giving it meaning. In turn, the culture gives religion its meaning and its legitimacy. Thomas contends that "the knowledge and rules of a particular institution [including religions] are an integral part of the cultural order as a whole. . . . Because the same ontology or underlying rule structure is being worked out and specified in each institutional sphere, there is a congruence or similarity of structures across diverse spheres."[4]

In this and the following chapters, I rely on this understanding of isomorphism, and in accord with it, I argue that revivalism appealed to lower-class, nearly stable,[5] and agrarian populations, usually "antiformalists" such as the Baptists and the Methodists. Revivalism, as an egalitarian expression of a lack of strict social rules and obligations, was isomorphic with these groups. Rule-bound, orderly, commercial, nonagrarian populations, however, shunned the revivals as unseemly. The Baptists and the Methodists, who were the most intensely interested in revivals, shunned reform. The "formalist" Presbyterians and Congregationalists expressed their religiosity through a concern for moral uprightness and in the support of reform movements, which were attempts to maintain the status quo.

The concern of this chapter is to identify the background to these social developments in Jefferson County and to locate the regions most hospitable to antiformalist inclinations, as well as those most hospitable to formalists.

Jefferson County's socioeconomic geography divides neatly into three regions, and each region's distinctiveness within the county derives from its particular historical circumstances. The agricultural northern section of the county had an immigrant European nobility dominating it and preventing it from developing a typical town structure. In the northern section, legal town structures did develop, but because of the much greater social prestige and power of the immigrant nobility, the town structures were devalued and overwhelmed by the nobility. The southern section of the county, also agricultural, demonstrated a town structure analogous to those of towns in New England; and the midsection of the county, the county seat, demonstrated an economy and structure verging on urbanism and commercialism.

A unique set of circumstances that distinguishes Jefferson County from other frontier settlements as well as better-known regions of New York State developed: the county's unusual combination of the extraordinary wealth of European investors residing in the county, along with the lifestyle of poverty of the average county farmer; its early position in the center of the most essential trade route (along Lake Ontario and the St. Lawrence River), while it was virtually isolated from much of the rest of the country, and even the rest of New York State; and Jefferson County's position as a major military encampment during and after the War of 1812. In the midst of this, only a small section of the county allowed American-born elites to rise to prominence. Only in the areas with noticeable mercantile economies—Watertown and to a small extent Hounsfield, Brownville, and Wilna (in which town many had invested at the turn of the century believing it would be the county seat)—did men achieve local notoriety, and with it the formalization of relationships.[6] These same areas, which allowed for formalization within their communities, were the same two areas that responded the least well to revivalism in the 1820s and which were some of the first to organize voluntary associations such as Masonic Lodges. In the southern and northern section of the county, on the other hand, where nonelites dominated, and where political and commercial activity was minimal, religious enthusiasm flourished.

Gordon's *Gazetteer of the State of New York* (1836) describes Jefferson County as "centrally distant N.W. from New York 305, and from Albany 160 miles." As the 1125-square-mile county runs for sixty-five miles along Lake Ontario and the St. Lawrence River, it thus indirectly borders Canada and was, in the age of water travel, more centrally situated among Canadian cities. Jefferson County also borders St. Lawrence County to the south, Oswego County to the north, and Lewis County to the west.[7]

However, before the political boundaries were set, Jefferson County first served as the hunting ground of the Oneida and Onondaga Indians, members of the Iroquois Nation. The Oneidas and Onondagas, though, were not living in the county in the midseventeenth century when the French first came through from Canada. Aside from missionaries, the next significant appearances of Europeans began in 1792 when surveyors came through for the land speculator Alexander Macomb.[8]

In 1788, the Oneidas had ceded their land to the state of New York—in exchange for perpetual fishing privileges along the local waterways. And in 1791 the state of New York sold the land to Macomb. Macomb's Purchase encompassed most of Jefferson County, aside from small areas such as Penet's Square and Tibbet's Point; all of St. Lawrence County; all of Lewis and Oswego Counties; and most of Franklin County: a total then estimated at 3,670,715 acres (although more accurately surveyed at 1,920,000), comprising the northern hump of New York State. Four-hundred-fifty thousand of these acres were in Jefferson County.[9]

The state wanted to settle the area quickly after the American Revolution in order to maintain a buffer zone with Canada. Hence, the state had originally planned to settle there soldiers from the war whose service made them eligible to receive western land. However, most of these men sold their land rights to Macomb. Meanwhile, homesteading had not yet come into favor as a means of settling western land, and the state of New York was not yet capable of managing the sale of numerous small parcels of land.[10]

Difficulties developed when speculating led Macomb into bankruptcy and subsequent arrest in 1792, meaning that he and his partner William Constable then had to sell large quantities of land quickly. They did so by attracting French noblemen who sought to escape from France during the Revolution. Constable contacted the Frenchman, James LeRay de Chaumont, an American citizen by 1788, who was the son of Jacques LeRay de Chaumont, a councilor to Louis XVI and supplier to General Lafayette, who had housed Benjamin Franklin and John Adams at various times.[11] James LeRay, who was familiar with the area as a result of his association with the colonial statesman Gouverneur Morris,[12] introduced Constable to his brother-in-law Paul Chassanis, who bought 210,000 acres in the future Jefferson and Lewis Counties.

Frenchmen settled quickly this area on the Black River, known as Castorland, and came with Morris's recommendation as valuable residents along the buffer zone:

> I understand that he [Simon Desjardines, one of the surveyors] will be followed by several of his countrymen, and I own to you that this appears to me a desirable circumstance not only for our state in particular but for the United States in general, because it will not only tend to the speedy settlement of our northern regions, but placing in the neighborhood of the ancient canadians, people of the same language, manners, and religion, render them a barrier so much the more useful for us.[13]

But most of those, who had not already left Castorland for France as the situation improved there, were forced to leave in 1798 when Adams signed the Alien and Sedition Act, and when the New York State Legislature denied to French citizens the right to own real property. This would not have posed a problem to LeRay, an American citizen, had he been in the United States; however, LeRay had not yet settled in Jefferson County and would not arrive as a permanent settler until 1816.[14] The influence of the European aristocracy in the northern section of the county ultimately created conditions conducive to Finney's earliest successes.

Most of the early American settlers of Jefferson and St. Lawrence Counties came over as families from western Vermont, a region notable for its extremist (as opposed to merely New Light) religious enthusiasm in the First Great Awakening, as it had then attracted those who opposed the standing order in New England, in addition to "'Rhode Island haters of religion'" and "recruits to the Methodist faith."[15] Northern New York was accessible from frozen Lake Champlain and indirectly by the St. Lawrence River. Moreover, the region was not threatening to most Vermonters, as its harsh winters and its land resembled the climate and topography of northwest Vermont.[16] These settlers achieved great social influence on the southern section of the county, where they set the religious tone while Finney was a young man.

In contrast to Jefferson County (and southern Jefferson County in particular) most of the early settlers of western New York—a region partially owned by the state of Massachusetts until 1786—had migrated directly west from Connecticut and Massachusetts. While Connecticut and Massachusetts maintained longstanding community control over excess excitement, and while the Connecticut River Valley area of eastern

Vermont managed to maintain some control over its population,[17] the future settlers of Jefferson County were engaging in the sort of wild behavior in western Vermont that would make them famous in the 1820s. One community of immigrants astonished George Gale (Finney's mentor), when he first visited Jefferson County in 1817:

> They were from Vermont and many of them were singular people. They had singular notions on the subject of religion. They were called rodmen from their using rods, as some do to determine whether there are courses of water under ground, and others where mineral exists. They would use their rods in selecting chapters in the Bible, as in looking for medicinal herbs. They rejected the ministry and were much like the Quakers in that respect. Any one might exalt as the Spirit moved. But they were not like Quakers in regard of ordinances. They maintained these but any of the brotherhood administer them [sic]. They were very much opposed to orthodox christians and their operations. I had left tracts to be distributed, and one of their leaders would destroy all he could find. This superstition was dying out. It did not spread.[18]

Although the "superstition" died out, it undoubtedly helped form the mentality of Jefferson County.

Following successful settlement, and the separation of Jefferson County from Oneida County in 1805, a third region was added to the county in addition to the northern, European-influenced section, and the southern, Vermont-influenced section: the county seat in the commercial midsection of the county.

At the time of earliest settlement, the future Jefferson County was considered part of Oneida County, which had been formed in 1798. However, the ninety miles from the future Jefferson County to Utica, the county seat, made conducting legal affairs difficult. Thus, already isolated in the nineteenth century by its location at the juncture of Lake Ontario and the St. Lawrence River, Jefferson County became even more isolated when it was created from the northern section of Oneida County on March 28, 1805. Jefferson County was named for Thomas Jefferson; while Lewis County, which was also formed from Oneida County, was named for Morgan Lewis, then governor of New York State. After much lobbying among residents of the various towns in the county, Watertown was chosen as the county seat, and thus the future financial center. If Lewis County had not been formed along with Jefferson County, Champion probably would have been chosen as the seat, as it would have been the most central location between Lake Ontario and Oneida County.[19]

These potential sites for the county seat all shared a significant portion of a local asset: the Black River. The rapids of the Black River, which run through Champion, Wilna, LeRay, Rutland, Watertown (named for its connection with the Black River), Brownville, and Hounsfield (where it empties into Lake Ontario), provided superb water power for mills running through the middle of Jefferson County. Of these towns, Wilna, Watertown, Brownville,[20] and Hounsfield were the commercial centers of Jefferson County. On the whole, the early economy of Jefferson County benefited from nearby midcounty sites for grinding lumber and for milling wheat. Easy access to Lake Ontario and what is now called the St. Lawrence Seaway meant that local products—which in addition to "barley, oats, rye, buckwheat, Indian corn, potatoes, and hay," as well as "horses, cattle, sheep and swine" included potash—could be easily transported to the nearest markets in Canada, and down the St. Lawrence to Montreal, the Atlantic Ocean, and ultimately New York City.[21]

Until the Erie Canal made this trade route obsolete, Jefferson County benefited from these fortunately placed waterways.[22] Only during the Embargo of 1807 when Congress interdicted commerce with the British—leading to a thriving smuggling industry in northern New York—and during the War of 1812 did trade across and via Lake Ontario and the St. Lawrence slacken.[23]

The first dam on the Black River was built in 1803 in Watertown in order to encourage industry. Three other dams followed in 1805, 1814, and 1835.[24] Franklin B. Hough indicates that in Watertown as early as 1827

> there were 321 buildings of which 224 were dwellings; 3 stone churches (Methodist, Universalist, and Presbyterian); court house, and jail; clerk's office; arsenal; 1 cotton factory with 1300 spindles, another (Beebe's) then building; 1 woolen factory; 3 paper mills; 3 large tanneries; 3 flouring mills; 1 furnace; 1 nail factory; 2 machine shops; 2 fulling mills; 3 carding machines; 2 distilleries; 1 ashery; 2 pail factories; 1 sash factory; 2 chair factories; 1 hat factory; 4 wagon shops; 2 paint shops; 4 cabinet and joiner shops; 8 blacksmiths; 4 tailor shops; 7 shoe shops; 3 saddle and harness shops; 8 taverns; 15 dry goods stores; 2 hardware stores; 2 hat stores; 2 book stores; 2 leather stores; 1 paint store; 2 druggists; 2 jewelers; 2 weekly papers; 7 public schools; 6 physicians, and 10 lawyers.[25]

These incipient commercial and industrial conditions in Watertown led to the encouragement of a formalist religious and moral perspective in Watertown, as well as in surrounding regions in the midsection of the county.

Early Settlers

In twentieth-century Jefferson County, the local historic figure of greatest prominence is Jacob Brown. Brown's significance in a study of the tripartite geographical separation in the social and religious history of Jefferson County lies in his participation with the European nobility in creating strict socioeconomic boundaries between the run-of-the-mill settlers and the great landholders in the northern section of the county.

Brown, the grandson of Joseph Wright, "a celebrated Quaker preacher," was born in 1775 to a devout Quaker family in Bucks County, Pennsylvania. While teaching at a Quaker school in New York, Brown met Gouverneur Morris and Rodolph Tiller, an agent for the Chassanis company, who encouraged him to settle in the North Country. He did so in 1799, as LeRay's land agent. By 1811, when the area needed leadership for the local militia, Brown, the former Quaker, was chosen to lead it. Thus, when the battles against the British at Kingston, Ontario, were raging in 1813, Brown led the local men to victory and achieved local heroic stature, as well as leadership of the army in the Northern Department. (Andrew Jackson led the Southern Department.) However, before leaving for Washington, the Quaker-turned-warrior did build a church for Brownville.[26]

The second stage of early French immigrants to Jefferson County did far more than did Brown to develop the region. By the time Brown arrived, Morris and LeRay owned most of the land in Jefferson County formerly held by Alexander Macomb; and another Frenchman, Pierre Penet, a slave trader, owned a small tract that had never been part of the Macomb Purchase. The Town of LeRay, where Finney first worked, was named for James LeRay; and the village of Leraysville in that town, where Finney also stopped, was the site of LeRay's mansion.[27]

James LeRay's father, Jacques, was the son of the mayor of Nantes, France, and slave trader, Rene LeRay, who once remarked, "What commerce can be compared to that which obtains men in exchange for commodities?"[28] James LeRay married in 1790 the American Grace Coxe to whom he had been introduced by Morris. At approximately the same time as his marriage, LeRay also attempted to arrange a treaty "of peace and commerce" with the Dey of Algiers during the Tripolitan Wars. He was unable to accomplish this, however. But such an endeavor did not far exceed the scope of LeRay's interests as he was also prodigiously involved in the Caribbean trade and would remain so involved, even when he was living in the northern, snowy, wilderness.[29]

While living in Philadelphia in 1802, LeRay began to prepare to settle in Jefferson County. This involved arranging to build his ornate mansion, bringing in French artisans, inducing other Frenchmen to settle in the area, and developing industry. He also continued to encourage settlement by selling a large portion of his land to a group of Philadelphia Quakers, whose village in the Town of LeRay would also be known as Philadelphia.[30]

Jacques Milbert, on a research trip for the Museum of Natural History in the King's Garden in Paris, traveled through northern New York in 1815 and described the results of this planning:

> In the remote wilderness, he [LeRay] has succeeded in creating an estate, which, for luxury, beauty, and comforts of every kind, could be compared with the most famous chateaux and parks in France. [The house] contained a large drawing-room, billiard and music rooms, a library, and two separate wings with guest rooms for visitors and friends. From the drawing room the windows overlooked a vast and magnificent vegetable garden, planted in French fashion and carefully tended.[31]

1815 was also the year of Mrs. LeRay's death and the beginning of the settlement of the estate of LeRay's "companion" Madame Janika de Feriet, also in Jefferson County. The estate was known as the Hermitage.[32]

Also in 1815, Napoleon faced defeat at Waterloo. He considered immigrating to the United States, but ultimately surrendered to the British. He allowed his brother Joseph, formerly king of Spain, Naples, and the Indies, to emigrate.[33] Bonaparte, known as the Comte de Survilliers in the United States, bought from LeRay 150,000 acres of land in Jefferson County in exchange for diamonds. He then built three houses, which he used for hunting expeditions when not traveling throughout America.[34]

In 1807 LeRay had already also sold 100,000 acres to the Belgian investor, business associate of Talleyrand, and fellow resident of Philadelphia, David Parish, who bought, in addition to this, a considerable portion of Morris's land along the St. Lawrence. Parish intended to raise sheep there, but the already financially burdensome effort became excessive when the War of 1812 obstructed his trade. Thus, in 1816 Parish abandoned the Town of Antwerp in Jefferson County for Austria, where he joined a bank run by Prince Metternich.[35] The town which he left, and which Finney would visit eight years later in its diminished spiritual condition "upon the borders of hell," had benefited materially from Parish's investment.[36] Along with a church, for which he had imported marble, Parish also built "stores, houses, mills . . . taverns, and roads upon endless acres of scrub and shale."[37] He left his brother George in charge of his investment.

LeRay also suffered setbacks, especially after the Erie Canal opened, causing the price of land to plummet and his lands to face foreclosure by 1835. Thus in 1832, LeRay returned to France, and left his son, Vincent, in charge of the land. The LeRay family land office remained open until 1910, and LeRay had so significantly influenced the region that the towns of Theresa and Alexandria were named for his daughters, the village of Chaumont for his home in France, the village of Cape Vincent in the Town of Lyme for his son, and the village of Plessis in the Town of Alexandria for his dog.[38]

Additionally, in the 1830s Jean-Frédéric de la Farge arrived from Philadelphia after having fought in Napoleon's army in Santo Domingo from 1802 to 1806. He settled in a mansion at least equivalent to LeRay's in a region in the far north of Jefferson County not included in Macomb's Purchase, and known as Penet's Square. La Farge's connections with the United States resembled LeRay's in that he had supplied ammunition to the Americans during the Revolutionary War. However, Mrs LaFarge was not happy in Jefferson County, as the other French nobles did not accept her and her husband as "social equal[s]." In 1837, he and his wife left the wilderness for Long Island, after having sold their land to the Archdiocese of New York which soon established there St. Vincent de Paul's Seminary, the predecessor to Fordham University.[39]

Jefferson County did have relatively illustrious American settlers and land agents in its southern and midsection, but none of them as significant as Brown, LeRay, or Parish. Several of them rose to prominence as legislators, as did, for example, Perley Keyes, who acted variously as sheriff, judge, and state representative for the early county. And as a good frontier representative, he, like many others, achieved his position without the benefit of education.[40]

Conversely, William D. Ford was educated as a lawyer. In 1817 he brought his family to Jefferson County from Herkimer County, where he had already served as a state legislator, and in 1819 he became a legislator for

Jefferson County. His greatest difficulty with the county was that he could find no other Episcopalians to form a church until 1828.[41] Hart Massey arrived in Watertown from Vermont in 1800. Like most early settlers, he held a variety of county offices. Moreover, in 1801 the first religious services in the town were held at his home, from which the First Presbyterian Church of Watertown later emerged.[42]

This disparity in the character and achievements of the residents in the southern and northern sections of Jefferson County is telling. In the northern sections wealthy landowners bought tracts that encompassed more than just one town. Their authority extended beyond their towns and dominated Keyes's, Massey's, and Ford's potential counterparts in the northern sections; and their authority even diminished what glory these three and others could garner from Jefferson County's residents.

Given these conditions, the standing order, which Randolph Roth speaks of in Vermont, never fully established itself in Jefferson County.[43] Granted, many Jefferson County residents who were former Vermonters had no desire to reestablish the standing order. Moreover, since disestablishment of religion in New York State, a standing order strictly resembling that of New England, could not develop. Nonetheless it was the societal order with which they were familiar. Thus, where these Vermont immigrants were able to recreate an order analogous to the standing order in New England they did so. Where they could not firmly reestablish a semblance of the standing order, the values of the nonelites flourished. This success in reestablishing the society with which most residents were most familiar expressed itself in gradations in the three areas of Jefferson County.

In the northern section of the county, home of the most elite of the local elite, LeRay, Parish, and Bonaparte managed to maintain order in the carrying our of their own affairs. Thus, LeRay's and Parish's business papers remain the most easily accessible and most well-preserved archival materials from early Jefferson County.[44] But these elite-elites did not take as close an interest in the daily affairs of the villages that arose surrounding their estates. Hence, beyond the confines of European mansions in the wilderness, popular values prevailed without hindrance from the elite local authorities. Additionally, New England town structure did not develop.[45] Even though the elites in the northern sections dominated the area with their extreme wealth, they did so on a grand scale, not at the level where most people carried out their business. This allowed nonelites to achieve preeminence at the most local level in the northern sections of the county. In effect, the enormous infusions of capital that these financiers provided for the northern regions of Jefferson County allowed for stable, though paternalistic,[46] development of the areas. No resident in the northern section could ever compete with the local European elites, thus all were nonelites.

LeRay de Chaumont and his colleagues in the northern section had the greatest influence on the northern section of the county, although their influence was still felt in countywide decision making. The middle sections though were able to recreate towns analogous to the ones with which they were familiar in New England. Watertown, Brownville, Wilna, and the village of Sackets Harbor in Hounsfield achieved importance as the commercial centers of Jefferson County as the Black River facilitated trade and industry in these areas. Thus, most local elites lived in these regions. Furthermore, Watertown's position as county seat meant that more local political and commercial elites lived there than in Brownville, Wilna, and Sackets Harbor.

The southern sections of the county—in particular the towns of Adams, Henderson, Ellisburg, Champion, Rutland, and Lorraine—without the influence of powerful European nobility, recreated towns analogous to the ones they knew in New England. However, they lacked a notable elite society. Their residents rarely achieved power at the county level, and most trade took place in the midsection of the county. Consequently, although the southern section mimicked the midsection's formation of a town structure, the society of the southern section more closely resembled the northern section's numerically superior marginal population.

Consequently, the southern and northern sections became the centers of fervor in Jefferson County. Methodists encouraged enthusiasm in their circuits through the northern section of the county, while Baptists encouraged fervor in the southern section. Meanwhile, Watertown as the county seat and the financial and formalist center in the county had revivals but did not express enthusiasm until the transformation and formalization of revivalism in the 1830s.[47]

Voluntary Associations

The formation of voluntary associations provides evidence of the nature and character of the settlements. In accord with Thomas's conception of isomorphism, institutions reflect the society. In the early stages of settlement, voluntary associations display the needs and values of a frontier society, and as the society develops, the voluntary associations reflect the needs and values of a settled and formalized society. Moreover, more formalized areas will develop more formalized associations. Thus, the chronology of the creation of voluntary associations portrays the development of the county, and it gives evidence of the effects of the tri-partite arrangement of the county.

Additionally, isomporphism in Jefferson County provides a contrast with Curtis Johnson's functionalist understanding of voluntary associations in Cortland County. Johnson notes that in Cortland County by the 1830s local churches and church-based societies no longer functioned as the only voluntary associations, and that as a result the churches secularized, or adapted to the competition. For example, Cortland County's Agricultural Society formed in 1838, while in the same decade "temperance, medical . . . educational, mechanic, [and] abolitionist," societies were also organized.[48]

Johnson's argument cannot be applied to Jefferson County, since Jefferson County's citizens preceded Cortland County's residents in the creation of such organizations, often by more than twenty years. The Bible Society of Jefferson County (originally the Bible Society of Rutland) was formed in 1817; the Jefferson County Union for Promoting the Observance of the Sabbath was created in 1828; and the Jefferson County Medical Society began in 1806.[49] The Jefferson County Education and Temperance Societies began relatively late in 1835 and 1846.[50] However, a benevolent organization to aid the Greeks' struggle for independence formed in 1826 and served as a precedent for a similar move to aid the Irish during the potato famine in 1847.[51] Masonry appeared in Jefferson County in 1805 in the village of Sackets Harbor in Hounsfield. Other lodges followed in Adams in 1806,[52] Watertown in 1806, Champion in 1807, Henderson in 1816, the village of Woodville in Ellisburg in 1817, Brownville in 1819, Cape Vincent (Town of Lyme) in 1822, Rodman in 1824, Theresa (Town of Alexandria) in 1824, and Antwerp and Evans Mills (Town of LeRay) in 1826.[53] What is remarkable about the geographical order of the lodges' formation is that the commercial villages and the southern religiously fervid towns tended to organize more quickly than did the northern nobility-controlled areas. A similar pattern holds for Baptist and Presbyterian church formation.

As evidence of the primacy of agriculture in Jefferson County, the Jefferson County Agricultural Society became the second agricultural society in the state of New York (after the Otsego Society) in 1817, two years before the passing of a state law providing $10,000 "to the encouragement of county societies for the promotion of agriculture and domestic manufactures." James LeRay was a pivotal force in the formation of statewide interest in agricultural societies.[54]

As a rule, LeRay's presidential addresses at the annual meetings of the Agricultural Society suggest that the society was interested first in furthering the interests of local farmers and in encouraging matchless agricultural productions:

> The object of our society and its more direct business is to encourage every branch of agriculture and rural economy best adapted to our soil and climate, by a well digested combination of science and practice. To promote enquiries, and receive information the most useful to agriculture; to suggest experiments and improvements which may tend to the amelioration and prosperity of our agriculture, and of course, our manufactures, of which they are the aliment and support.[55]

Second, the society sought to entice other farmers to settle in Jefferson County. LeRay's former land agent, General Jacob Brown, served as vice president of the society, thus implying that their motives were at least partially self-serving.

> We hear with satisfaction, that Joseph Bonaparte, after having traveled through a great part of this country, has expressed in the most lively terms to different persons, how much he admires this part of the United States, and wishes to give it the preference for his residence, if his lady consents to come.[56]

The existence and success of the society indicate that Jefferson County had, at least by 1817, a stable enough agricultural economy that the local farmers could form an association. And the early creation of other voluntary associations indicates that Jefferson County had developed in certain regions greater formalization of activities and relationships than had Cortland County at the same time.

One factor—but certainly not the only one—that appears to have promoted "secularization" in Jefferson County was population increase, an apparent indication of population diversity and a loss of the New England cultural monopoly.[57] From 1820 to 1830 the population grew by 68 percent and from 1830 to 1840 by 80 percent.[58] This does not compare well with the figures Cross gives for other areas: 96 percent in Albany, 183 percent in Utica, 282 percent in Syracuse, 314 percent in Buffalo, and 512 percent in Rochester.[59] However, this was enough to redefine the character of the region. The Roman Catholic population in the region, for example, swelled between 1820 and 1840 with the arrival of Irish and French-Canadians; and the Universalists in the county had by 1823 established a Universalist Association, whose geographical boundaries were redefined in 1829 in response to continued growth.[60] And it was Watertown, which had a consistently higher population than any other town in the county, that evidenced, by the mid-1820s, earlier than other regions of the county, a tendency toward "secularization."[61]

But given Johnson's criteria for "secularization," it appears that Watertown "secularized" in the 1820s; as organizations besides the evangelical churches were already common and, unlike Cortlanders who did not balk until the 1830s, communicants of the First Presbyterian Church in Watertown were frequently disregarding the disciplinary pronouncements of the session as early as the 1820s.[62] (While in Roth's Vermont the height of disciplinary content came before 1811, more than twenty years before the success of voluntary associations or Arminianism.)[63] Areas outside of Watertown did not experience a redefinition of churchly activities until the 1830s. Nevertheless, I do not view this redefinition as secularization. Henderson had numerous evangelical and nonevangelical societies in the 1820s, as well as a Masonic lodge in 1816, and residents who belonged to the Agricultural Society. The changes in the 1830s, as I will demonstrate in chapter 4, appear to have been a sharing of values on the part of formalist and antiformalist churches.

In sum, then, Finney's unstructured youthful home in southern Jefferson County was dominated by an agrarian, egalitarian, nonhierarchical population, which favored antiformalism. The structured central region of the county, with which Finney had minimal contact, was dominated by the formalist Presbyterian church. Meanwhile, the northern section of the county developed unique conditions. It had an agrarian, egalitarian American population, and a dominant, elite, European-immigrant, ruling class. Hence, it demonstrated neither formalism nor antiformalism. As I will note in the following chapter, Finney was fortunate in his assignment to the northern section of the county, which he received for his first preaching, since he opposed the standard of formalism in Presbyterian churches; but, as a former attorney, he did not condone the extremes of

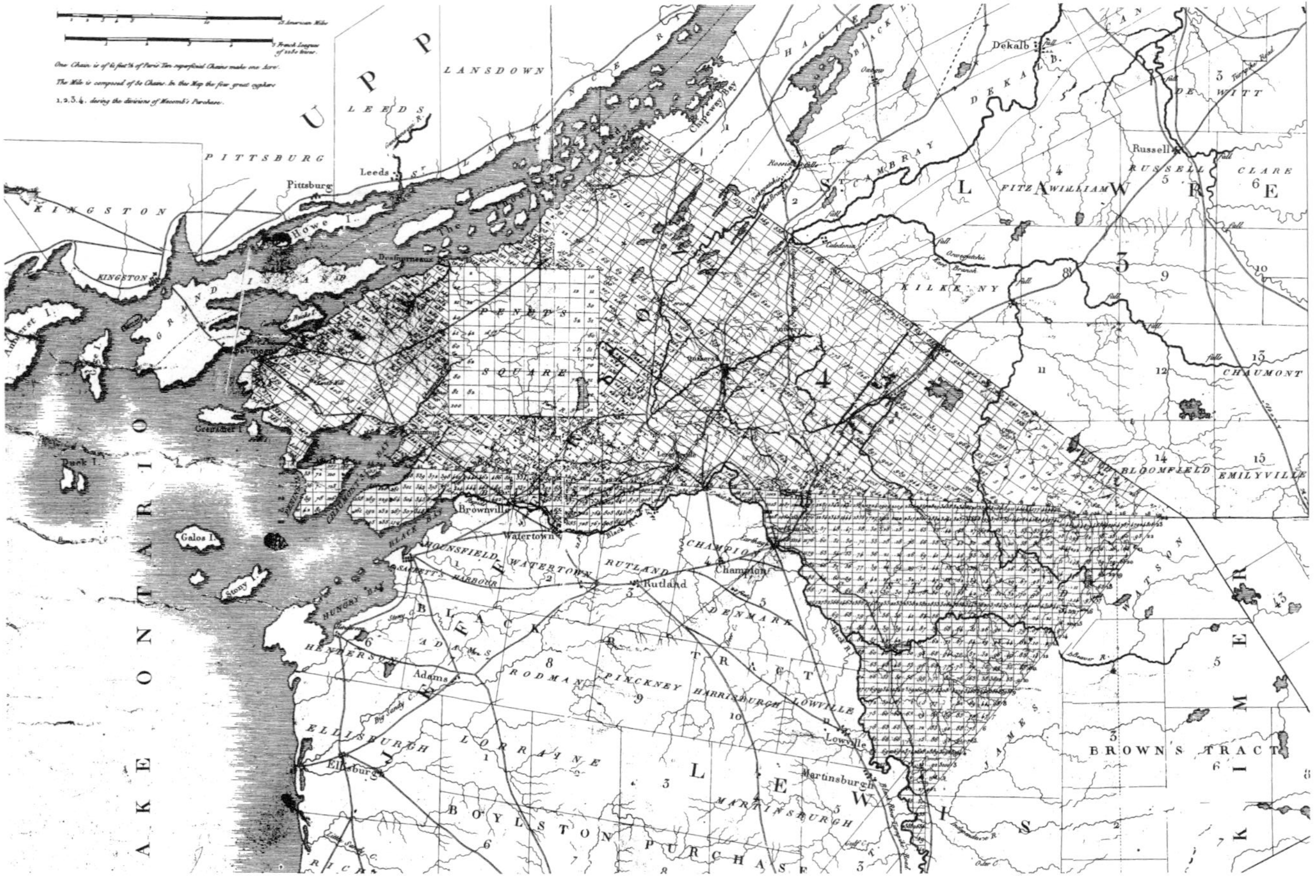

Map 2.1 Map presented by James LeRay to cartographer Oliver Child in 1816.

antiformalism. Such a mix was exactly what the churches in northern Jefferson County required. The following chapters provide a closer look at how the populations of these geographic divisions expressed their formalism and antiformalism.

Map 2.1 indicates the differences in town structure between the northern and southern sections of the county. The northern region of the county, owned by LeRay and other European immigrant nobility, failed to form definite town structures. Thus, the northern section on the map appears as crosshatching representing the division of LeRay's lots, while the southern and midsections show large squares marking the county's earliest ten towns. LeRay presented the map to the cartographer Oliver Child in 1816. Child apparently intended to include the map in an atlas.

The original 2′ × 2′ map is on display at the Jefferson County Historical Society, Watertown. The photograph from which this copy derives was made at the *Watertown Daily Times,* Watertown.

Appendix: New York State Census of 1835 and 1845

The following tables distinguish between the tripartite divisions of Jefferson County.

Table 1 Home manufactured cloth[64]

Whitney Cross has remarked that "When the farmer could sell rather than eat his crops, his wife could buy textiles instead of spinning and weaving."[65] In Jefferson County, the quantity of home manufactured cloth is a helpful indicator of the level of commercial activity in a region. A high number indicates a low level of commercial activity. The figures are for yards of cloth manufactured per capita.

TOWNS IN SOUTHERN JEFFERSON COUNTY

Ellisburg	6.69
Lorraine	7.74
Rodman	9.40
Henderson	6.29
Adams	5.91
Rutland	7.69
Champion	5.87
average	7.08

TOWNS IN MID-JEFFERSON COUNTY

Hounsfield	3.37
Watertown	3.38
Wilna	2.99
Brownville	3.32
Lyme	2.71
average	3.15

TOWNS IN NORTHERN JEFFERSON COUNTY

Pamelia	6.36
LeRay	4.71
Philadelphia	6.44
Orleans	5.30

Alexandria	4.67
Antwerp	5.92
Clayton	3.34
average	5.25

Table 2 Farmers per 1000 people; merchants and professionals per 1000 people; and inns, taverns, and stores per 1000 people.[66]

A low number for farmers indicates low agricultural activity, while a high number for merchants, manufacturers, and professionals and inns, taverns, and stores indicates high commercial activity.

	Farmers	*Merchs/prof'ls*	*Inns/taverns/stores*
TOWNS IN SOUTHERN JEFFERSON COUNTY			
Ellisburg	133	35	4
Lorraine	163	18	4
Rodman	132	43	4
Henderson	204	63	3
Adams	180	52	4
Rutland	175	58	4
Champion	206	42	2
average	170	44	4
TOWNS IN MID-JEFFERSON COUNTY			
Hounsfield	85	32	7
Watertown	50	105	14
Wilna	134	38	7
Brownville	163	55	5
Lyme	151	38	5
average	117	54	8
TOWNS IN NORTHERN JEFFERSON COUNTY			
Pamelia	138	32	3
LeRay	598	51	4
Philadelphia	129	46	5
Orleans	163	29	3
Alexandria	163	30	5

Antwerp	172	34	4
Clayton	142	38	6
average	215	37	4

Table 3 Quantity of total agricultural production per capita.[67]

Towns in Southern Jefferson County

Ellisburg	169.30
Lorraine	266.81
Rodman	282.43
Henderson	123.68
Adams	149.90
Rutland	308.83
Champion	303.49
average	229.21

Towns in Mid-Jefferson County

Hounsfield	99.05
Watertown	80.55
Wilna	84.48
Brownville	88.49
Lyme	89.78
average	88.47

Towns in Northern Jefferson County

Pamelia	189.13
LeRay	132.93
Philadelphia	136.83
Orleans	94.15
Alexandria	58.30
Antwerp	124.28
Clayton	87.16
average	117.54

Table 4 Summary: Combined per capita agricultural values, minus merchants and inns per capita.[68]

High numbers indicate high agricultural activity, and low numbers indicate high commercial activity. Towns from the northern section of the county—LeRay, Pamelia, Antwerp, Orleans, Philadelphia, Alexandria, and Clayton—are dispersed throughout this spectrum of agricultural activity. By contrast, towns from the southern section are bunched at the top of the spectrum, while towns from the mid-section are bunched at the bottom.

LeRay	680.64
Champion	471.36
Rutland	429.52
Lorraine	415.55
Rodman	376.83
Pamelia	298.49
Adams	279.81
Ellisburg	269.99
Henderson	267.97
Antwerp	264.20
Orleans	230.45
Philadelphia	221.27
Lyme	200.49
Brownville	194.81
Alexandria	190.97
Clayton	188.50
Wilna	176.47
Hounsfield	148.42
Watertown	14.93

3
The Foundations of Fervor

Fervor arrived early in Jefferson County as a normal expression of piety. This chapter describes two aspects of the environment in which fervor throve. The first section describes the backgrounds of the revivalists who worked in Jefferson County, among whom Charles Finney was the most prominent as well as the only one to achieve great fame. Finney dominates much of the narrative, as he was the only one to achieve great prominence outside of Jefferson County. Certainly, none of his counterparts were ever his equals outside of Jefferson County, but Finney was by no means alone in Jefferson County. And unlike some other regions of New York State that imported revivalists, Jefferson County did not. What is most remarkable in the biographies of Jefferson County's revivalists of varying levels of fame is that all of them had experienced notable formalist and antiformalist influences.

In most cases, the names of these revivalists do not reappear often in the rest of the narrative. Most of them worked in Jefferson County only a short time before moving to other areas. Although they clearly had an impact on Jefferson County, and although they provide a clear context for understanding Finney's work as well as the mentalities of the churches throughout Jefferson County, their names do not reappear frequently or consistently in the church records. Finney's name, for example, only appears in the records of the church in LeRay for a short time.

The second section of this chapter backtracks from the time of the revivalists' prominence to the formation of the churches in Jefferson County in order to describe the interest of some churches in fervor, and the interest of others in orderliness. The tripartite organization of Jefferson County played a notable role in determining which churches favored fervor and which favored orderliness. By and large, Presbyterian churches were formalist, and they favored orderliness and orthodoxy; and by and large, Baptist and Methodist churches were antiformalist, and they encouraged fervor and egalitarian relationships. Hence, in accord with George Thomas's conception of isomorphism, Presbyterians dominated commercial areas where orderliness and correct behavior were valued the most highly; while Baptists and Methodists dominated egalitarian, agrarian areas. However, Baptists and Methodists did thrive in the commercial centers where they allowed for some formalism, and Presbyterians did succeed in agrarian areas where they did allow for some antiformalism.

This lack of a strict and constant delineation between formalists and antiformalists is important to recognize, since, as I note much more completely in the next chapter, the delineation began to crumble after 1830.

Revivalists in Jefferson County

Charles Grandison Finney

Finney's family moved from Warren in Litchfield County, Connecticut and from Paris, in Oneida County, New York to Henderson, New York in Jefferson County in 1802. Finney received his education in Connecticut, taught in New Jersey, and eventually returned to and remained in Jefferson County at his mother's request because of her ill health. He moved to Adams, a town adjacent to Henderson, and studied law under Benjamin Wright.[1] In the course of these years, Finney heard the preaching of the staid Calvinist preachers of New England and of a rural Baptist minister in Henderson in Jefferson County, Emory Osgood.

Although Osgood's influence on Finney's life occupies little space in Finney's *Memoirs,* it is important not to diminish the significance of the influence of the preaching of an ignorant Baptist minister on Finney's early development. Although Finney later is supposed to have ridiculed the ignorant preacher, Osgood no doubt provided an example of the value of lively preaching.[2]

While working under Wright, Finney led the choir in the First Presbyterian Church of Adams, and attended prayer meetings regularly. Nonetheless, the local church-going population and their pastor, George W. Gale, regarded him as an unlikely convert and a hindrance to the religious development of the choir members. The time he spent with the church, however, did influence him, and after two or three years, in 1821, he experienced a sudden conversion experience, during the course of which he prayed, "If I am converted, I will preach the Gospel."[3] On

December 31, 1821, Finney went before the church session, where he and nine other people "were examined as to their hope in Christ & knowledge of his gospel"; they were then "propounded for admission to the communion of [the] church."[4]

Soon afterward, Finney began his studies for the ministry in 1822 in the Presbytery of St. Lawrence under the care primarily of Gale, but also of Rev. George S. Boardman of the First Presbyterian Church of Watertown. Gale was experienced in training ministers by this point as he had also earlier taken Jedediah Burchard under his care.

Finney contends that he did not wish to attend any seminary, Princeton in particular, as he felt the seminaries destroyed ministers' capacities to preach. But Gale asserts that he wrote to Andover, Princeton, and Auburn, and that he received "no encouragement" to enroll Finney.[5] Finney remained under Gale's care until 1824 when Gale left Adams for reasons of health for Oneida County. As a result of an earlier, politically motivated controversy concerning Jedediah Burchard's lack of qualifications for licensure, the Presbytery licensed Finney to preach in 1824 despite his similar lack of qualifications. Nonetheless, he had never read the Westminster Confession and its article concerning unconditional election, which the Arminian Finney never accepted—even after reading the confession.

His ignorance of the confession marked the difference between Finney, the revivalist, and his colleagues in the Presbytery of St. Lawrence who did not encourage enthusiastic revivals. Finney, as I will later demonstrate, developed in Jefferson County the bridge between the Methodists' successful Arminianism, the extemporaneous preaching of the Baptists and Methodists, and the law-oriented theology of the Presbyterians. This bridging ultimately culminated in the formalization of revivals and benevolence among denominations in the 1830s, in other words a balance between the methods of the Methodists and Baptists and the conservative benevolent ideology of Lyman Beecher.[6]

Finney's first experience as a preacher was in Gale's pulpit in Adams, after which, because of Finney's casual manner of speaking to the congregation, Gale remarked that he would be embarrassed to have anyone know that Finney had studied under him. Nevertheless, before Gale succumbed to his ill health and left Jefferson County for Oneida County, he obtained for Finney a position as a missionary in the village of Evans Mills, Town of LeRay.[7] The Female Missionary Society of the Western District, based in Utica, with auxiliaries throughout Jefferson County, financed Finney's work.[8]

In the *Eighth Annual Report* (1824) of the society, Finney describes at length his plain and simple preaching and the hopeful conversion of two hundred people—a number which he admits may be high—as well as the successful proselytization of a community of German immigrants to the north of Evans Mills.[9] Undoubtedly, Finney's simple form of preaching had much to do with the awakening in Evans Mills, and much to do with the local Baptist minister's praise of his preaching.[10]

However, the population must have helped. They were not fighting his efforts. In fact, in the *Sixth Annual Report* (1822), Adams W. Platt, who performed the marriage for Finney and his wife in 1824, remarked:

> I have a few times visited a church in Leray's-Ville, about twelve miles from Watertown, at a place called Even's [sic] Mills. It is small and the membership generally poor. They need assistance at this time very much. There is some considerable seriousness among them at present. A large church under the blessing of God might be collected there.[11]

Thus, Finney began his work in an area perhaps more willing to experience conversion than he initially suggested in referring to it as a "burnt district." Probably the situation in Evans Mills was similar to that of DeKalb, Finney's last stop in the North Country before he left for Oneida County to aid Gale. Finney wrote in his *Memoirs:*

> A few years before there had been a revival there [in DeKalb] under the labors of the Methodists. It had been attended with a good deal of excitement; and many cases had occurred of what the Methodists call "*falling* under the power of God." This the Presbyterians had resisted, and in consequence a bad state of feeling had existed between the Methodists and the Presbyterians; the Methodists accusing the Presbyterians of having opposed the revival among them because of these cases of falling under the power of God.[12]

In both Evans Mills and DeKalb the populations were eager to participate in Finney's religious meetings, but they resisted what they viewed as the fanatical improprieties of the Methodists. Thus, it is likely most accurate to assume that in referring to Evans Mills as a "burnt district," Finney meant that the residents of the village evidenced the same wariness as did the residents of DeKalb.

In any case, while Finney was at DeKalb the Presbyterians also began "falling." However, he takes great pains in his *Memoirs* to present himself as far less fanatical than the Old School Presbyterians considered him—and perhaps he was sufficiently less exuberant for the Presbyterians in DeKalb to consider "falling" tolerable. Finney also apparently managed to overcome wariness of the Methodists in Evans Mills, as he introduced the use of the anxious bench there, before his more famous use of the bench in Rochester in 1831.[13]

At this early point, he also satisfied the wish of the people to have sermons delivered spontaneously. This Baptist and Methodist method, according to Gale, was expected by the residents of Jefferson County when he arrived there. Gale satisfied the requirement by writing his sermons ahead of time and then memorizing them.[14] Finney preferred at this time not to write his sermons ahead of time, not even to think about what he would preach on, only to wait for the inspiration of the Holy Spirit. This resembled the preaching of the "ignorant Methodist ministers" who "produced so much more effect than our most learned and splendid divines."[15] After leaving Jefferson County, and after his methods and the revivals themselves became generalized, he wrote "skeletons" of his sermons, and he solidified what he had developed in Jefferson County.[16]

Hence, this half-way point between Finney and the Methodist revivalists is another indication of his position as a bridge between the Methodist and Baptist revivalists and the New England revivalists, Beecher in particular.

But before facing Beecher and his counterparts at New Lebanon in 1827, Finney labored until 1825 in the North Country, where he developed his methods and theology. On the whole, he proceeded freely and was able to discover in an unimpeding and welcoming environment how best to encourage conversion experiences.[17]

His still somewhat pliable understanding of his profession allowed him while at these early posts to experiment: to baptize by immersion,[18] to allow people to "fall," to use the anxious bench, and to deliver sermons extemporaneously. Essentially, Finney's theology represents at this point Henri Bergson's "open" religion, or Victor Turner's "antistructure." On Ernst Troeltsch's continuum ranging from church to sect, from sect and to mystic, Finney's theology qualified as mystical. And in terms of formalists and antiformalists, Finney was an antiformalist. In accord with the assumptions which Bergson and Troeltsch, in particular, use with these terms, Finney gradually organized his methods, and his theology slowly became more formal, more "closed," and more "church"-like. Still, although he lost some of his youthful enthusiastic charisma after he left his earliest pulpits, the fruits of that initial enthusiasm remained with him.[19]

Garth Rosell considers Finney the leader in American revivalism from the New Lebanon Conference until 1832 when Finney traveled through Boston, New York City, Philadelphia, and Rochester. Finney's successes were halted, however, when he fell ill with cholera in 1832 and when he accepted a settled position as pastor of the Chatham Street Chapel in New York. In 1835, he began teaching theology at newly created Oberlin College. From 1851 to 1866 he served as president of Oberlin. In his later years, his evangelistic efforts consisted chiefly in teaching his "theology" to students at Oberlin and in occasional itinerant preaching, as in his voyage to England in 1850. As Finney's theology formalized he recorded the routinization of his beliefs in methods in several treatises: most notably *Sermons on Various Subjects* (1834); *Lectures on Revivals of Religion* (1835); and *Lectures on Systematic Theology* (1846).[20]

George Washington Gale

George Washington Gale did not experience a tumultuous conversion experience as did Finney. After finishing common school, he taught for awhile and then attended Union College in Schenectady, near his home in Troy. After giving several years' consideration to his ultimate profession, he entered Princeton Theological Seminary in 1815. He spent a year there and was then licensed to preach near his home without having been ordained.

He decided to become a missionary for the Female Missionary Society of the Western District, in order to be near his sister in Cayuga County. However, in 1817 the society sent him far from Cayuga County to the Town of Henderson in Jefferson County. Gale encountered there a newly settled society with few ministers. In fact, the ministers he met were strongly antiformalist Baptist. Thus, the congregations he served desired that Gale not prepare his sermons ahead of time. Although many of these people were Congregational and Presbyterian, they had grown used to the methods of the Baptists and the Methodists.[21]

Whiskey drinking was a social expectation of this group which Gale met with misgiving, but for which he, nonetheless, made a concession in an effort to sate the religious needs of the community.[22] Though Gale did find it difficult to adapt to this condition, the requirements of the community may not have shocked him as much as they might have a minister with a strict New England upbringing; Gale could not and did not expect to maintain control or exert great influence over the actions of the frontier community. Although the frontier communities of Jefferson County maintained the forms of eighteenth-century New England communities,[23] they could not police the actions of their entire population. And since Gale's family was virtually split in its Baptist and Presbyterian allegiance in New York State, Gale had developed a less restricted understanding of the place of religion and of his role than he probably would have had he grown up an adherent of state-supported New England Congregationalism.[24]

After spending 1817 preaching in Henderson and its vicinity, Gale left for Princeton. He returned to Jefferson County in 1819 and "supplied" the First Presbyterian Church of Adams as its first steady pastor after the congregation's years of contention with its former pastor.[25] He arrived several months before his fiancee, Harriet Selden of Troy, during which time they exchanged several letters, notable chiefly for their concern for Harriet's soul, as Harriet's father was an Episcopalian and had himself not urged her to convert.[26]

Although the church in Adams did occasionally experience "seasons of refreshing" as any evangelical church must, none of these seasons satisfied Gale's wishes entirely; as Gale's method for achieving the revivals was conservative: he urged the church only to fast and pray.

Gale's position on revivals in Presbyterian theology did ultimately change as a result of the influence of his student, Finney, but Gale was probably more open to this change than were many of his colleagues. After all, Gale's familiarity and openness to Baptist methods led him to bring Finney and Jedediah Burchard up for consideration by the presbytery—despite their deficiencies. A stricter minister would not have done so.

When Gale's poor health made it impossible for him to continue his work, he left Jefferson County in 1824 and moved to Oneida County where he eventually established the Manual Labor Institute, which was meant to provide for the education of young men who could not afford the cost of ministerial education. Essentially, Gale planned to accomplish on a larger scale what he had already done with Burchard and Finney. He later moved to Illinois, where he developed his Manual Labor Institute into Knox College in Galesburg.[27]

Thus, Gale's fame is not merely a product of his accidental association with Finney, although his association with Finney certainly plays a significant role in any fame Gale might still have. Still, his willingness to adapt put him in a position to succor those who could accommodate to the tastes and needs of their religious audiences. Despite Gale's Old School training, he opened the way for the form of Presbyterian preaching—most resembling that of the Baptists and the Methodists—that the rural Presbyterians of Jefferson County expected. It was also Gale who made concessions for Finney's form of preaching and who urged Finney to encourage a revival in Utica.[28]

Jedediah Burchard

Jedediah Burchard probably set an example of correct preaching for Finney, before Finney converted. According to Gale, Burchard was originally a merchant in Albany, who apparently led what was then known as a dissolute life. However, when his business failed he grew serious and, after his conversion, began to consider joining the ministry. The presbytery in Albany, for reasons Gale had not determined, refused Burchard licensure. Burchard then went to Sackets Harbor in Jefferson County, where he lived with friends and family, and spent his time reading his Bible.[29]

Gale heard Burchard preaching in the Village of Smithville, near Adams, and was favorably impressed, although he could not ascertain to which denomination Burchard belonged. (He discovered that although Burchard was a Presbyterian, he had been raised a Baptist.) Gale later requested Burchard to read the prayers at the church in Adams while Gale went to Albany to be with a sick relative. But he did not allow Burchard to give sermons "to prevent him from assuming duties which did not belong to him, and which also might give offense."[30] When Gale returned, he found that numerous people had become interested in converting while Burchard was there. So Gale invited Burchard to remain in Adams for awhile. He assisted both Gale as well as the local Baptist Church, and he demonstrated to Gale that "he was possessed of talents to render him useful, and that he had very correct views of the doctrines of the Gospel and an uncommon tact at reaching the conscience of sinners."[31]

Accordingly, Gale urged Burchard to seek ordination. But Gale realized that most members of the presbytery would not be open to an ignorant and excited preacher, so he suggested to Burchard that he seek ordination from the Black River Association, a remnant of the Congregational association of ministers in Jefferson County, all of whose members were also members of the St. Lawrence Presbytery. When Burchard went before the association in 1822, he knew almost nothing about church history and theology. Fortunately, what the association quizzed him on, he had learned from Gale on the buggy ride to the meeting. Like Finney, he did not prepare his sermons ahead of time. Hence, he shocked the members of the association by giving his sermon to them extemporaneously.

Because Burchard had no education but had a large religious following in Jefferson County, the association agreed to license him temporarily while he studied under Gale. Although Burchard proved resistant to studying, the association continued his license, and ultimately, the association dismissed (or transferred) Burchard to the presbytery at his request. The presbytery had no choice but to accept a member of the association in good standing. Consequently, when Finney went to the presbytery for ordination, they accepted him then, fearing that he might eventually join their ranks haphazardly through the association, even though the presbytery had complained to the synod about the association's laxness in admitting poorly prepared candidates.[32]

Like Finney, Burchard served several Jefferson County churches before laboring as a Presbyterian circuit rider.[33] However, because he was more extravagant than Finney and because, unlike Finney, he never tempered his extravagance, he was never as successful among the urban upper classes. While Finney was encouraging the 1842 revival in Rochester among the lawyers and merchants, Burchard was working among the lower classes in the same city.[34] Contemporary discussions of Burchard follow a pattern of mentioning that he was vulgar and unrefined:

> Many of the most important churches in these districts [the state of New York including New York City] were opened to him, and wherever he went large congregations came out and great interest was awakened. He cannot be judged by ordinary rules. Constitutionally eccentric, he was irresistably erratic. A thorough Presbyterian and a hyper-Calvinist, he was of a mercurial disposition and a brilliant genius. His power of description has been seldom surpassed, and his fund of anecdote and fountain of humor were so overflowing that he could not seal them. Without culture and often crude and coarse, his picturing was always vivid and occasionally beautiful, and his delivery, though too obviously acting well befitted it. His preaching would have drawn crowds irrespective of its spiritual impression.[35]

In this description, the nineteenth-century Presbyterian historian P. H. Fowler accepted the New School developments and continued to refer to its adherents as Calvinist, or even "hyper-Calvinist." George F. Wright,

Finney's nineteenth-century biographer, made similar remarks regarding Finney. Their goals as apologists were more to argue for the orthodoxy of the revivalists than to indicate their actual fidelity to the Westminster Confession.[36]

As in Finney's case, attacks against Burchard issued from outside northern New York, Vermont in particular. Russell Streeter, a Universalist, writing in Woodstock, Vermont, in 1835, used "Calvinist" as a term of opprobrium against Burchard, while, C. G. Eastman, an Old School adherent in Vermont, wrote a tirade against Burchard's Arminianism.[37] And James Hotchkin, writing the western New York equivalent of Fowler's history, did not treat Burchard's eccentricity kindly:

> The writer has no personal acquaintance with Mr. Burchard, and does not know that he ever saw him, but if he can credit testimony which appears to him undoubted, there must have been very much in the course pursued by him, and in his instructions, which was exceedingly reprehensible. It would seem to have been his grand object, by every variety of means to bring the impentitent to say that they gave their hearts to God.[38]

Regardless of the difference of opinion on the courses taken by the newer revivalists, Burchard did represent the new wave in the ministry of the nineteenth century. In fact, Luther Myrick—who was eventually excommunicated by the Oneida Presbytery for his enthusiasm—considered Burchard's methods excessive, though his opinion of Burchard's methods did not prevent him from seeking admittance into the organization that admitted Burchard to the ministry, the Black River Association.[39]

What little is available on Burchard indicates that he provided a nonconformist model during Finney's early development, one which Finney later repudiated along with Burchard.[40] Burchard remained separated from the values of the larger culture, and he remained a marginal, though enormously successful revivalist.

Daniel Nash

Daniel Nash experienced a second conversion experience after meeting Finney and gave up his farm in order to devote himself entirely to his ministry. According to Cross, "the likelihood is that Finney learned more from this old veteran of the backwoods than he taught in return."[41] Finney first saw him at a meeting of the Presbytery of St. Lawrence praying very loudly, with his eyes open, as if he were talking to the congregation. This intensity appealed to Finney, while Finney's willingness to devote himself to conversions appealed to Nash. Such was Nash's allegiance to Finney that while Finney was serving in Evans Mills, Nash was serving for the Female Missionary Society of the Western District in the village of Carthage and the Town of Wilna, and aiding Finney.[42]

Nash's fervency is representative of the revivalists in early nineteenth-century Jefferson County, and of Finney's early preparation. For example, John Humphrey Noyes described Nash as "the highest type and best representative of the old revival spirit. In him the faith of the New Measures school reached its highest point."[43] Hence, while Nash was as exuberant as the early Finney, Nash, like Burchard, never lost the exuberance. For example, Nash urged Finney in 1835 very strongly against using "skeletons" or outlines in preparing his sermons, as Nash feared it would destroy Finney's spirituality.[44] The change in Finney meant that although Finney and Nash were frequent companions while in Jefferson, St. Lawrence, and Oneida Counties, when Finney moved to more cosmopolitan congregations, he abandoned his association with the coarse Nash. Nash and Luther Myrick responded to Finney's assimilation of his methods to the standards of the middle class by urging Finney in letters to return to his previous methods of preaching.[45]

Jacob Knapp

A footnote in the preface to Jacob Knapp's *Autobiography* indicates that "while holding a meeting in the Mulberry Street church, in the city of New York, a young man rose in the presence of a vast congregation, and requested prayers for the *devil.* Elder Knapp quietly remarked, 'Brethren, this young man has asked you to pray for his father.' "[46] This anecdote is identical to one also told about Finney. Descriptions of Knapp's career in the *Autobiography* could also pass as descriptions of Finney's career: "Posterity will speak of Elder Knapp as the pioneer and champion of modern evangelism"; and "He was perhaps the first man, at least in the Northern States, who devoted himself exclusively to the work of conducting protracted meetings."[47] However, Finney and Knapp were not identical, they were mirror images.

Finney encountered a significant Baptist influence in his youth, while the Baptist Knapp was raised an Episcopalian in Otsego County, New York. Finney disdained the influence of ministerial education on preaching, while Knapp went against his father's wishes in order to attend the Hamilton Institute. Finney paid little attention to reform, especially in his years in Jefferson County, while Knapp was "among the pioneers in the temperance movement," "an avowed anti-slavery man," and "the consistent friend of missionary enterprises and ministerial education."[48] The most significant similarity between the two is that Knapp also repudiated the doctrine of unconditional election.

Furthermore, whereas Finney arrived in Jefferson County early in the revival cycle and labored in the most sparsely settled regions, Knapp did not appear in Jefferson County until 1830 when he "accepted a call from the Baptist Church in Watertown," the most populated town in Jefferson County.[49]

Yet, Knapp's position in the formation of the expression of nineteenth-century evangelical piety is just as important as Finney's. Finney represents a transition in Presbyterian expression more closely related to Baptist and Methodist preaching; and Knapp represents the later Baptist acceptance of the Presbyterian concern with moralism. And like Finney Knapp did get his start as an evangelist in Jefferson County, when in 1833 he left to preach to others in the simple language that had succeeded for three years in the First Baptist Church of Watertown.[50]

Nathan Bangs

Despite Nathan Bangs's work just across the river from Jefferson County, the Methodists in Jefferson County were not distinguished. However, these circuit riders and the local Baptist preachers provided the standard against which Finney's, Burchard's, Nash's, and Knapp's followers judged preaching. Sometimes the Presbyterian congregations sought to restrain themselves from what they considered Methodist excesses as in the case of Finney's congregation at DeKalb; and sometimes they urged their ministers to accept the ways of the Methodists, who for example, disdained prepared sermons.

This lack of ministerial distinction within the ranks of the most naturally revivalistically inclined denomination is telling. Whereas Finney, Burchard, and Nash were developing new measures among Presbyterians in the northern wilderness, the Methodists—who provided a model for these measures—were continuing to foster and encourage enthusiasm without measurable outside interest. The excitements they engendered were not as notable or controversial for them as for the Calvinist denominations.[51] Eventually, Bangs, more so than Knapp, formalized. Thus after he moved to New York City, he took over the *Methodist Quarterly Review* and turned it into a respectable, elite publication. Furthermore, Bangs, unlike Knapp, did not continue his career as a popular-but-formalized revivalist and, hence, did not achieve popular renown as did Knapp.

It is difficult, however, to gauge the possible influence of Bangs on Jefferson County, and Jefferson County on Bangs. Although correspondence does indicate that he crossed the border into St. Lawrence County in 1818, nothing demonstrates a direct influence, merely great proximity and the possibility for frequent contact.[52]

Jefferson County was unusual in the large number of revivalists who lived there in the 1820s and 1830s. Among them, none achieved fame equivalent to Finney's. But they tell us something about revivalism, Finney, and Jefferson County. All of the revivalists of varying degrees of fame and success combined antiformalism and formalism. Antiformalism on its own among Baptists and Methodists, could not appeal to the larger population; and formalism on its own, did not resemble revivalism at all. Finney's methods did not develop out of a vacuum. These revivalists influenced the early development of his revival methods, certainly as much as he influenced theirs. Moreover, their presence and Finney's suggests an openness to revivalism in the county. Finney and his colleagues slip into the background in much of the following narrative, but their importance does not diminish.

With a few exceptions, the names of these revivalists do not appear in extant church records. Still, what we do know about them confirms what follows. Revivalism (or any antiformalist behavior) before 1830 occurred in the southern and northern sections of the county. The only revivalist to appear in the commercial midsection of the county was the Baptist Knapp, who encouraged revivals among the formalizing Baptists after 1830. Finney had his conversion experience under Gale and Burchard in the southern section of the county, and he began his labors in the northern section of the county. And Nash worked in the northern section. The factors that led and kept these men in revivalism are the social and cultural issues in Jefferson County that now concern us.

Orderliness and Fervor in the Churches

The following section distinguishes between formalist and antiformalist churches and isomporphic formalist and antiformalist secular societies;

and it distinguishes between the levels of formalism and antiformalism among same-denomination churches across regions. In order to accomplish this, this section surveys the chronological formation of the churches within each denomination, and it emphasizes the contrast and interplay among these churches. This serves two purposes. It identifies the characteristics of churches in rural and commercial regions and elite and nonelite regions, in order to clarify the definitions of formalist and antiformalist and in order to use these definitions as standards against which to identify changes that appear after 1830.

Presbyterians

Protestant missionaries began visiting the future Jefferson County in 1802. The Reverend John Taylor of Westfield Massachusetts, a 1784 graduate of Yale, was sent to the western sections of New York State by the Missionary Society of Hampshire County, Massachusetts.[53] Taylor entered New York State near Albany, and began by visiting the Towns of Amsterdam and Johnstown on the Mohawk. He then headed up the Mohawk to Utica. His first encounter with enthusiastic religion was at Floyd, eleven miles north of Utica. He found some Presbyterians among the population, but the majority of the eight hundred residents were Baptists and Methodists, who practiced a form of piety significantly different from Taylor's.

He found no Presbyterian minister in Floyd, and one local member of the Baptist congregation who acted as their minister. The Methodists, meanwhile, were then apparently experiencing a revival, which probably was not an exceptional event:

> The last meeting was on the 4th of July—had their sacrament in the woods—began their meeting on Saturday morning, and continued until Sunday night. There were 6 preachers present. In this meeting 6 persons fell down—in a manner similar with the falling down in Kentucky—and after lying 20 or 30 minutes, rose, crying glory to God. . . .
>
> Conversed with two of the persons who had been struck down. There is a very strong resemblance between the conversion and those which I suppose to be genuine yet there is a great mixture of passion and of something unaccountable.[54]

The Methodist tendency to fall down, which the Presbyterians in Evans Mills and DeKalb disdained, had a long history in the wilderness, and it is likely that after twenty years in the wilderness, Presbyterians in Floyd and Jefferson County were beginning to expect experiences somewhat similar to those of the Methodists. Finney satisfied that expectation in Jefferson County before he did in the vicinity of Utica. Twenty-two years before Finney began his labor, however, Taylor, who had a strict New England upbringing, found the excitements in Floyd and the prominence of Baptists and Methodists in Jefferson County great religious abominations.

In fact, Taylor's description of Jefferson County suggests that Jefferson County would be less prone to act in accord with Taylor's New England expectations than was Floyd. Taylor followed the route of the Black River loosely toward Jefferson County, arriving first just south of the future Jefferson County in Sandy Creek. There he found the Presbyterian Hackly family. Mr. Hackly was once a minister, but in the desolate wilderness he found himself preaching only to his family on the Sabbath. The rest of the community according to Taylor were "in general nothingarians or fatalists—or Methodists and baptists who are the worst of all." Nonetheless, Taylor and Hackly arranged for Taylor to preach to and visit the community.[55]

By 2 September, Taylor was in Town No. 7, or Adams, where he found no church, two or three families of Baptists, and three or four deists, although he preached to approximately forty people:

> The people stand in special need of assistance, and most of them are very thankful for everything which is done for them in a religious way. The people meet every Sabbath, and perform regular exercises, by praying, reading, and preaching. I have seen no people who I think stand in more need of the cultivating hand of the Societies than this, unless it be Camden [north of Utica]. They have no proper books to read upon ye Sabbath, and indeed nothing but a few ordination sermons.[56]

Although the residents were indeed deprived of the sort of civilization to which Taylor was accustomed, and although they did not worship in ways familiar to Taylor, he did find that all of them—including the Baptists—were interested in supporting his work. The denominational divisiveness that he voiced in denouncing the Methodists and the Baptists for their "great mischief" was not apparent among the residents of the wilderness areas, as the Baptists, Methodists, and even "a considerable number of Universalists" were pleased to have him preach for them.[57]

And as a result of this ecumenism, by the time Finney arrived the Presbygationalists in these areas had grown gradually more willing to accept certain diluted practices—such as falling—of the antiformalists. Taylor discovered this in Lowville in the future Lewis County, as he headed back toward the Mohawk; the town had both Baptists and Congregationalists, but, as the Congregationalists had no meeting house or minister, they gladly met with the Baptists. He also noted in the midst of his travels that despite what he considered abominable religious practices, the residents all had Bibles and were not as destitute of religion as the eastern regions believed. Thus, he suggested that no more Bibles be distributed in these areas, as the Baptists were using them to further their own religious views.[58]

Around the time Taylor was exploring the religious condition of the wilderness, the communities he had visited, as well as others in Jefferson County, were beginning to form the first churches in Jefferson County.

The Town of Champion held religious services in 1801, with the aid of a Massachusettsan, Rev. Bascomb, and of the Ladies' Charitable Society of Connecticut. However, the first settled minister in the county, Nathaniel Dutton, did not arrive in Champion until 1807. Dutton, like Taylor, was a missionary from the Hampshire Missionary Society. Dutton was educated in a less strict environment than Taylor's, and thus was apparently less distressed by the social and religious environment in Jefferson County. Dutton grew up in Hartford, Vermont, and graduated from Dartmouth College in 1802. He then taught in Hatfield, Vermont, for a year before spending a year studying for the Congregational ministry with "Dr. Lyman," also of Hatfield, Vermont. In 1804 Dutton was ordained by the Hampshire Missionary Society. He then traveled to northern New York along the same path followed by Taylor. In addition to the towns visited by Taylor, Dutton traveled through most of the settled areas of the county, where, despite Taylor's counsel against doing so, he distributed Bibles and tracts.

But Dutton did not merely travel through northern New York; he was the first settled pastor and the most consistent ministerial presence in Jefferson County until his death in 1854. While other ministers regularly left for more populated areas, Dutton remained in the area and established, in addition to his own church in Champion, a Congregational Church in the village of Carthage, the Presbyterian Church in Gouverneur, and Finney's eventual church in LeRay. At his first religious service in Champion, three or four hundred people attended. Dutton also taught the classics in his home at Champion to future ministerial students, and he resumed work for the Hampshire Missionary Society in 1813–14 by making a second extended tour of the county.[59]

In 1819 Dutton's work in bringing 150 people into the church in Champion was recorded in Joshua Bradley's *Accounts of Religious Revivals in Many Parts of the United States from 1815 to 1818.* Although Henderson, Ellisburg, Lorrane [sic], Denmark,[60] Rodman, Lowvillle, Brownville, Watertown, Rutland, and Adams are also mentioned in the account, which estimates that one thousand people joined churches in Jefferson County in 1815, Bradley refers specifically only to Dutton's church in Champion and Emory Osgood's Baptist church in Henderson.[61] As usual the nucleus of the enthusiasm was around the southern towns in the county, Henderson and Ellisburg.[62]

The Congregational Church in Adams (which later became Finney's Presbyterian Church) first worshiped in 1800 or 1801. With the arrival of the missionary Rev. Woodward in 1802, the first sermon was preached among the residents. And in 1804 Taylor arrived to establish the group officially as a Congregational Church consisting of "4 males & 5 or 6 female members 2 children."[63] Taylor, like his successors until George W. Gale's arrival, did not last long. Preaching at the Congregational Church in Adams, as in many other formalist churches in Jefferson County until the 1820s, was sporadic and inconsistent, frequently not lasting more then a few months. Also, it was not until the arrival of Gale that additions to the church became consistent and heavy.[64]

In 1803, the residents of Watertown and Rutland also formed a Congregational Church (later the First Presbyterian Church of Watertown), which during the nineteenth century acted invariably as a reliably stable force in Jefferson County. Unlike other local churches, even without a resident minister the church kept detailed records of its activities and maintained and developed a significant enrollment.[65] And although their first "stated" minister, Daniel Banks, did not arrive until 1815, he remained until 1821 when "financial embarassment" (apparently not directly related to his salary) finally forced him to vacate his position.[66] Immediately after his departure, the trustees of the Watertown Ecclesiastical Society (the society connected with the church) voted to place the church under the local presbytery, and then hired Rev. George S. Boardman, D.D., who remained with the church until 1834.

Boardman was as well suited for the church in Watertown as Gale was to the church in Adams. While the church in Adams maintained close contact with the local Baptist Church; while Taylor found in Adams Universalists, Presbygationalists, Methodists, and Baptists supporting each other's worship; while the church in Adams shared its building for a few years with the Methodists; and while the church in Adams expected Gale on his first visit in 1817 to approximate closely the preaching of the Baptists and the Methodists, the church in Watertown instead expected Boardman to maintain strict orthodoxy. Gale had not been raised in a strict Presbyterian environment, and he had not even completed his studies at Princeton. And Gale was, as a result, willing to compromise with the desires of the church in Adams.

The First Presbyterian Church in Watertown, on the other hand, developed and maintained more formalization than did any other church in the area. Their session and society records indicate such formality that the church seemed to feel itself reestablishing the standing order of New England by considering itself *the* Watertown Ecclesiastical Society, as if there could be no other.[67] No other church in the area took such a liberty until 1851.[68] Most societies referred to themselves as the society of the church of a certain town, as did for example the First Associated Congregational Society of the Town of LeRay and the First Presbyterian Society of Antwerp. Furthermore, the session of the First Presbyterian Church of Watertown adhered so closely to the rules that the presbytery's examination of the session records, unlike those of the other churches in the county, never mentions improprieties in the recordkeeping.[69] In fact, the most significant trouble the session evidenced with the presbytery was in the case of an excommunication when the presbytery felt that the session (not uncharacteristically) had acted too quickly and too harshly.[70] Rigidity and a concern for making quick and unambiguous judgments typify formalist churches, and accord with an isomorphic understanding of religion which sees a rule- and achievement-oriented congregation in the commercial center of the county enforcing behavioral standards. In contrast to this, the session of the First Presbyterian Church of Adams frequently dragged out its disciplinary proceedings for months, and then made its final decision only after consultation with the presbytery.[71] As a Presbyterian church, Gale's church in Adams was formalist, but as a church in a rural town it allowed for antiformalism. It was not as quick in making decisions, nor did it see issues as unambiguously as did First Presbyterian in Watertown.

For example, the case of Mrs. Elizabeth Rosa, begun under Gale's successor, John Sessions, endured for almost three years, while the session waited to see whether she would be worthy to return to the church. It is unlikely that Boardman's church would have progressed as slowly. Mrs. Rosa first appears in the Adams church records during the tenure of Gale on 6 January 1824 as the plaintiff against Mrs. Sylvia Morton a member of the Adams branch of the Female Missionary Society of the Western District. Mrs. Rosa accused Mrs. Morton of falsely asserting that Mrs. Rosa's baby was not Mr. Rosa's but Mr. Chittenden's. The church ultimately found against Mrs. Morton, and disciplined her lightly with a public admonishing on 9 January 1824.

The possible truth of Mrs. Morton's statements became evident in 1825 when Mrs. Rosa confessed before the church that she had engaged with Mr. Benajah Phelps in a "species of intercourse, which, under existing circumstances is highly improper & disreputable, [and] calculated to dishonor the cause of religion." She had received Mr. Phelps in her home when her husband was not there and she had exchanged letters with him, but she insisted that she and Mr. Phelps had never engaged in any "criminal" activities. The church was pleased with her willingness to confess, though it believed that since she had acted dishonorably for so long that it would have to suspend her nonetheless.[72] Mrs. Rosa demonstrated that this decision distressed her greatly, and she endeavored to have her case reconsidered for three years before the church, without finding that Mrs. Rosa had continued in illicit relationships, decided to excommunicate her.[73] Boardman's tendencies in disciplinary proceedings in the Watertown church indicate that he would have excommunicated her far sooner, despite her confessions.

In contrast to Gale, Boardman, who was placed in charge of Finney's education along with Gale, and who was a classmate of Charles Hodge, did graduate from Princeton Theological Seminary.[74] And although P.H. Fowler credits Boardman with beginning a revival in 1821 in Watertown (at approximately the same time as the revival in Adams in which Finney was converted), Boardman was not a revivalist. Boardman's formalist understanding of Presbyterianism pleased the church in Watertown, and would have pleased Hodge, as a revival in Boardman's case meant merely an unusually large number of conversions to the church, rather than an emotional outpouring as an expression of piety. Given Boardman's formality, and despite reports that the revival began in Watertown, the increase in conversions was likely the residual result of Burchard's work in Adams in initiating the revival, or the result of the efforts of the Baptists or of Methodist circuit riders.[75]

Boardman's severity in implementing disciplinary proceedings indicates that he had a strong antipathy to any disorder or commotion whatsoever. Not unjustly, Frederick H. Kimball has referred to Boardman's years at First Presbyterian Church as "An Era of Discipline," as he determined that "the Session appointed committees . . . at almost every meeting for 16 years to investigate the wrongdoing of someone."[76] In the space of that time, the session excommunicated twenty-seven people. A few times Boardman encouraged the session's vigilance to the point that the session even considered cases of members of other churches or other towns. For example, in 1828 the session considered the case of "Mr & Mrs Gates, members of the church in Brownville," who were residing in Watertown and who were known to "live in contention with one another." The session resolved to request that Mr. and Mrs. Gates not "[come] to the Lords Supper on the following Sabbath—and the Moderator was directed to notify the church in Brownville." Another church would have informed the church in Brownville of the problem before acting. On the same day the session made the Gates decision, it also resolved to notify the church in LeRay that "Mr. Nathan Goodale & wife, members of the church in LeRay, have resided in this place for some time & have not connected themselves with this church, although, they have, as it is said, a letter of Dismission from that church."[77] And in 1835 the session appointed a committee "to visit Catharine Smith of Brownville on account of alledged [sic] misconduct & authorised to act as a commission."[78] In 1829, an effort to discuss the conduct of men in the Town of Theresa (which had its own Presbyterian church) proved particularly difficult, because of the great distance.[79]

Additionally, Boardman's stringency resulted in the charge from Archelaus Fuller and Noah W. Ripley, two members of the church, that he "did not preach the gospel—that he did not preach the truth & was afraid to use those passages that sent sinners to hell"; and that "if all Mr Boardman's preaching since he had been in Watertown had been blessed, it could not have been the means of saving one soul."[80] When Fuller went on trial he was not allowed to call any witnesses to prove that Boardman did not preach the gospel so as to send sinners to hell, as the church deemed that such testimony would not have been proper. Fuller thus went without defense testimony. Meanwhile the prosecuting testimony commonly went as follows:

> *Mrs Little* being duly sworn testified that she had heard Mr Fuller say that the Members & Minister of this church were corrupt—I understand him to mean that there were few members who were christians & he doubted whether Mr. Boardman was one. He said he disapproved of his preaching & of the doings of the church—& that Mr. Boardman's preaching would not

> feed him more than to eat an old disch cloth. He said the General Assembly was the great beast mentioned in prophecy, which is to be destroyed.
>
> Questions by Mr. Fuller. Did you not understand me to approve of the Presbyterian church, as the church of God, that it had become corrupt & must be overthrown as was the Jewish Church.
>
> Ans. Sometimes of this church in particular & sometimes of the Presbyterian church in general.[81]

Further testimony, which neither man contested, asserted that they felt that another local minister, Reverend Ingersoll, preached more satisfyingly.[82] The impression is that Fuller and Ripley sought less legalism and more revivalism:

> When asked what he meant when he said that Mr. Boardman did not preach the gospel. He said, he meant, that he did not preach the doctrines of the gospel—such as the doctrine of atonement, of the saints perseverance, election, justification by faith—such doctrines as were calculated to edify christians [sic] & lead them to a correct knowledge of God. That he left out the substance of the gospel & therefore leanness has come among us. He preaches in a strain of morality that we should neglect certain things & perform others—He comes short & holds back those doctrines which are calculated to awaken sinners & edify christians. He supposed Mr. Boardman did this from fear of disaffecting some of the people—Mr F. considered the Minister & church practically corrupt.[83]

As the trial progressed, it came to light that Fuller and Ripley disdained the stringency of the session, and expected that the session would eventually call them up for something.[84] Thus, Fuller and Ripley ultimately concluded that the colorful local Universalist minister, Pitt Morse, was more morally sound than the session, though they did not want to join Morse's church. Instead they organized a meeting to form a separate church not under Boardman. The Second Presbyterian Church was formed in Watertown in 1831,[85] but by then the church had excommunicated Ripley and Fuller. The resolution to suspend Fuller before proceeding to excommunication was particularly censorious:

> It was resolved that Mr. Fuller having perseveringly defended himself even to the attempting to impeach the credibility of a witness [Mrs. Little] &

> then having confessed the whole—has manifested a spirit of vexatious litigation as well of contumacy & that thereby he has rendered himself obnoxious to severe censure.[86]

Ripley was not as outspoken as his colleague:

> The reasons of Mr. Ripley were considered insufficient & his statements [that Boardman did not preach the gospel so as to send sinners to hell] incorrect—It was therefore resolved that Mr Noah Ripley be excommunicated from the church of the Lord Jesus Christ.[87]

Nonetheless, before the excommunication was put into effect on 31 October 1829, the church gave Fuller's family two dollars because it was "afflicted & needy."[88] Ripley and Fuller apparently did not fit into the social niche of the Watertown church that disdained unseemly religious enthusiasm. They were also unlike many other defendants in disciplinary proceedings at the church in Watertown in that they attended their trials and tried to defend themselves; and in that they attempted to challenge their excommunications all the way to the Synod of Utica on the grounds of a "manifest prejudice of the session."[89] The presbytery, however, which had already denied their appeal, concluded that a technicality rendered these appeals procedurally invalid:

> Presbytery are decidedly of the opinion that the admission of these appeals by the Presbytery & their doings thereon are unconstitutional because the appeals were not presented to the session within the constitutional time. The consequence of this is that the appeals of these persons to Synod are unconstitutional & therefore no barrier in the way of infliction of the sentence of excommunication upon them.[90]

When the appeals failed, Ripley and Fuller confessed and were ultimately dismissed from the church.[91]

The level of watchfulness and formality in the Watertown church went unmatched in other churches, and explains Daniel Nash's 1830 report to Finney regarding a local man:

> During the 14 weeks that I have been here, I have not seen Ballard of Brownville; but I hear that he has become worldly, & carnal, is Boardmanized, & rails against me, tho' I have not seen him for more than 3 years.

> I have been told that his wife has become gay and fond of dress—wears false curles, & does not know whether she should be glad to see Finney or not.[92]

Boardman would have disapproved strongly of any worldliness or carnality, but Boardman among the wealthy in Watertown, and Ballard in the second most significant commercial center in the county were more susceptible to the interests of the wealthier classes who sought isomorphic respectability in their churches. Boardman as a minister and Ballard as a local churchgoer depict the relation between a church's religiosity and its ministers' actions. Just as it would be impossible for Finney to have succeeded in LeRay and Antwerp if the residents entirely opposed him, it would have been impossible for Boardman to have succeeded if his congregation opposed him.

Neither Finney in LeRay nor Burchard in Ellisburg prosecuted any disciplinary proceedings.[93] They both, however, did provide an outlet for the latent fervor in those towns, while Boardman provided an outlet for the legalism in Watertown. Ballard's "Boardmanization" in Brownville is notable, because the church in Brownville was not as openly legalistic as was the church in Watertown.

Boardman's church evidenced no interest in the excitements of 1824 and 1825 that appeared in the northern towns of Jefferson County and the southern towns of St. Lawrence County. However, Finney did appear in Brownville in 1824. Essentially, Finney destroyed the Brownville church, as the "influential citizens," including Jedediah Burchard's merchant brother, Peleg, left the Presbyterian Church in opposition to Finney's enthusiasm and then formed St. Paul's Episcopal Church, also in Brownville. And since these defectors owned the bulk of the stock in the Presbyterian Church, the church was reconsecrated as an Episcopalian Church.[94] The Presbyterian church in Brownville, which did not form until 1818, did not demonstrate the stability of the Watertown church, and lost its long-time pastor, Noah Wells, in 1825, soon after the Finney inspired dispute over the appropriateness of enthusiastic preaching.[95] As the Finney-followers remained in Brownville, Burchard successfully replaced Wells, although in 1826 Boardman "acted as Moderator of [the] Session and administered the Sacraments," for ten months.[96] Areas with commercial economies, such as Watertown, were less interested in revivals than were rural areas. Thus, Brownville, with a semicommercial economy as well as a farming economy, was a central point between the legalism and formality of Watertown and the openness to enthusiasm in areas such as Henderson, Adams, and

LeRay. Brownville's church had a substantial though uninfluential number who accepted Finney's enthusiastic means, as well as an influential, commercially successful group who opposed Finney's apparently unseemly techniques.

The next in formation among the Presbygational churches were in Rodman and Rutland. In both cases, the ministers from Watertown promoted the creation of these churches. The Rodman church was formed in 1805 under Rev. Lazelle of Watertown and then supplied by Rev. David Spear, who like Dutton was from Vermont and remained with the church faithfully.[97] The Rutland church was an outgrowth of the Watertown church, as the Watertown church was originally based in Rutland. After the Watertown church moved away from Rutland, a separate church was also formed in Rutland. Daniel Banks was concurrently installed as the pastor of the Rutland and Watertown churches in 1815. The Rutland church—which, aside from a short visit from Finney, never exhibited remarkable fervor—did exhibit some of the same stringent legalism as the Watertown church, as it denounced the choice of the unmarried Amos Mallory as a deacon in 1815. Church law required that deacons marry.

No other Presbygational churches were formed again until 1814, when the residents of LeRay formed a Congregational Church. They did not have a steady minister until Finney's arrival ten years later.[98] And aside from the Sackets Harbor Presbyterian Church and a second Congregational Church in Adams, which were organized in 1816, the remaining Presbygational churches in the county were created as Presbyterian churches in the 1820s and 1830s in the northern sections of the county. Although these areas were not settled twenty to thirty years later than the southern towns, their churches were formed twenty to thirty years later, and their settled ministers arrived even later. The few ministers who did work in the northern regions before the arrival of a settled ministry were missionaries for the Female Missionary Society of the Western District, whose branches in the southern section of Jefferson County helped support the missionaries' work.

Gale did first supply the church in Adams under the auspices of the Female Western Missionary Society, but the church in Adams soon supported him financially. The Presbyterian church in Watertown, as well as the churches in Rodman and Rutland, supported their ministers on their own—though occasionally with difficulty. As I indicate later in this chapter and as Finney contended in his reference to the "spurious" revivals of the Methodists in LeRay, the northern sections of the county embraced

Methodist enthusiasm more thoroughly than did the other regions. This is likely to be partially a result of the lack of a town structure that would encourage the development of nonstructured religious quasi-institutions.

Church records indicate moreover that only nonelite churches in nonelite-dominated regions would experience revivalism. Boardman's overly formalized church in the center of commercial and political power did not participate in the fervor. However, Boardman's church and most other local churches did frequently have an increase in accessions immediately after the arrival of a settled minister: Champion did so apparently only in 1815 after Dutton finally settled permanently after a few years of itinerant preaching in the county; Adams did in 1821 when Finney converted; Watertown saw a sudden increase in accessions after Banks's replacement by the stern Boardman in 1821; and Evans Mills and Antwerp did so after Finney's arrival in 1824.[99] Thus a sudden increase in accessions does not necessarily indicate the continued and consistent presence of fervor. Although in the case of the churches Finney visited, and in many other cases, especially after 1830 when churches were firmly established, large accessions did frequently coincide with fervor.

Sackets Harbor presents the exception to this model, as it did not have a revival after the creation of the church and the arrival in 1816 of Reverend Samuel F. Snowden of the Female Missionary Society of the Western District. Two reasons make Sackets different in this respect. The first and most obvious reason is its distinctiveness as a military town and a stringently run investment of some unseen New Yorkers. Although some of the local soldiers became the "praying regiment," the presence of the military necessarily prevented stability. George W. Gale indicated the second reason for a lack of fervor in Sackets Harbor:

> Mr. Samuel Snowden, of Sacketts Harbor, had an air about him that rendered him unpopular. It was the buckram preciseness and aristocratic air of the city where he had been reared—Philadelphia. The fault was more in the man than in the place. But he was companionable and agreeable to those with whom he associated.[100]

Fowler notes that Snowden graduated first in his class at Princeton Theological Seminary and that he was even the first settled pastor in Princeton, New Jersey. Additionally, Fowler remarks that Snowden's "great elegance of person and manners were his introduction to circles of refinement."[101] These appraisals of Snowden are corroborated by Snowden's reports to the

Female Missionary Society in 1824 and 1825. After eight years in Jefferson County, Snowden accepted a commission from the Female Missionary Society to visit the destitute regions of the county. This meant visiting, in particular, Henderson, Ellisburg and Cape Vincent. Snowden devoted most of his time to Henderson and Ellisburg, and is possibly the only minister ever to enter either of those towns without causing the populations to erupt in enthusiasm. Snowden indicated in 1823 that Henderson was more prone to error than was Cape Vincent, especially as Henderson had no Presbyterian or Baptist minister when he visited. Furthermore, since the Presbyterians of Cape Vincent were expecting Vincent LeRay to build a meeting house soon, and since the citizens of Cape Vincent were not as disorderly as those of Henderson, Snowden did not devote as much effort to Cape Vincent as to Henderson.

Although Snowden demonstrated a greater liberality than had John Taylor in 1802 in hoping that Henderson would have at least a Baptist minister to evangelize, Snowden, as Boardman would also have, misread the instability in Henderson and the pleadings for preaching in Henderson as signs of infidelity. On the other hand, because Vincent LeRay was building a church in Cape Vincent, Snowden considered it less needy. Meanwhile the residents of Cape Vincent complained to Snowden that missionaries ignored them.[102] Cape Vincent never received the support it was seeking, but Evans Mills, also a LeRay-controlled region, would receive Finney as a settled minister in 1824 and then would explode with enthusiasm.

Snowden remarked that Henderson was "much distracted with sectaries, and exposed to alarming and fatal errors. It is distressing to learn with what readiness many imbibe them, when left without the constant and vigilant care, of the able and faithful pastor."[103] Cape Vincent, lacking ministerial support more than was Henderson, did not exhibit such bedlam. In Snowden's next report to the society (which differed from his others only in his failure to visit Cape Vincent at all), his description of Henderson as "surrounded by enemies, whom error and prejudice have armed in the service of the adversary,"[104] and the fact that within two years of his first visit Henderson had a Congregational church in addition to its Presbyterian church, a new Baptist society, a Universalist church, and a Swedenborgian society[105] is indicative of Henderson's proximity to the state, which Whitney Cross identified as ultraism and with which I concur:

> The stage of religious emotionalism immediately preceding heterodoxy was that which contemporaries called ultraism. An amorphous thing in an intellectual sense, it can scarcely be considered a system of belief. It is better described as a combination of activities, personalities, and attitudes creating a condition of society which could foster experimental doctrines.[106]

Henderson's marginal, nonelite population put Henderson in a prime position to erupt in emotionalism whenever a minister open to enthusiasm arrived, and its antiformalist tendency away from moral and doctrinal stringency allowed it to accept heterodox movements such as Universalism and Swedenborgianism. (Similar circumstances led Henderson's neighbor, Adams, to organize a Seventh Day Baptist Church in 1822.)[107] Snowden viewed all of this as an indication of irreligion surrounding Henderson and its neighbors.

From the first report of the Female Missionary Society of the Western District to the ninth, assessments of the religious condition of Henderson, Ellisburg, and Adams are constant. Generally, missionaries were concerned that the areas were disorderly and thus possibly immoral. However, few express as great a concern as does Snowden, which is likely the reason for Snowden's failure to foment a revival. Moreover, no other region of Jefferson County received as much attention from missionaries as did this area. Ellisburg and Henderson (as well as Adams, which Snowden did not visit) had definite town structures, which provided the missionaries with a base from which to evangelize a region. Constant evangelization in the hundreds of lots in the northern towns (before the mid-1820s, when Finney arrived) would have proved far more difficult for the orderly Presbyterian ministers. Missionaries did appear in the northern regions, but with less frequency.

Ellisburg, Adams, and Henderson appear in the first report of the society in 1817. Reverend David R. Dixon reported that in addition to forming the Congregational Church of Ellisburg he encouraged the formation of branches of the society in all three towns. He also noted that Henderson would be a worthwhile site for a stationed missionary, who might from there extend his labors to the other local towns.[108] Thus, in 1818, Gale was stationed in Henderson. Once again a relation between a missionary's apprehension of immorality and the tendency toward revivalism prevailed:

> Ellisburgh, although a large and populous town, and one which has been settled as long as any in this part of this country, has never had the gospel regularly established in any part of it. All the unhappy consequences which usually result from a want of regular preaching of the gospel are here to be found. There are some professors of different denominations, who have refused to connect themselves with any church. There are a few who lament the state of things, and who use all their influence to effect a reformation. This is properly missionary ground. At Wood's Settlement [a village in the Town of Ellisburg] there were very favorable indications of a revival of religion. Meetings were uniformly full, and a number appeared unusually serious.[109]

Although Gale proved himself receptive and adaptable to some antiformalist beliefs and practices, he still expressed a formalist perspective. Surprisingly, Gale asserted that he "was denied the pleasure of communicating intelligence of extensive revivals," even though one hundred people joined the Congregational Church in Henderson in 1817.[110]

These towns, the sites of the earliest branches of the society in Jefferson County, continued to receive inordinate missionary support as Amzi Benedict related in his report, the only one to appear in the third report (1819). Like Gale, he visited families and schools, and he preached extensively. Additionally, he organized Sabbath schools in Henderson and Ellisburg, tract societies in Ellisburg and Little Sandy Creek, and a "society of youth for the study of scriptures," in Henderson. Nonetheless, despite the interest evinced by the population in his work and the fact that a notable revival had taken place there, he too found that "the morals of the people have suffered greatly for a want of religious instruction."[111] Benedict also visited Cape Vincent, Brownville, and Penet's Square and reported more extensively on the natural beauty of these areas than on the religious condition.[112] He closed his report with a postscript: "I would add likewise, that I know of no place where more good might *continually* be expected from missionary labor, than Ellisburgh."[113]

Although reports continued from Henderson, Ellisburg, and Adams in the next few years until Snowden's arrival, the missionaries noted little change except occasionally to remark, for example, that Henderson and Ellisburg had "seasons of refreshing," and "would form an interesting station for a missionary,"[114] or to remark, as Rev. Oliver Ayer did that

> while travelling over the various parts of this widely extended region, in a moral point of view, it appeared to be the region and shadow of death.

> Where Churches had been formed, religion was in a languid state, and the Sabbath almost totally disregarded; children and youth were growing up ignorant of God and the Saviour, imitating the vicious examples of their ungodly parents; and profaneness, intemperance and a black train of other immoralities greatly abounded. In my visitation among the people, and public discourses to them, on the Sabbath, and other days of the week, I made it an object to develope [sic] the deplorableness of their condition, and to point to them the wretched consequences, which would be the unavoidable result of their practices, in the great day of retribution.[115]

After visiting Cape Vincent, however, Ayer remarked that the condition of the citizens there was exceptional, even though "no religious society nor church is yet organized."[116] And when he described religious "excitement" in his report from the northern section of the county in 1821, he indicated that he "baptized two adults and seven children,"[117] a number that would not have impressed the Baptists as excitement.

As a formalist denomination, Presbyterianism in the 1820s and earlier was not prone to religious enthusiasm. "Seasons of refreshing" generally, and especially in the cases of Watertown and Sackets Harbor, referred to a high point on the bell curve denoting admissions to a church. Some years had large numbers of admissions, some low; the high years were considered revivals. Furthermore, cases in P. H. Fowler's history of Presbyterianism, in which he stresses revivals in Watertown and Sackets while entirely ignoring revivals in Henderson, indicate that the "orthodox and orderly" clergy of the Synod of Utica[118] disdained the excitements that frequently led to enormous increases in congregational populations.

Although indications from the missionary reports of the Female Missionary Society are that Henderson experienced fervent outpourings, the lack of an established ministry[119] in the region prevented it from receiving credit for its distinctiveness in the records of the Presbytery of Watertown.[120] Moreover, the heterodoxy and disorder in these towns led ministers from other areas to believe that Henderson, Ellisburg, and Adams must have been immoral.

George Boardman's term at the First Presbyterian Church and Samuel Snowden's experiences in Ellisburg and Henderson indicate that the maintenance of "orthodoxy and order" and moral stringency were opposed to religious enthusiasm. Although religious enthusiasts were not necessarily immoral, the structured and formalist way of life necessary to maintain moral stringency prevented spirited outpourings.

These circumstances suggest the reasons behind the common use of the term "burnt district" as an indication of opposition to revivalism stemming from the belief that moral desolation followed an enthusiastic revival. Opponents of fervor—generally Presbyterians with a strong sense of a need for moral probity—saw that Finney, Burchard, and Nash, as well as the Methodists against whom the term "burnt district" was most often used, did not encourage moral rigor but, rather, an experience of grace. Old School opponents of Burchard, such as James Hotchkin, complained that Burchard strived to have people submit to a conversion experience whether they were actually penitent or not, and that Burchard and his counterparts were not interested "to sit down with a church through all the vicissitudes which might occur in a period of time."[121] Church records demonstrate that, typically, "vicissitudes" meant problems with the maintenance of morality within the church community. In fact, Hotchkin closes his chapter on the "Character of Modern Revivalism" by indicating that the antiformalist genre of revivalism was leading to exactly this problem:

> In conclusion, on this particular subject, there can be no reasonable doubt, that there have been of late years, in the Presbyterian churches of Western New York, most glorious outpourings of the Holy Spirit, by which the kingdom of the Redeemer has been greatly enlarged. At the same time, it must be acknowledged that there, as well as in other parts of the moral vineyard, many circumstances have occurred, which have given pain to the heart of the enlightened Christian, marred the good work, and hindered the salvation of precious souls. The revivals in many places have been of a less pure character than those of preceding years, and many professed converts have been introduced into the churches who give no evidence of piety, some of whom have long since been cut off by the process of discipline, and others hang upon the church a dead weight, crippling its energies, marring its beauty, and affording an occasion for the enemies of the Lord to blaspheme.[122]

The phenomenon of enthusiastic revivals incited by itinerant evangelists was depicted most sensationally and fearfully in Presbyterianism because enthusiasm differed so significantly from orderly and orthodox ways.

Baptists

When John Taylor traveled through Jefferson County in 1802, he remarked that no Presbygational churches yet existed, although in Sandy Creek, as in many areas in the southern section of Jefferson County, "The people are baptists, and are a most wretched people—the filth of the world."[123] Accordingly, because Baptists made up the bulk of the population, and because of the simplicity of forming a Baptist church by calling a Baptist minister out of the congregation, the Baptists easily established the earliest churches in southern Jefferson County. Like Taylor, the earliest Baptist missionaries, Peter P. Root and Stephen Parsons, came through Jefferson County in 1802; and the first Baptist Church—where Finney later heard the "ignorant" Emory Osgood preach—was also formed in 1802 at the house of David Grommons in the village of Smithville, Town of Adams.[124] Not surprisingly, Henderson, Lorraine, and Ellisburg followed with churches in 1806 and 1807; in 1809 a church in the Town of Watertown was organized, and in 1811 Rutland also formed a Baptist church.[125] None of these ministers achieved even the local renown of the Presbyterian ministers, and none of them enforced the stringent moral standards advocated by the most orderly and orthodox of their Presbyterian neighbors.

Generally, because of Baptist concern with maintaining the covenant among church members, and because of their strong disapproval of taking one another to civil court, cases of discipline involved personal disputes and failures to keep the sabbath holy.[126] At the church in Rutland the earliest case of discipline involved a charge

> that Br James Murr[e]y had said many and [illeg] obvious words against Br Johson [the pastor] to Br Joseph Mal[t]by in Br Lothrop's Mill when people were coming into the Mill and appeared to say it without reason and also in Br Lothrop's House before his family and representing that Br Johnson was seeking for a salary.

The church decided that "Br James Murrey was rong [sic] in talking to Br Joseph Mal[t]by as he did as it was calculated to injure Elder Johnsons Character and his influence and union in the Chh."[127] Murrey confessed rapidly, and the issue was then forgotten. On the whole, the charge that Murrey spoke against his minister was handled with much less reproach than was the charge against Ripley and Fuller in the Presbyterian church in Watertown.

On the other hand, Baptist records do frequently fail to mention any charge, and when they do mention the charge they assert only that the charged failed to "walk" or "travel" with the church. Many of these cases were probably problems with intemperance or sabbath breaking, which were frequently resolved. Proceedings of trials (as in the case of all their meetings) are not carefully or fully recorded. Moreover, few proceedings ever endured for as long as the Presbyterian disciplinary proceedings; Baptist proceedings were normally begun and finished on the same day, as in the case of James Murrey. Unlike the Presbyterians, who placed all disciplinary proceedings and church decisions in the hands of the session, the entire Baptist congregation participated in meetings. In cases of discipline the church usually sent women to speak with other women.

One of the few extended Baptists trials that I have seen took place at the First Baptist Church of Marion in Ontario County. Two women in the church both claimed ownership of a "fine" shawl and both claimed that the "coarse" shawl belonged to the other. The difficulty was first heard in the church on 2 September 1826. By 17 February 1827, the problem was known as "the Shawl controversy." On 2 August 1827 the church called a conference with the church of Palmyra and the Second Church of Phelps to make a decision in the case. The church decided in favor of Sister X, who on 16 August 1828 brought charges against Sister Y for claiming that Sister X and the entire church had wronged her and cheated her out of her property. On 15 November 1828, the records report that the two had finally on their own settled their differences "amicably." Although the duration of the difficulty is unusual, the nature of the problem, a personal dispute, is common.[128]

The only case resembling this one occurred at the First Presbyterian Church of Watertown and involved Mr John Gotham who "dishonestly obtained possession of a certain piece of land" for less than its value, who held "the belief of salvation of all men," and who denied "the essential divinity of all men." The trial proceedings lasted from 1 June 1825 to 5 July when the session found Gotham guilty of the latter two charges. However, the session found that there was insufficient evidence to convict him of the charge of buying land for less than its worth. The session was clearly more interested in the charges regarding his moral character than with the personal dispute. Furthermore, although the trial was concluded in one month at the Watertown Presbyterian church, as opposed to three years at the Baptist church in Marion, the session spent far more time in initial deliberations than did the church in Marion.[129]

The records of the Black River Baptist Association indicate that the churches were concerned with using discipline when necessary and in living correctly. But their description of living correctly differs from the Presbyterian concern with strict moral rectitude; where Presbyterians stress not doing the wrong thing, the Baptists stress doing the right thing. Fowler, for example, describes the synod's performance as follows:

> Irregularities occurred and errors sprung up about it [the synod] that were not chargeable upon it, and in the excitement of the hour, individuals and communities identified with it from time to time, were carried away into abnormal movements and acts; but as a whole, its constituency has preserved a remarkable propriety of deportment and correctness of doctrine. The fact, in general, is demonstrated by what has already been related—the instruction and training it so diligently gave; the carefulness with which it organized its churches, and the cautiousness with which it received them, and the faithfulness with which it warned and reproved and directed them; and its constant effort for stability in the pastoral office. Still more clearly does it appear in specific actions on current extravagancies and heresies.[130]

Fowler demonstrates the overriding Presbyterian concern in correcting wrong action in his final sentence; for even though the synod had on the whole acted with order and orthodoxy, "still more clearly" had it shown its condemnation of wrongdoing in the actions it had taken against "extravagancies and heresies." No description of this nature appears in Baptist histories or minutes. The history of the Black River Baptist Association is a litany of revivals. Whereas Fowler includes in his history the statements that "Ministers were brought to account with even more stringency than communicants," and then describes the censure of every minister in the synod, the Baptists choose in their own history to discuss the periods of greatest accessions to their churches.

In Baptist discussions of discipline, stress is placed more strenuously on prayer and the avoidance of the violation of the sabbath. Actually, the urgings for prayer in the Circular Letter sermons of the annual meetings read much like Daniel Nash's discourses on prayer.[131] Although in 1826 the association did take up the problem of discipline, the "Circular Letter" of that year urges the administration of discipline when necessary (but refuses to define when that is, as the letter says these cases are sufficiently clear in the New Testament) and deplores the practice of ignoring a wrongdoer's actions from the belief that everyone is fallible. But the letter is also careful to explain how to avoid excessive discipline.

> Another evil against which we would have you carefully guard is an unwarrantable and restless spirit to make much of every little offence, and convert

> every indiscretion into a case of discipline. . . . Such spirits can discover wrong in every action, find cause of condemnation in every word, and have a peculiar faculty to magnify every trifle into a most heinous crime. . . . Against such we feel it our duty to warn you; and to caution you against indulging such a spirit in your bosoms. It is a deadly viper which seeks your ruin, and which if cherished will inevitably destroy you.[132]

It is unlikely that this passage was directed against a clearly defined problem with excessive severity in the churches of the association, as it is an indication of the Baptist concern that discipline when used can be as dangerous as the sin it is meant to correct. Moreover, the figures in the minutes given for exclusions in the individual churches are consistently the lowest of all the figures, aside from deaths. In the years surrounding the publication of this letter in 1826, the largest number of exclusions was twelve out of forty-seven members in the church in New Haven in Oswego County.[133] And the largest number of exclusions from a Jefferson County church is eight out of 140 members in the church in Ellisburg.[134] Most typical is Adams, which in 1826 out of 107 members had three exclusions.[135] Generally, in the years when certain churches have an unusually strong demonstration of discipline, they also have very few admissions to their churches; and when they have many admissions to their churches, they have few exclusions.[136] On the whole, the Black River Baptist Association demonstrated in its first thirty years an interest in the value of "fervor," "zeal," and "fervency" over orderliness and orthodoxy.[137]

Methodists

From all appearances many of these same values also applied to the other antiformalist evangelical denomination, Methodism. Like the Baptists, they were not concerned with maintaining "order and orthodoxy," as they approved of fervor in their camp meetings to the extent that one of their great revivalists, Jesse Lee, asserted that "It has been frequently observed, that there was never any remarkable revival of religion, but some degree of enthusiasm was mingled with it."[138] Nor would the Puritan-descended Presbyterians of northern New York have tolerated the camp meeting philosophy that produced the verses:

> Come hungry, come thirsty, come ragged, come bare,
> Come filthy, come lousy, come just as you are.[139]

Fowler in fact notes that Methodist "crudities" were common in northern and central New York as early as the beginning of the century:

> A special reason for the frequent mention of the orderliness of the revivals here, during the first ten years of the century, and of the Calvinistic type of the preaching, was not so much the 1740 extravagancies in New England, or the Kentucky extravagancies and errors in 1800, as the extravagancies of Methodism then common here, reports of which were likely to give repute abroad to the operation of grace in our own churches. Methodism had not then passed out of its early crudities and excesses, examples of which are noted in the Rev. John Taylor's journal of his missionary tour through this region in 1802. They acted as checks and cautions to Presbyterianism and Congregationalism, and so saved them from the looseness of doctrine and uncouthness of measures to which a new community is liable, and made our early churches and ministers the best of progenitors.[140]

Fowler's desire to refute reports that the northern region fell into "excesses" is clear in this passage. Although early ministers such as Taylor did fend off the "uncouthness" of the Methodists, Finney did not. As I will indicate in the next chapter, the end of the Methodist "extravagancies" came in the 1830s.

Hough indicates that the earliest Methodist circuits ran chiefly through the northern sections of Jefferson County. Although in 1815, the Sandy Creek circuit did run through part of the southern section of the county, in 1818 a circuit was formed around Watertown; in 1821 in Indian River (Town of LeRay); 1826, LeRay and Watertown; 1827, Cape Vincent; 1829, LeRay and Carthage, as well as Brownville and Sackets Harbor, and eventually Adams in the same year.[141] The earliest Methodist churches and societies were also in these areas: Watertown, 1821; LeRay, 1824; Champion, 1825; Adams, 1828; and Brownville, 1829.[142] Methodist churches did not form in Henderson and Ellisburg until 1830 and 1832.[143] Basically, the Methodists did the least well in the southern towns that most closely resembled New England villages. In the northern towns upon which structure slowly trickled down from the top, the Methodists were the most successful as itinerants. They were also successful in Watertown, the most formalized and populous community in the county. Not surprisingly, the Methodists established their first formal church in Watertown.

Unfortunately, however, Methodist records have not been preserved. As antiformalist records, they were never kept as exactly as were Presbyterian records. Thus, an exact count of Methodist converts is impossible, as it was probably never made. *The Methodist Magazine* (later *The Methodist Quarterly Review* edited by Nathan Bangs) regularly carried reports of unusually successful revivals until the formalization of the revivals in the 1830s. However, there were only two reports that appeared regarding revivals in this area. One, in 1818, reported that during the 1815 revivals the "Black River Circuit has been highly favored of the Lord; about three hundred have been added to the societies on that circuit this year."[144] And in 1827 the Reverend Isaac Puffer reported that the circuit had been "generally blessed."[145] Reports in the *Methodist Magazine* are not concerned with improvements in the moral character as a result of successful camp meetings.

The lack of material on the Methodists should not be construed as an indication that the Methodists were not active in Jefferson County, as Finney's references to the Methodists' work in Evans Mills (and in DeKalb in St. Lawrence County) indicate that the Methodists did in fact labor vigorously in the northern sections. However, the Presbygationalists in these areas were seeking in their religious services a little more structure than that found in a camp meeting. Finney provided this when he arrived in Evans Mills as the first settled minister.

Essentially, using the paradigm of the head versus heart or piety versus moralism dichotomy, in the 1820s the Presbyterians were intellectual and moralistic; while the Baptists were less head-oriented and more pietistic.[146] Nonetheless, almost all historical studies of evangelical denominations during the Second Great Awakening have asserted that revivalism fueled the reform impulse.[147] As I will demonstrate, these denominational differences of opinion with regard to discipline carried over into reform movements and indicate in the 1820s an indirect association between revivalism and reform.

Conclusion

Three distinct regions with isomorphic religious and social structures formed in Jefferson County. The first region was comprised of the northern towns, such as LeRay, Cape Vincent, Antwerp, and Theresa, where residents bought land from the holders of immense tracts of land, such as LeRay, Parish, LaFarge, and even Bonaparte, who allowed greater freedom for nonelites. However, the unusual strength of the elites over residents of these areas left the nonelite residents with a poorly structured society. As the map following chapter 2 indicates, in the northern section town structure was secondary to the numerous minute separations of lots. This poorly structured society was not conducive to productive missionary labors or to the firm establishment of churches. Aside from the Catholic Church in Cape Vincent and LeRay's own Catholic Church at his estate, the only noticeable religious presence in the northern towns was Methodist. Until the 1820s, these areas had no settled Presbyterian ministers. Thus, when Finney came through in 1824, the nonelite, non-Methodist, non-Catholic residents, who showed some concern that they not fall into the "crudities" of the Methodists, responded enthusiastically to Finney's urgings that they convert in the manner with which they were most familiar.

The southern towns more closely approximated New England town structure. However, they too had a large number of Vermonters and "Rhode Island haters of religion." And because they did not have the opportunity to achieve prominence at the county level, the southern areas were left with marginal populations. In their efforts to recreate New England towns, they established churches and voluntary associations earlier than the northern regions, but their lack of prominent men to manage the churches and associations made these areas marginal.[148] The constant flow of missionaries noticed that these areas were responsive to their labors, though disorderly and consequently, in their missionaries' views, immoral. Also in the midst of this disorder were the problems caused in the southern section by the opening of the Erie Canal. And as a result of their marginality, Henderson, Ellisburg, and Adams became the chief centers of fervor in the early 1820s, though Adams with the most commercial economy of the southern regions and hence more formal churches was generally less fervid than were Henderson and Ellisburg.[149]

Watertown had the most significant commercial economy and the least fervor. Even the Methodists in Watertown created the first settled Methodist church in the county. Brownville's church, on the other hand, split as a result of Finney's introduction of fervor. Similarly, Brownville's economy was split between the commercial elites and the large number of nonelites. Sackets Harbor and Champion, like Brownville, also had a higher proportion of commercial elites because of the towns' proximity to the Black River. These towns also did not express pronounced fervor, nor did they have occasion to split, since Finney never appeared in Sackets or Champion.

In sum, there were three distinct areas in Jefferson County: the elite-controlled north, with a large population of nonelites; the commercial center in the middle; and the nonelite-dominated south. The south and the north conjoined when Finney traveled to LeRay.

4
The Maturation of the Churches

Around 1830 something happened. Presbyterians suddenly experienced a surge of conversion experiences within their churches throughout New York State in areas with and without professional revivalists. Even George Boardman conducted "conference" meetings. On the other hand, Baptists began to demonstrate more interest in moral order and reform movements within their churches. In terms of Victor Turner's structure/antistructure dichotomy, which assumes that structure will at some time require the infusion of fervor in order to prevent succumbing to deadening rigidity, the structured, formalist Presbyterians allowed for a period of antistructure. However, Turner does not provide for the reverse case; that is, where an antistructural or antiformalist group such as the Baptists experiences bureaucratization. Henri Bergson's distinction between open (antiformalist) and closed (formalist) religions that do experience aspects of each other works best here.

Finney's role at the First Presbyterian Church of LeRay and other Protestant churches in the northern section of the county foreshadowed what happened in the 1830s. In 1824 and 1825 at the church in LeRay where antiformalism and formalism had long mixed, Finney encouraged antiformalist expression among formalists, six years before such expression became commonplace among formalists. His experience with the openness of the church in LeRay provided him with an opportunity to refine his methods of bringing antiformalism to formalist churches so that by 1830 he was one of the leaders in the urban, northern, Second Great Awakening. Finney did not cause or create antiformalization of the formalist churches, but he was one of its most notable proponents. Finney's experience in the northern section of Jefferson County had prepared him to successfully bring antiformalism to eager formalist churches after 1830.

According to David L. Rowe, the presence of antiformalism in the newly settled areas of New York State was inevitable:

> With few preachers on the frontier, with clerical authority far removed, and with emotion in religion high, the door was open for individual initiative, for reliance on the Bible and direct personal revelation rather than on doctrine, and for volunteerism in the calling of churches and pastors rather than formal ordination.[1]

However, as the frontier matured, the antiformalists were bound also to mature or formalize; in Ernst Troeltsch's terms "sects" unavoidably bureaucratized to form "churches."[2] Formalization began in the 1820s and arrived in the 1830s. But as Rowe is more concerned with the Millerite backlash against formalization than with the "dynamic" association between formalists and antiformalists (which he nonetheless considers essential to "pietism"), he does not discuss the infusion of antiformalism into formalist denominations that also occurred in the 1830s.

Rowe does indicate that by the 1830s, when the antiformalists were losing the element of strain that fed their antiformalism, the Baptists were beginning to encourage their ministers to receive educations. Moreover, they were also ordaining ministers rather than licensing them, so that whereas previously all ministers were licensed rather than ordained, by 1836 81 percent of Baptist clergy were ordained while 19 percent were licensed. This also meant, as he notes, that the clerical life had become a profession instead of a sideline.[3]

The churches' bureaucratization struck many diehard antiformalists as devotion to materialism, as did the increased interest in benevolent movements, chiefly missionary work and eventually, in many Baptist churches, antimasonry. In the meantime, revivals were no longer considered surprising manifestations of God's grace; they were expected and regular occurrences. Furthermore, the Baptists became more concerned with disciplining moral and doctrinal offences. However, aside from Millerites and Antimission Baptists who opposed the transformation, most Baptists viewed the changes as signs of progress.[4]

Among the Methodists similar formalization developed. Revivals became for them expected occurrences, while their ministers also began to receive educations and circuit riding was replaced by the formation of churches. All that remained of the early antiformalism were books giving instructions for the replication of camp meetings.[5] And in 1830, when during the era of formalization the *Methodist Magazine* became the *Methodist Quarterly Review,* reports of revivals gradually disappeared altogether while essays on benevolence became more common. Nathan Bangs, the enormously successful minister on the Canadian side of the St. Lawrence River, who had himself been formalized (or made urbane), became the editor of the magazine and formalized its content as well. Nathan Hatch notes that Bangs's formalization and his interest in making Methodism respectable represent the overturning of the original values of the church, a disavowal of Francis Asbury's concerns and essentially a form of secularization.[6] The Methodist Protestant Church was the response against this adaptation to the larger culture.

The formalization of the Baptists and the Methodists, as both Rowe and Hatch demonstrate, was less the result of market forces and urbanization than of a collective movement within "revivalistic Protestantism" from youth to adulthood.

Finney and Jefferson County

Hatch notes that antiformalization, which he refers to as the "quest for respectability," occurred when the revivalistic groups moved from "alienation to influence."[7] As they formalized, their methods and beliefs became more acceptable to the formalists who then adopted some of them. On a microcosmic level, and at the earliest point, this transformation is apparent in Finney, whom Hatch refers to as a "transitional figure";[8] and although I do not view Finney as the creator of the New Measures, I do view him as an example of early antiformalization. As the Presbyterian bearer of enthusiasm from southern Jefferson County to the northern towns of Jefferson County, Finney represents spatially the bridge connecting formalist Presbyterian orderliness and orthodoxy with antiformalist Baptist and Methodist enthusiasm. Thus, Finney's effect on Jefferson County was to help to begin there the process of antiformalization, or to allow antiformalization to blossom in Jefferson County. It probably would have gone forward had Finney not appeared on the scene, but Finney certainly aided it in its development, as much as Jefferson County's early antiformalization aided in his development.

Finney did not force this process on the Presbyterians of the northern part of the county. Jefferson County had created Finney, just as much as Finney had created antiformalization there. For while the Presbyterians in the northern sections understood intellectually that Presbyterian orthodoxy required certain formalist practices, after years of separation from formalist controls, they were prepared to accept an approximation of enthusiasm.

In the meantime, the already noticeably antiformalized southern section set an example for the northern section and for Finney. When Finney was growing up in Jefferson County in Henderson, and when he heard Emory Osgood's Baptist preaching, he became accustomed to emotion in preaching rather than to intellectualism and moralism.[9] And he became accustomed there to constant heavy admissions to the church, as well as to the Baptists and Congregationalists' sharing preaching, since he notes that the denominations in Henderson met together once a month.[10] The unusual strength of fervor among formalists in Henderson is especially apparent in Finney's description of the Congregationalist Deacon Montague of the Congregationalist/Baptist Church in Henderson in 1821 immediately after Finney's conversion:

> He read a passage of scripture according to their custom. They then sung a hymn, and Deacon Montague stood up behind his chair and led off in prayer. The other persons present, all of them professors of religion and younger people, knelt down around the room. My brother said that Deacon Montague began as usual in his prayer, in a low, feeble voice; but soon began to wax warm and to raise his voice, which became tremulous with emotion. He proceeded to pray with more and more earnestness, till soon he began to rise up on his toes and come down upon his heels more emphatically. And as the Spirit of prayer led him onward, he began to raise his chair together with his heels, and bring that down upon the floor; and soon he raised it a little higher, and brought it down with still more emphasis. He continued to do this, and grew more and more engaged till he would bring the chair down as if he would break it to pieces. In the meantime the brethren and sisters that were on their knees, began to groan, and sigh and weep and confess, and all melt before the Lord. From this meeting the work of the Lord spread forth in every direction all over the town. And thus it spread at that time from Adams as a center, throughout nearly all the towns in the county.[11]

Because of this and other experiences in Henderson while growing up, when Finney was living in Connecticut and attending school he was more likely than others also listening to the staid minister Peter Starr to be distressed by Starr's complete failure to move his hearers.[12]

Finney's decision to settle in Adams was providential. Adams was among the southern towns that consistently demonstrated enthusiasm, but unlike the other churches in the southern region it maintained by 1821 a stable Presbyterian church. As a lawyer, Finney probably would not have been drawn to convert to an antiformalist Baptist church, but because of the force of early Baptist influence, Finney would not have been drawn to convert to either Boardman's or Snowden's churches either.

Hence, when Finney returned to Adams and heard Gale's preaching he was probably not distressed by Gale's apparent orthodox formalism, since Gale remarks in his autobiography that he had made some adjustments to the unorthodox demands of the residents of Henderson in 1817. But Finney was disappointed by the failure of Gale's church's prayer group to achieve its goals, and he surmised that the members of the group were not sincere in their prayers. His concern regarding their failure to have their prayers answered led him to begin considering the place of religion in his life and the correct methods involved in having one's prayers answered.[13]

Finney's hearing Jedediah Burchard's preaching within a month of his conversion was probably for Finney reassurance that his ideal minister did exist in the church with which he was associated in his adulthood. Burchard's exhortations in prayer came much closer to Osgood's fervency than Gale's preaching could have, and probably reminded Finney of Osgood's effective methods. When he converted and became a minister, he emulated the fervor he had seen in Emory Osgood, and he expected the congregations to which he preached to react as he had seen the Henderson Baptist congregation respond to Osgood. Finney also emulated the Baptist preacher in not going to seminary and in believing that a seminary education could have harmed his ability to preach effectively.[14] Moreover, although Finney has long been identified as the reification of the connection between revivalism and reform, Finney himself was never very interestd in reform.[15] Furthermore, the reforms with which he most closely identified himself were the reforms that appealed most to the antiformalists, such as abolition. (Although the truth is that Finney was indeed antiformalist in his general lack of interest in reform and in his lukewarm interest even in his greatest reform interest, abolitionism.) Finney, therefore, is the reification of antiformalism.

His methods and his successes were remarkable only because they had been imported to a formalist denomination. None of the other ministers in the Presbyterian church with him could have accomplished the transfer to the northern towns of the county as well as he did. Boardman, Snowden, and Gale had been educated at Princeton and understood correct religious practice differently than did Finney. However, neither Burchard, Myrick, nor Nash was as well educated as he, and consequently were incapable of bringing antiformalism to the formalist denominations as early as the mid-1820s. Thus only Finney could appear to maintain Presbyterian orthodoxy while also conveying to frontier residents in the northern sections of the county on the edge of stability the correct measure of orderliness and Arminianism.

Jefferson County and Finney had a symbiotic relationship. Jefferson County's diversity and paradoxes provided a stimulating environment for Finney's development; and in return Finney, and to some extent the other revivalists, reinforced the antiformalization begun in Jefferson County in the early 1820s. Reports from outside Jefferson County of Finney's early revivals in Jefferson County as raucous events reflect the formalist concern that antiformalist methods were infecting Presbyterianism. However, the Methodist-wary LeRay residents, who at first questioned Finney's methods, soon realized and appreciated the distinction, subtle though it was.

Antiformalization in the Presbyterian Churches of Jefferson County after 1830

After 1830, Finney's kindling of antiformalization became apparent in all the churches in Jefferson County, including Samuel Snowden's church in Sackets Harbor and George Boardman's church in Watertown. Moreover, formalist churches outside of Jefferson County also began to show significant signs of antiformalization begun by Finney and the "New Measures Men," as well as by years of contact with antiformalist denominations. P. H. Fowler, for example, contends that from 1829 to 1839 revivals appeared in the Synod of Utica more constantly, consistently, and widely than in the previous ten years.[16] And James Hotchkin notes that "it was in the year 1831, that the most extraordinary displays of the power and grace of God, in reviving his work and converting souls in western New York, were exhibited."[17] He notes that in this year evening prayer meetings of three or four days, known as "protracted meetings," in which "a spirit of fervent prayer, deep humiliation, and active effort in the churches, and a course of devoted, persevering, and judicious labors on the part of the ministry, uniformly preceded the displays of pardoning mercy."[18] Nonetheless, what particularly pleased Hotchkin was that as a result of the revival the moral character of the citizens of western New York also improved.

In 1831 the lawyers and merchants of the Third Presbyterian Church in Rochester requested that Finney begin a revival there. The only difference between Third Presbyterian in Rochester that year and most other churches was that Third Presbyterian deemed it necessary to bring in outside help to foment the enthusiasm, for revivals throughout western, central, and northern New York were rife in 1831.[19] Had the members of Third Presbyterian not been influenced by the antiformalists they would never have been willing to bring in Finney, yet, as Paul Johnson has noted, the Third Presbyterian congregation still maintained its formalist interest in moralism.[20] Meanwhile, the Presbytery of Watertown reported the highest accession figures in the synod in 1831: "from two to three thousand additions" to its churches as a response to protracted meetings.[21]

The fact that these post-1830 revivals were planned and that some churches sometimes intentionally brought in outsiders to foment enthusiasm indicates that the revivals were no longer spontaneous developments. Given the forethought that went into these later revivals, it is not possible to argue that they were the products of a culture near stability; they were the result of years of living in proximity to antiformalist enthusiasm and the belief that the formalized methods of the enthusiasts could benefit formalist denominations by increasing additions to the church and by increasing morality in the community. These new revivals were intentional, planned, uniform, and much less enthusiastic than the spontaneous revivals of the 1820s. And unlike the revivals of the 1820s, the revivals of the 1830s lasted for five years under the constant efforts of the churches to continue them.

In Fowler's description of the successful revivals in the Presbytery of Watertown, he does not mention Henderson (which did not have an established Presbyterian church), and he does not give special attention to the village of Belleville in Ellisburg, despite the fact that Burchard worked in 1831 as "stated supply" and brought 108 people to the church.[22] The results in Ellisburg were not remarkable, but the successes at George Boardman's church were.

The first and most obvious post-Finney sign of antiformalization in Jefferson County came in the fall of 1831 when protracted meetings became common in Presbyterian churches in Jefferson County. The Presbytery of Watertown indicated to the synod that, although the means were apparently antiformalist, formalist values were maintained:

> The plain preaching of the law and the gospel, preceded, accompanied and followed by fervent, effectual prayer, has been the chief instrumentality employed, and especially has this been so in meetings frequently protracted for many successive days; and in connection with this, has been affectionate

> and urgent conversation with individuals. . . . A more general attendance at the sanctuary, a more general interest in religion throughout the community, a better observance of the Sabbath, a more obvious distinction between the righteous and the wicked, are among the results that have followed . . . and the circulation of the Scriptures, the distribution of religious tracts, the support of Home and Foreign Missionaries, the education of young men for the ministry, instruction in Sunday schools and Bible classes, and the promotion of the temperance reform, engage Christians and many also, who make no profession of religion.[23]

These are essentially the same values Paul Johnson found expressed in the Finney revival at Third Presbyterian in urbanizing Rochester. However, rather than social control, these assertions in the case of the Presbytery of Watertown demonstrate that the formalist churches had maintained their same understanding of the essential relationship between law and gospel but that they had adapted some antiformalist methods in order to compete with antiformalist successes.

Aside from the unusually heavy additions to all of the churches in 1831, the only other indication of the protracted meeting in the records of these churches comes in the 1833 trial of Mr. Bennet Rice, who was brought up by the First Presbyterian Church of Watertown on charges of neglecting public worship. As evidence of Rice's failure to worship, witnesses came forward to testify that when they had been at the meetings they had not seen Rice. It is likely that Boardman held other meetings as the reference to a meeting in Adams was meant as an indication that Rice, who lived in North Adams, was using distance from the church and other excuses (one of which involved working on the sabbath) as excuses to avoid public worship.

In testifying against Rice, Solon Massey also noted that in the same fall there was a "great excitement" about religion for two or three months and that he did not see Rice in North Adams at the "conference meetings" (as opposed to camp meetings). Moreover, he supposed that Rice did not take any interest in the "revival." Revivals apparently had become so commonplace by this time that even Boardman felt compelled to lead protracted meetings, and he expected full members of the church—who had already had conversion experiences—to attend the meetings for worship. This may explain why the church reported only twenty-one admissions in 1832, as opposed to sixty-two in 1831; evidently in 1831, the Presbyterian congregations whom Boardman served developed a "great excitement," which he then institutionalized by hosting "conference meetings" that served more as church services than as meetings to exhort sinners to convert. By 1832 interest was down, but Boardman was attempting to maintain the interest by holding the meetings.[24] Unfortunately, this involved disciplining those who did not show an interest in the revival. Significantly, the session did not reintroduce stringent discipline until 1832, when "interest in religion" had diminished. Ultimately Rice was admonished and suspended for his negligence.[25]

The condition of the Second Presbyterian Church, formed in 1831, was noticeably different from that of First Presbyterian. Interest in forming a separate Presbyterian church in Watertown first surfaced in the records of the First Presbyterian Church of Watertown in the trial of Archelaus Fuller and Noah Ripley in 1829. The men had instigated a meeting to form a separate church in Watertown in order to escape the stringent legalism of the First Presbyterian Church. However, this effort resulted in their excommunications from the church (which were later rescinded.) Nonetheless, they never joined the Second Presbyterian Church.

Second Presbyterian's different agenda was evident immediately after its formation. For their first minister, they hired Jedediah Burchard away from the church in Ellisburg. Burchard remained for a year before returning to his circuit. Although First Presbyterian experienced a short respite in disciplinary proceedings during their period of greatest admissions in 1831, Second Presbyterian did not have its first trial until 1834. And despite Burchard's presence at the formation of the church, Second Presbyterian did not experience a revival until 1833. Given that most of the churches in the Presbytery of Watertown experienced the height of interest in 1831, it is remarkable that Second Presbyterian reacted so slowly. This may have been a result of the church's need to establish itself solidly in order to arrange "protracted meetings" for the interested. And Burchard may not have wanted Boardman to think he was intruding on Boardman's territory in Watertown.[26] Moreover, the post-1830 revivals were exceptionally successful in the churches that were the least excited in the 1820s. Although Adams, Ellisburg, and Evans Mills were among the churches that increased in 1831, their counterparts in this success in 1831, according to Fowler, were Brownville, Watertown, and Sackets Harbor.

Those churches in the Presbytery of Watertown whose records are extant did have remarkable increases in additions to their churches in 1831. The church in Watertown reported to the presbytery in February 1832 that it had sixty-two additions in 1831 while for the next few years it maintained additions in the twenties; Adams reported eighty additions during 1831 and none during 1832; Evans Mills did not report the number of additions to the church, but it lists the names of sixty-two new members in 1831, and indicates a remarkable decline in admissions in 1832.[27] And like Second Presbyterian in Watertown, the church in Theresa did not have a revival until 1833, two years after the arrival of its second pastor, Roswell Pettibone.[28] In the years preceding 1831 these churches rarely had more than ten additions; and even during the revivals of the 1820s, the names included in the records (a not entirely precise guide to the number of additions) never matched the number of additions in 1831.

In the next few years, antiformalizing attempts to maintain the original "interest" continued but never matched the successes of 1831, except in Second Presbyterian and Theresa in 1833. Some of the effort to maintain the interest of 1831 resulted in attempts to bring in outsiders to rekindle the area. Luther Myrick, for example, reported to Finney in 1832 (before Myrick's excommunication) that the residents of Jefferson County had requested that he help organize a protracted meeting in Adams.[29] He was unable to attend then but hoped to attend later. In 1833, Jacob Knapp, in an example of the success of antiformalization and formalization, traveled through Jefferson and Lewis Counties encouraging conversions even among Presbyterians.[30] Fowler indicates that after 1832 efforts to sustain the interest were fruitless. However, what is notable is the effort to sustain the interest, which was not apparent after the revivals of the 1820s. It is likely that despite these efforts the enormous numbers of conversions in 1831 severely diminished the population interested in converting and willing to convert.

A counterpart to the antiformalization of these churches was the increased formalization of the First Presbyterian Church in Evans Mills, which had already experienced antiformalization when Finney was there. Until 1831, Evans Mills conducted no disciplinary proceedings, but beginning in 1831 after the revival-related accessions, the church began to prosecute wrongdoing regularly. And in 1841, the church in Evans Mills became the only church in the Presbytery of Watertown to separate from it and to join the Old School Presbytery of Ogdensburg in St. Lawrence County.[31]

Formalization in the Antiformalist Churches of Jefferson County

In addition to the indications Rowe gives of the results of formalization among the Baptists, one of the most obvious is a change in the Baptist understanding of the relationship of faith to practice. With formalization, practice became a more significant indication of faith. The minutes of the Black River Baptist Association indicate that, in the same way that the Presbyterian churches did not lose their interest in discipline as they antiformalized, the Baptist churches maintained their interest in fervor as they formalized. The 1849 history of the fortieth anniversary of the Black River Baptist Association dwells on periods of "refreshing" and not on the moral usefulness of the churches; nor does it describe missionary conventions or other benevolent institutions, whose work was greatly encouraged by the association.[32] Although the association developed a vigorous interest in moral usefulness and in benevolence in the 1830s, the association continued to define itself as it had during its frontier period. Nonetheless, the association and the individual churches had undergone significant changes.

As among the Presbyterian churches in 1831, the 541 baptisms of adults (the equivalent to additions in Presbyterian churches) far outweighed baptisms in any other year in the history of the Black River Baptist Association from its formation until 1883.[33] Money and property donated for benevolence rose steadily in the 1830s, as did interest in benevolence, chiefly missionary work, in the circular letters of the association.[34]

Disciplinary proceedings, the simplest indications of formalization, are present in the records of Baptist churches in Jefferson County from their formations. The earlier interest in discipline among antiformalists as compared to formalists is apparently less a result of a more intense interest in discipline among these churches than among the Presbyterians, who do not become seriously concerned with discipline until the 1820s, than it is an indication of the greater ease with which the Baptists could conduct disciplinary proceedings. Whereas the practice of Presbyterian polity required that a member's wrongdoing be a matter of "common fame" and that a committee composed of session members be sent to discuss the matter with the offending member, the Baptists would generally initiate disciplinary proceedings when one member brought a charge, frequently unnamed, against another. Often the member would begin on his own what the Baptists referred to as the first two stages of labor with an offending member. If these earlier stages did not succeed, members of the church would then be sent to discuss the matter with the member. Moreover, while Presbyterian trials resembled civil proceedings, Baptist transactions of proceedings leading to the decision to "withdraw the hand of fellowship" are not included in the records. Typical of these early proceedings is the case of Sister Darby, Sister Crowel, and Sister Grommons on 29 March 1808. When the unnamed difficulty came before the church, seven members of the church, including three women, were appointed to "labour" with the women to solve the difficulty. The next reference to the difficulty was on 7 May 1808, when the church, without giving a reason, voted to give a letter of admonition to Sister Grommons.[35] A formalist church would not have considered a purely personal difficulty an appropriate concern for the session; as the disciplinary interests of formalist churches dealt more with legalistic (or formal concerns) than with personal disagreements. A formalist church would have taken pains to spell out the offense clearly in all its manifestations, and a formalist church would not have allowed members facing disciplinary proceedings to choose four out of the seven members of the committee to labor with them as did the Baptist church in Adams.

The disciplinary proceedings of the Baptist churches became a regular occurrence around 1814, a decade after the organization of the first churches in the county and immediately after the War of 1812, when the churches approached stability. In those years, on the rare occasions when charges are mentioned, the most common charges in addition to personal difficulties were breach of covenant, sabbath breaking, and disorderly walk. From 1814 through the 1820s, disciplinary cases became more common. Most churches had zero to two exclusions, although a few churches had as many as twelve or sixteen.[36] In the 1830s, the formalization grew more severe, and as in the case of George Boardman's church ten years earlier, disciplinary proceedings begin to appear in the records of every meeting of the church. Although "withdrawing the hand of fellowship" does not as a result become more common, the association also begins to evince greater interest in formalist concerns.

In 1831 the association quoted from Titus 1:13 in urging that those who did not adhere to the faith be "rebuke[d] sharply.[37] In 1832, the association denounced ignorance and noted that its ministers had to be educated in order to work effectively. The association also resolved to consider whether intemperance should be considered just cause for excommunication, though the Presbyterians had been considering it just cause since the 1820s. They published their decision in 1833:

> Ardent spirits possess no nutritious properties—that they act as irritants and not as nutriments—that they are always useless when even used in the smallest quantities, except as medicine—that in most instances they have a

> most decided injurious influence, converting a regular drinker into a monster of wickedness, exerting the most disastrous influence upon the morals of community, filling the land with brutality, licentiousness and wo—that they are the principal and prolific source of profanity, sabbath-breaking, and debauchery—that the evils they engender are the greatest scourge which ever afflicted our country; and that every effort should be adopted for their suppression.[38]

The association also resolved that the member churches should encourage their congregations to join temperance societies, although, as I will note in the next chapter, there is no evidence that this suggestion was acted upon or that temperance societies among Baptists prospered. And in the same year it advised against wearing mourning apparel, as its use was usually a display of worldliness. They also advised churches to form laymen's associations for the promotion of "evangelical piety." In these cases, the formation of societies is less an indication of the loss of the churches' societal power, as in Cortland County, since it was an indication of formalization, or the Baptist churches' attempt to establish ecclesiastical authority more widely in communities, as the formalists already had.

In 1836, both the Black River Baptist Association and the Jefferson Baptist Association wrote circular letters concerning the "DUE OBSERVANCE OF THE LORDS SUPPER,"[39] and urged strict adherence to standards regulating who would be admitted to the Lord's Supper, and to the correct administration of the ordinance.[40] Thus, the Jefferson Baptist Association noted that

> it appears that to give the communion to an individual out of the church however ardent his piety, or to those who walk not in the fellowship of the church, is a departure from apostolic example.
> . . . We remark that this order is essential to the maintaining of the discipline of the church. A *constitutional* article of a church must be scrupulously regarded by its members. If not, the existence of such church is at once endangered.[41]

Finally in 1838 the association published a circular letter that in strong terms advocated strict adherence to the administration of discipline:

> The subject to which we would call your attention is, *the importance of a strict and well directed discipline.*

> . . . In pursuing our subject, we shall speak first, of the evils of a lax discipline: *First,* many are delinquent in duty, who would otherwise remain steadfast. It is true, a spirit of benevolence and cheerful obedience, should stimulate the christian to faithful discharge of duty. Still, such is the propensity, even of true christians, to neglect the cross, that, like the wayward child, they need the rod of faithful discipline, constantly applied. Hence, let it be known that members can hold their standing, and habitually absent themselves from the church, on the Sabbath, and on other occasions; that they may or may not contribute to the support and extension of the gospel; that it matters not whether they do or do not pray in the closet, with the family, watch their tongues, curb their passions, or attend to the various relative duties of religion, and how often will frivolous excuses present themselves as insuperable barriers to the discharge of duty? But, let it be plainly understood that, in neglecting any of these duties, the delinquent incurs the disapprobation of the church, and subjects himself to strict and unwavering discipline; obstacles otherwise great, would be surmounted, a disposition to slothfulness overcome, and the public and private duties of religion faithfully discharged.[42]

Additionally, the Association noted that personal offences were not the only issues that should come before the church: "The expression, 'if thy brother trespass against thee,' not only implies personal injury, but also sins that come within our knowledge."[43] The letter closed with the assertions that the "strength of the church" and the honor of Christ depend on the correct use of discipline.[44] And while the association did not, as it did in 1826, caution against excessive discipline, it did note that the point of discipline should be to redeem the wrongdoer and not to exclude him.

This letter apparently represented the prevailing mood rather than an urging to those who found discipline distasteful, as was the case with the circular letter in 1826; for in 1835, the First Baptist Church of Rutland was already taking discipline more seriously when it accused its pastor, Elder Elisha Morgan, with unlawfully charging interest and with violating the sabbath several times. Morgan confessed to the accusation of illegally charging interest, but before confessing he provided excuses for breaking the sabbath. He admitted that he had chopped wood on the sabbath, but that he was out of wood and a member of his family was ill; that he did once carry hay home from Sunday preaching, but that he had had no hay to feed his horses; and that he had carried a horse poke and pumpkins on the Sabbath out of necessity.[45] After this difficulty with Elder Morgan was resolved, the church called a council with other local churches on 9 May to consider whether Morgan had acted dishonestly in the sale of two barrels of pork. The council decided that, although he did not intentionally act dishonestly, he had nonetheless acted in such a way that the suspicion of dishonesty could justly be brought against him.[46] Elder Morgan was replaced by Elder Joshua Freeman in 1836.

At the height of disciplinary concern in the mid-1830s, the churches of Jefferson County complained distressingly of the lack of interest in baptisms in their churches and indicated in 1836 that they had added by baptism seven people and excluded (or excommunicated) thirty-five.[47] Thus, the increase in church trials among the Baptists does not indicate an increase in sinful behavior among Baptists, since after all their Presbyterian neighbors had been accused of similar charges ten years earlier. Furthermore, the disorderliness of frontier society makes it likely that more wrongdoing occurred before the 1830s than after. The increase in church trials does indicate the formalization of the Baptists; even if there were actually fewer cases of wrongdoing in the 1830s than during the frontier era, the formalized structure made every case more susceptible to investigation by the church.

Schismatic Ultraisms in Jefferson County

The Mormons and the Universalists qualify as the ultraisms of Jefferson County. I find two reasonable nineteenth-century connotations for "ultraist" (as opposed to "perfectionist," the term with which ultraist is too often confused). First, ultraist suggests what today we refer to as a fanatic or an extremist. The Taliban or David Koresh and the Branch Davidians would certainly qualify as ultraists, but probably not perfectionists. Second, "ultraist" may refer to an extreme lack of structure in an archetypically enthusiastic and antiformalist group. The groups under discussion fall under the first definition of this term. In the twentieth century, we do not equate Mormons and Universalists or any of the other groups I list below as ultraisms. However, where today we would use the terms "extremist" or "fanatic" for a new religion, nineteenth-century Americans seem to have favored ultraist.[48]

In addition to the Mormons and the Universalists, several heterodox movements, such as Swedenborgians in Henderson,[49] Free Will Baptists in Alexandria,[50] Seventh-day Baptists in Adams,[51] Disciples of Christ in

Adams,[52] Fourierists in Watertown,[53] members of the Zoar Society,[54] and Millerites[55] appeared in the county. However, only the Mormons and Universalists established themselves as a significant presence in Jefferson County.

The Mormons established themselves in the county in 1835, while the Universalists were well represented by 1822. And although the organization of the Universalists preceded formalization and antiformalization in the 1830s by almost a decade, both denominations represent a balance of formalism and antiformalism as a protest against the dominant religious trends.

The Luff family, the first Universalists in Jefferson County, left England in opposition to taxation for the Church of England and arrived in Sackets Harbor in 1805. Immediately after arriving they established a Universalist meeting house that stands as a home on the corner of Broad and Washington Streets and at which Edmund Luff preached until 1822. Luff allowed other denominations to use the church, and the church also served as a hospital during the War of 1812.[56]

In 1814, Pitt Morse arrived in Jefferson County as the area's first settled Universalist minister. Morse's impassioned preaching and his written rhetoric are the nonevangelical equivalent of Finney's. Morse was born in Brooklyn, Connecticut, in 1796, but accounts of Morse's life from 1818 to 1820 are contradictory. Some say that he preached in Madison or Monroe County from 1818 and was then ordained by the Genesee Branch Association of Universalists in 1820. Others indicate that he was in Jefferson County by 1818 and was ordained by the Black River and St. Lawrence [Universalist] Association in 1820. None of the sources mention that Morse attended a college or a seminary. All sources agree that Morse's youthfulness caused great concern among local Universalist ministers and congregants. However, Morse's capacity to preach astonished them all and resulted in general agreement in favor of his ordination.[57] No records indicate that he took up Luff's pulpit in Sackets. Instead he itinerated between Henderson, Brownville, and Watertown. Eventually, he devoted all of his time to Watertown and Henderson. And in 1824 Morse began to make arrangements for Hosea Ballou to preach at the dedication of the first church of the Universalist Society of Watertown. Ballou wrote to Morse on 29 July 1824 and remarked that he was gratified that "we have no small resources in that vicinity, which are affording generous support to the desired increase of Zion's provision." Nonetheless, Ballou was unsure that his health or his congregation in Boston would allow him to attend.

Ultimately, Ballou did preach at the dedication, with the understanding that the Watertown congregation would cover his expenses of one hundred dollars.[58]

The expense of bringing Ballou to Watertown proved worthwhile, since soon after his departure local evangelical churches experienced a sudden surge in trials against members seeking dismissions to the Universalist church.[59] The most acrimonious trials occurred in the Presbyterian churches. And Morse responded by printing the transcripts of the trials, with his commentary, in his semiquarterly journal *The Herald of Salvation,* which he began in 1822. It was the only religious periodical in Jefferson County in the 1820s and one of 138 Universalist periodicals in the country.[60]

On 9 May 1823, a year before Ballou appeared in the county, Morse printed Mrs. Roxanna Woodruff's letter to the session of the First Presbyterian Church of Watertown. The records of the First Presbyterian Church in Watertown show that Morse faithfully reproduced the contents of the letter that Roxanna Woodruff wrote to the session requesting a letter of dismission to the Universalist church after members of the session had visited her regarding rumors of her heretical tendencies. In requesting her dismission she noted that many members of the church would consider her new beliefs in opposition to Calvinism and in opposition to a belief in "eternal misery" "erroneous and fatal to the spiritual welfare of mankind"; and she remarked that she expected that the church would censure her if she did not leave it. The session responded by indicating that it could not dismiss a member of the church to anything other than "[an]other branch of the Christian church."[61] The session continued to visit Mrs. Woodruff only to learn that she "was tenacious of her opinions though she supported them very feebly—instead of giving a candid consideration to observations adduced against her opinions, appeared to be desirous of evading them, & to be unwilling to be convinced."[62]

Morse's commentary accompanying the published letter typified his writing:

> The following letter, from Mrs. Woodruff, to Mr. Boardman, contains a request for a dismission from the church. . . . To her letter a *verbal* answer was given, which was that her request could not be granted—that *excommunication* is the only, and of course the most friendly manner in which Presbyterians can proceed against those who think for themselves—act conscientiously—and walk uprightly. . . .

> It is fortunate for mankind that excommunications have lost their awe-imposing influence—and every vestige of disgrace, since members of the most unexceptionable moral character, must be given over to satan, merely for exercising their own understandings, and avowing their honest opinions.[63]

Morse frequently italicized and underlined his writing, probably in an attempt to approximate his spoken emphasis. He was also commonly sarcastic and vitriolic.

Additionally, Morse demonstrated a strong concern with morality as an indication of a religion's worth. Morse printed the trials and letters of suspension of Jerusha Torrey of the First Presbyterian Church of Brownville, Ezekiel Robbins of the Congregational Church in Adams, and Mr. and Mrs. Levi H. Pierce of the First Presbyterian Church in Adams. As in the case of Roxanna Woodruff, and in all of Morse's written commentaries on these cases, he dwelled on the moral uprightness of the accused heretics:

> We have at length arrived at the *conclusion* of these painful if not worse than useless proceedings [leading to the excommunication of Jerusha Torrey]. . . . How long shall the peace of the moral world be disturbed by proceedings so intolerant, anti-social, and unnecessary?[64]
>
> Some time during the winter past, *Ezekiel W. Robbins*, a young man of unblemished moral character, was excluded from the Congregational Church in Adams, merely for believing in the fulfillment in the divine mission of Christ.[65]

In his commentaries, Morse responded to Presbyterian attacks on Universalist morality as much as he indicated his own concern with morality. The Baptists, like the Presbyterians, excommunicated those attracted to Universalism, but Morse did not print their proceedings, apparently because they did not impose trials of long duration and because they did not attack the Universalists in the course of the proceedings. When the Baptists did excommunicate Universalists, they indicated that they were merely resigning themselves to what they viewed as an unfortunate circumstance, while the Presbyterians' actions suggested that they were punishing the "heretic" for his or her dissident stubbornness and lack of a Christian moral character. The Baptists simply did not have as many opportunities to "withdraw the hand of fellowship" from Universalists, since from 1822 to 1834 only two cases of Universalist departures occur in extant local records. Thus, the

Baptists did not provide as fruitful a forum for Morse's commentary, and the Baptists did not have occasion to excommunicate Universalists as often as did the Presbyterians.[66]

Additionally, Morse's concern with the morality of converts from Presbyterianism to Universalism is not only a response to Presbyterian animadversions, for despite the apparently correct perception that generally Universalism was antiformalist[67] or an example of the "democratization of American Christianity,"[68] Morse's articles in the *Herald of Salvation* and his sermons provide a sense of the importance of such formalist concerns as education and morality. Moreover, the attraction of Universalism for Presbyterians suggests that, in Jefferson County, Universalism was more attractive to formalists than to antiformalists. In Jefferson County, Presbyterians had the most to lose from Universalist success, and Universalists reacted most virulently against the denomination from which the bulk of the new membership derived.

Universalism in New England, as opposed to Unitarianism and as opposed to Universalism in Jefferson County, attracted former Baptists. Thus, Universalism is generally considered antiformalist. New England Unitarianism, on the other hand, separated from the established Congregational organization and attracted former Congregationalists. In the fight for separation of church and state, Universalists and Baptists frequently united in their efforts to end ecclesiastic establishment in New England.[69] Moreover, in the early nineteenth century, most Universalist clergy and congregants came from among the antiformalist Methodists and Baptists.[70] However, Universalism grew closer to Unitarianism under Ballou's influence and in fact led Robert Baird in his history of American religion in 1844 to refer to Ballou as a Unitarian.[71] Universalism had developed a sympathy to the other historically antiformalist denominations, while it had a history of antipathy for formalist denominations.

Given Morse's affinity for Ballou, the Universalism that Pitt Morse brought to Jefferson County more closely resembled a frontier Unitarianism than it did standard Universalism. Most of the converts were from among the formalist Presbyterians, and all of them rejected the Trinity. The necessary denial of pietist enthusiasm among Universalists meant that the denomination naturally tended to formalize more quickly than did other denominations and that Universalism stressed morality above all other concerns, such as conversion experiences. Morality was a prominent concern among Universalists; since Morse, like Ballou, held that people paid for their sins during their lives on earth rather than afterwards, Morse and his followers believed that moral transgressions would lead to punishment on earth. Also because the Universalists believed that traditional Presbygationalist doctrines such as the Trinity and Calvinism were superstitions, the Universalists praised education as a means of escaping delusion. Although Morse was apparently uneducated, he frequently drew from the Greek New Testament and wrote knowledgeably of the theologies of the Calvinists and Arminians;[72] and his numerous writings convey a concern with presenting Universalist beliefs as more intellectually consistent than evangelical beliefs, as he does in the following letter to the Reverend John Dempster:

> The intellectual powers of man are bestowed upon him, by the infinitely beneficent parents of his existence, for the obvious purpose of their *exercise* in drawing consolation and instruction from the exhaustless fountain of Truth; in the amelioration of his condition; and in all the duties of social life.[73]

Morse continues by urging Dempster to help him "promote knowledge" by answering Morse's questions regarding one of Dempster's sermons that attacked Universalism. And in his "Address on Education," Morse argues:

> He who would make the greatest possible progress in the knowledge of the various relations he bears to his Maker & his fellow creatures, & practice the duties which those relations impose, instead of pertinaciously adhering to some time-honored speculative theory must listen to reason, the language of experience, & carefully notice matters of fact, & be ready to renounce all the favorite opinions of infancy the moment *truth* clearly demands the sacrifice.[74]

Morse contends in the rest of the "address" that even the "common" classes should be educated in order to prevent "rapacity, lying, cheating, theiving [sic], drunkenness & sensual low pleasures." He thus combined his formalist concerns for morality and education in one address.[75]

A strict formalist view is also apparent in Morse's and other local Universalists' positions on revivalism. The first and most strident opposition appears in Morse's response to Finney's assertion that his horse had more religion than Morse.

> If I am correctly informed, you, sir, are supported, wholly or in part, by a *Female Missionary Society,* who, through your instrumentality, are

> literally sending the *gospel of eternal misery to the destitute!*—Through your thundering denunciations of the vindictive, unceasing, vengeance of the Almighty, I understand you have succeeded in producing a great commotion in certain neighborhoods within this county, and have made many proselytes. Furthermore, I am informed, from a source which is entitled to the fullest confidence, that you have recently made the following statements concerning me, viz.: "*That I have no more religion than your horse; that I am the wickedest man in all this county; that I do not believe what I preach; and that I told you I did not believe what I preached.*"[76]

Morse responded first by denying the charges, and then by asserting that he "could name facts which would cause you [Finney] to crimson with *shame;* but I spare you."[77] Morse then condemned the "frantic fury of fanaticism" and he demanded an apology from Finney, which demand he would renege if Finney were "subject to paroxysms of *insanity.*"[78]

Later, in a sermon, Morse decried the suicides that resulted from revivals in Jefferson County.[79] And in 1831, when all the churches in Jefferson County, including First Presbyterian in Watertown, began to enjoy numerous converts, the local Universalists, sounding very much like Samuel Snowden almost ten years earlier, condemned the "whirlwinds of moral desolation" that would result from the enthusiasm. It is unlikely that George S. Boardman allowed the "interest" his congregation demonstrated in religion to sink into enthusiasms, but his kind of formalist interpretation of revivals reappeared in the commentary of the Universalists:

> We regret that in the prosecution of any inquiry or investigation, it should be taught that Reason should be silenced and that any system, doctrine or faith should be established on other ground than a conviction of its truth and propriety; and should the very large and respectable meeting who instigated this address thereby incur the imputation of being enemies of Religion, it will be because in their consideration of this subject they consulted that 'still small voice' which is not heard in the 'whirlwind' of fanaticism, or discovered in the fire of religious bigotry. Moral and religious sentiments lose none of their force in being expressed in good language in a temperate manner, and at a suitable time and place.[80]

Thus the Universalists, whose origins were antiformalist, formalized to the point that they were reacting to Boardman's "conference meetings" the way Boardman's counterpart Snowden had reacted to the excitements in Henderson. As a result the Universalists asserted as had the Presbyterians before antiformalization that revivals created "burnt districts," or areas that suffered "moral desolation" from the intensity of revival emotions.

Formalization among the Universalists of Jefferson County began with Morse's arrival and Ballou's visit, just before Finney brought antiformalism to the formalists of the northern sections of the county. Aside from atypical Henderson, the centers of Universalism in Jefferson County were Watertown and Brownville, the formalist, commercial regions. Essentially, although Universalism was ostensibly an antiformalist denomination, Universalism in Jefferson County resembled New England Unitarianism more than it did Universalism in most other frontier areas, for in the Black River Valley, where formalization and antiformalization began earlier than in most other areas, the antiformalist Universalists began to resemble Unitarians sooner than in other areas. This position on the edge of formalism and antiformalism proved profitable to Jefferson County Universalists, as a writer to the *Herald of Salvation* remarked in 1824 in response to Baptist assertions that the Universalists in the Black River Valley were renouncing Universalism:

> The fact is, the cause of Universalism is as prosperous, (if not more) in the Black River Country, as in any section of the United States. It is impossible to form a just estimate of the numbers, respectability and ability of the believers in that part of the state, by any casual observation. In the county of Jefferson, there were no less than *seven* preachers of the gospel of universal grace, last July.[81]

Pitt Morse remained in Jefferson County until 1825, when the *Herald of Salvation* merged with *The Universalist* in Utica, and when he moved to Philadelphia. In 1827, his former congregation in Watertown convinced him to return. He then remained in Watertown until his death in 1860. Unlike other areas, where the Unitarians lived alongside Universalists, Universalism held a monopoly in Watertown as both the formalist and antiformalist alternative to the evangelical denominations. Unitarianism did not arrive in the county until the unification of the Unitarians and Universalists in 1961.[82]

While the originally antiformalist Universalists sought more formalization than the evangelical denominations could provide, the Mormons appealed to those who sought an antiformalist reaction against formalization in the 1830s. Rowe indicates that the Millerites, Mormons, Christian

Unionists, the Perfectionists, and the adherents of the new form of Shaker spirituality all wished to return their churches to a primitive innocence that they felt formalization was hindering.[83] Hatch demonstrates further how the apparently authoritarian Mormons appealed to those seeking "democratization." Even though the Church of Jesus Christ of Latter-day Saints bureaucratized quickly and thus appeared to formalize, it, like other antiformalist denominations, attracted the "marginalized," and "challenged common people to take religious destiny into their own hands, to think for themselves, to oppose centralized authority and the elevation of the clergy as a separate order of men."[84] The Mormons made every man a priest and a prophet, but placed formalist controls over these offices in order to prevent chaos. For example, the Mormon doctrine that any man could receive revelation appealed to many who would otherwise be borderline members of formalist and formalizing mainline churches, but it had to be kept under control, as in the case of John Elmer of Jefferson County:

> John Elmer was charged with holding very incorrect principles; such, for instance, that the Spirit of God sometimes took him and threw him down, and that he could die the death of the righteous, and of the wicked; and in order to show his power with God, he also stated that he had passed through a kind of death so as to become immortal, and would exist forever without any other death or change, only growing brighter and brighter eternally.[85]

Even though the Mormons as antiformalists believed that any man could become like God and that God was once like them, beliefs such as Elmer's would have led to anarchy. Additionally, the Mormons spurned the institutionalization of the mainstream churches and offered a faith derived, they said, from the primitive church that exalted the common person over the powerful. Furthermore, one should not assume the Mormons are formalist because of their hierarchical government, since, Hatch argues, "the conjunction of democratic aspiration and authoritarian style is a characteristic pattern of populist cultures."[86] Because Joseph Smith and other populist leaders appealed so strongly to the longings of the "marginalized," it was natural for them to rise to powerful positions. Nonetheless, the appeal of Mormonism was its espousal of antiformalist values.

Thus, unlike the Universalists who appealed to the prominent, chiefly in the central regions of Jefferson County, the Mormons found converts among the common people, chiefly in marginal regions. The traveling High Council of the Church met in Pillar Point on 19 June 1835 and gave the following tally:

> The church at Pillow [sic] Point numbered twenty-one, but did not generally observe the Word of Wisdom. The church at Sackets Harbor numbered nineteen; Burville [sic], seven; Champion, six; Ellesburg [sic], thirty-three; Henderson, four; Alexandria, four; Lyme, four; and two in Orleans, three in Potsdam, and six in Stockholm.[87]

The final two towns in the report, Potsdam and Stockholm both in St. Lawrence County, were the homes of Joseph Smith's paternal grandparents and paternal uncles.[88] In addition to these areas, the council noted that five more conversions took place at the end of their meeting. But there is no indication that the church ever prospered in the commercial center, Watertown. In fact, extant documents indicate that ultimately the two areas in which the Mormons did best were Theresa and Henderson.[89]

Legends in Jefferson County assert that Brigham Young appeared in Theresa in 1832. However, there is no hard evidence to support this, only an indication that Young crossed over to the United States from Kingston, Ontario, in 1832. Young probably landed in Sackets Harbor and may have traveled to Theresa.[90] In any case, missionary activity in Theresa achieved more local renown than it did in other regions of the county. Mormon missionaries allegedly built a bridge just underneath the water of the Indian River, and thus convinced residents that Mormons could walk on water, and the Mormons cured a feverish boy in Theresa, also leading to the conviction that the Mormons could work miracles.[91]

The Huntington family, achieved renown after leaving Jefferson County. Indications are that William Huntington, a veteran of the fighting in 1813 at Sackets Harbor, was a marginal figure in Henderson when he joined the Presbyterian church in Adams in 1816, partly from the hope that church membership would improve his fortunes, which had slumped during the trade embargo of the War of 1812.[92] He began to become disillusioned with membership in the Presbyterian church when his life did not improve; and even before the arrival of Mormon missionaries in 1832–33, he had begun to accept beliefs that would later be codified in the Mormon Word of Wisdom: he opposed alcohol, as did many others, and he began to believe that the use of tobacco was evil. Thus, when the missionaries did arrive, Huntington and his family left the Presbyterian church and joined the Mormons. In 1835 Hyrum Smith baptized them.[93] Soon after that

Huntington sent his son Dimick and daughter Prescindia to Kirtland, Ohio, to join the trek west. He and the rest of his family followed in the same year. In the ensuing years, Huntington became one of the earliest settlers of Nauvoo, Illinois, a member of the High Council, and a presiding elder at Mount Pisgah, Iowa.[94]

His daughters, Prescindia and Zina Diantha, achieved greater acclaim in the church as two of Joseph Smith's first plural wives in Nauvoo. Both were already married when Joseph Smith asked their husbands if he could marry their wives spiritually, so that he would be with them in heaven. Both husbands consented. When Joseph Smith was assassinated, and after Prescindia's original marriage collapsed, she became a plural wife of Heber Kimball, a member of the First Presidency.[95] And when Brigham Young took control of the church, he married Zina, without her husband's consent. Zina eventually became the third president of the women's Relief Society in the church, as well as an ardent suffrage supporter.[96]

Although the prominence of the Huntington family in western Mormon history does not illustrate the significance of the success of the antiformalizing tendency inherent in early Mormonism, it does indicate that anyone could achieve eminence in the church, even the apparently socially marginal Huntingtons of Jefferson County.[97] Notably the antiformalist Mormons of Jefferson County generally came from the marginal areas of the county that were formalizing in the 1830s, while the subtly formalist Universalists did best in the central and dominant areas of the county that were antiformalizing in the 1830s.

The dynamic between the antiformalists and the formalists was inevitable, since the two groups lived as neighbors and since the enthusiasm of the antiformalist evangelicals naturally became an expected and bureaucratized occurrence. For the antiformalists this meant a loss of spontaneity in their pious outpourings and a bureaucratization that led to more formalistic disciplinary proceedings; while for the formalists, antiformalization meant an acceptance of some of the formalized antiformalist practices, such as the camp meeting transformed into a conference meeting. But reactions against formalization and antiformalization were also inevitable, as in the cases of the apparently-formalist-but-actually-antiformalist Mormons and the apparently-antiformalist-but-actually-formalist Universalists.

As I will demonstrate in the next chapter the transformations within the denominations in the 1830s were also apparent in the reform concerns of the same era.

5
The Progress of Reform

Historians have long recognized a connection between Second Great Awakening religious interest and benevolent reform. Most interpretations of the antebellum reform impulse assert that revival fervor drove an interest in perfecting society. However, fervor had been surfacing in the Northeast since after the War of 1812, and in the Southwest since Cane Ridge in 1801. These earliest, most antiformal revivals did not produce reform interest, nor did the revivalistically inclined antiformal denominations before 1830 encourage the sort of reforms with which Second Great Awakening fervor is generally identified. In fact, the revivals of the First Great Awakening did not produce any reform movements either. Thus, the historiographical association between revivalism and reform is a result of a failure to distinguish between antiformalist and formalist revivalism, for revivalism and reform are not associated until after 1830.

It is common to contend that Finney brought about the new interest in an association between reform and revivalism, but Finney himself never encouraged aggressive participation in benevolent movements. Assertive reform movements require formalization and bureaucratization, as well as a population genuinely interested in furthering the reform cause. Finney, as William McLoughlin has remarked, more closely resembled the antiformalists. And antiformalists were generally more interested in increasing evangelical efforts or, in other words, increasing accessions to the church, as through revivals. They used this as their primary means of improving society, since they assumed that increased accessions would improve the moral tone of the community. Finney, as an antiformalist, did denounce intemperance, for example, but he did not encourage temperance reform. Instead he asserted essentially that the primary goal of a congregation should be to encourage a revival in order to convert sinners but that, if the congregation actively opposed temperance reform, it would diminish the success of the revival.[1] Formalists, on the other hand, were more interested in diminishing the frequency of the appearance of sin in the society. Thus, they hoped that their revivals would engender interest in their benevolent reforms. In other words, the formalists' chief goal was reform, while the antiformalists' chief goal was evangelization. As a result of antiformalization and formalization, after 1830 both sides advocated revivals, but they continued to do so for different reasons.

The simplest way to understand a denomination's reform interests is to refer to what each denomination considers worthy of discipline. As I indicated in chapter 3, although the Baptists and Presbyterians ostensibly maintained similar moral and doctrinal concerns, they actually demonstrated different priorities through their choices of problems worthy of discipline. The Presbyterians sought to maintain order in their congregations and in their communities. Thus, they overwhelmingly stressed doctrinal and moral concerns in their disciplinary proceedings. The Baptists, on the other hand, considered maintenance of the covenant among themselves the highest priority, and consequently they sanctioned far more disciplinary proceedings concerning personal difficulties among members than they did moral concerns.

Although both denominations strongly disapproved of sabbath breaking and intemperance, the Presbyterians before 1830 were far more likely to prosecute a violator or to name these violations than were the Baptists. Additionally, as Curtis Johnson indicates, by the 1820s Presbyterians were generally more interested than were Baptists in total abstinence from alcohol.[2] Because of this tendency, T. Scott Miyakawa asserts that Presbyterian churches devoted a remarkable portion of their time to discipline, and analogously that Presbyterianism in general on the frontier was marked by "an orderly system of government, and . . . respect for law and order."[3] Meanwhile, the Baptists defined themselves through their missionary activity. Just as most of their activity on the level of the congregation was devoted to conversions, so was their benevolent activity concerned with conversions through missionary activity. Hence when the Baptists formalized and devoted more time to benevolence, the antiformalist schism was among the Antimission Baptists.

These differences are apparent furthermore in the records of the Female Missionary Society of the Western District and Fowler's history of Presbyterianism in central and northern New York, as well as in the records of the Black River Baptist Association. The Baptist's records indicate that Baptist benevolent concerns attempted to improve the condition of the downtrodden, with whom the Baptists identified. And improving the condition of others often meant merely encouraging them to convert. Meanwhile the Presbyterians sought to maintain "law and order." Thus, the Presbyterian concern with discipline on the congregational level reappeared as a concern for encouraging reform within the community in order to maintain a disciplinary presence in society.

Presbyterians

As well-organized formalists, the Presbyterians most easily formed benevolent movements, while they had the greatest initial difficulty in forming churches. Just as Presbyterian churches did not immediately manifest strict formalism after they were formed, the earliest benevolent organizations were not as strictly formalist as later organizations. The most antiformalist of benevolent organizations are missionary societies. Consequently, from their earliest appearance in Jefferson County, the Presbygationalist missionaries encouraged additions to both newly formed churches and missionary societies, as did the supplies sent by the Female Missionary Society of the Western District. Miyakawa indicates that Presbygationalists frequently considered it their duty not to seek new additions to the Presbygationalist churches, but to organize Presbygationalist churches.[4] Thus, the Female Missionary Society differed from its antiformalist counterparts in that it sought to prevent moral decay by aiding the formation of churches. It was not attempting to ameliorate the condition of the downtrodden. The clearest indication of this concern is the frequency with which missionaries, such as Samuel F. Snowden, referred to the moral condition of an area rather than to its religious enthusiasm. While the churches in the southern towns of the county effusively welcomed missionaries and responded unusually positively to their pleas to join churches, the residents of the southern towns impressed the missionaries with their moral desolation. On the other hand, the missionaries praised the residents of northern towns who were not joining churches in droves, but who were nonetheless demonstrating the sort of order that bespoke morality and religiosity to the Presbyterians.

Apparently, the missionaries hoped that by encouraging the women of the southern towns to join the Female Missionary Society they would augment the morally beneficial effect of church membership. Even Finney's account of his mission in Evans Mills, while portraying an antiformalist interest in "outpourings of grace," nonetheless noted that "wickedness abounded among them to an alarming degree, and they seemed generally to suppose that to belong to the church, be baptized, and partake of the Lord's Supper was religion enough." Nevertheless, although Finney used the rhetoric of the formalists, he did not urge the residents of Evans Mills to supplement their religious practices with benevolent work, as would have a true formalist. Instead Finney more strenuously urged the people of Evans Mills to be born again.[5]

Other missionaries manifested their formalism more clearly. Adams Platt, despite other descriptions of Ellisburg as morally desolate and chaotic, remarked approvingly in describing Ellisburg in 1822 that he had maintained solemnity (rather than excitement) in the meetings and that he had seen the moral condition of the people improve.[6] Henry Smith had a similar experience in Adams in 1822; "solemnity," he said, was maintained, and he noted that one of the effects of the revival was a "genuine reformation of morals."[7]

In effect, the Presbyterian missionary societies sought to improve morality along the frontier by providing missionaries who could gather Presbygationalists into well-established churches, and who could encourage women to join the effort to supply missionaries to other destitute areas. The one exception to this understanding of the missionary's purpose was Finney, who realized the formalist concern with morality, but whose primary interest was in converting people, while the average formalist was interested in converting or gaining accessions to churches in order to improve morality.

The last extant report of the Female Missionary Society appears in 1825. Seemingly, this was in fact the last report of the society, which had succeeded in establishing churches and had thus aided the Presbygationalists on the frontier in achieving a level of formalism and stability that precluded the need for missionary societies.[8] At the same time disciplinary proceedings became commonplace in Presbyterian churches also denoting increased stability and formalism. Hence, at that point, benevolence among Presbyterians became more formalist too and even more open in its concern for moralism, especially temperance reform and sabbatarianism.

However, before the mid-1820s, the first county-based benevolent society in Jefferson County, the Bible Society of Rutland (later the Jefferson County Bible Society), formed in 1816 as an auxiliary to the American Bible Society. Like the Watertown Ecclesiastical Society, which reflected the social hegemony of the Presbyterians in Watertown in its assertion of its position as the "Watertown Ecclesiastical" Society rather than the First Presbyterian Society of Watertown, the Bible Society of Rutland did not identify itself as a Presbyterian organization. The Bible Society also defined itself in the early stages of developing formalism as a missionary society, but like the Female Missionary Society its chief concern was with the morality of the population.

The auxiliary of the nondenominational American Bible Society did not profess Presbyterianism or hope that those to whom it supplied Bibles would become Presbyterians. Nonetheless, almost all of the membership was Presbyterian, and almost all of them were either ministers or members of local sessions. The names of Baptists and Methodists did appear as members, as, for example, did Emory Osgood from Henderson, but as a rule the meetings of the society were dominated by the orthodox and orderly George S. Boardman and Samuel F. Snowden.[9] Unlike a missionary society the goal of the organization was not to encourage Presbyterians to form and maintain Presbyterian churches; the Bible Society asserted itself into the population in general by urging that all people have Bibles. As usual the goal of the society was to improve morality:

> Though small, it is yet a tributary stream which will assist in swelling that mighty tide of benevolence, which is beginning to flow broad and deep, and is destined to water and refresh the earth, and to make ever "the wilderness bud and blossom like the rose." Wherever the pure unadulterated word of God comes, it brings with it a holy, a reforming, a regenerating influence, which raises higher the standard of morals, and thereby ameliorates the condition of man.[10]

Additionally, the records of the society exhibit the formalist tendency toward legalistically and conscientiously recorded minutes. These notes demonstrate that the investment that the Presbyterians of the Bible Society made in the moral condition of the county as a whole was regularly supported by all the local Presbyterian ministers except for Finney. Finney's name does not appear in the membership list of the society during the period from 1824 to 1825 when he was working as a missionary in Jefferson County. His only contribution to the society was to recommend that its work of visiting every family in the county and determining whether it was "destitute of the Scriptures" would be more easily carried out if the society were split into branches in each town.[11] The society did this, but unlike other ministers, Finney's name does not appear either among the names of the members of the branches in Antwerp or LeRay. The extent of Finney's participation reflects the level of antiformalist interest in the Bible Society; although Baptists and Methodists attended the meetings and rose to the level of officers of the society, the orthodox, formalist Presbyterians and Presbyterian concerns dominated the earliest years of the society, if only because the Presbyterians were the wealthiest members of the community and thus the most likely to dominate an ecumenical organization.

Just as the Female Missionary Society had seen its purpose disappear in the mid-1820s, the Jefferson County Bible Society also changed in the mid-1820s. The society lost its earliest urgency and lost its sense of moral necessity, while meetings became less frequent. Jacob Knapp joined the society in 1830 as Baptist membership rose and as the Baptists formalized, but Presbyterian interest diminished. In fact in 1832, a year after the widespread revivals that indicated Presbyterian antiformalization, the society decried the sudden lack of interest:

> It is a matter of regret that for about two years past, the interests of the Bible Society have excited but little attention in this County. Prior to that period, the destitute families of the County were reported to have been supplied. To this circumstance, and the general belief, that the future increase of the destitute would not be rapid, we attribute, in a great measure, the subsequent remissness that has prevailed in relation to this truly benevolent cause. It seems to have been taken for granted, that all which can be reasonably expected of this section of country, has been already accomplished; that there is no further need of effort for our own benefit, and that we have not the means of doing any thing to extend the circulation of the Bible beyond our own bounds. Accordingly, not a single report from an Auxiliary was received at the last annual meeting of the County Society, and we fear that many, if not all the Auxiliaries have ceased to exist.[12]

After 1830 benevolence took on a different character. Paradoxically, while Presbyterian churches were demonstrating their antiformalization in their advocacy of conference meetings, they were also expressing increased formalization in their clear and precise opposition to specific moral ills. In the mid-1820s, when most Presbyterian churches in Jefferson County were beginning to take a tougher stance against disciplinary infractions, the churches and their populations had reached a point of stability that allowed them to recognize and oppose societal ills more efficiently. Although these ills had existed before, and although the sessions had opposed these ills before, the sessions had not had the structure to check them. In 1831 the churches added conference meetings as a means of answering the desire for antiformalization among the overly structured Presbyterian congregations and as a further means of combating moral wrongs. Even though the Bible Society was an institutional hold-over from the period when the Presbyterians were not fully formalized in Jefferson County, and even though in its infancy it had opposed general moral delinquency, by the mid-1820s, when the Presbyterians had the means to fight particular moral wrongs, the Bible Society no longer sufficed to fight the moral wrongs. As a result the Presbyterians quietly withdrew their support and joined organizations targeted expressly against moral infractions.

Moreover in 1828, the session of the most exemplary of local formalist churches, First Presbyterian of Watertown, after years of suspending and excluding intemperate members, voted that Reverend Boardman give a sermon advocating abstinence from "ardent spirits" and that the Session should attempt "to form the Church and Society into a Society for the promotion of Temperance."[13] In 1829 the session decided that all candidates for admission should have to take a pledge renouncing "ardent spirits" except for medicinal purposes.[14] And in 1831, the session voted to extend the pledge to all members of the church who had joined before the institution of the pledge.[15] After these actions, many of the members suspended or excommunicated before the institution of the pledge requested to be reunited with the church, and cases of intemperance brought before the session disappeared almost entirely, despite the fact that the Session had recently created a special committee to examine accusations of intemperance. Not surprisingly, all of the actions supporting the Temperance Society preceded the 1831 revival, which did not develop until the summer months.

W. J. Rorabaugh notes in *The Alcoholic Republic* that cases of intemperance actually increased in the mid-1820s and then declined again in the 1830s. The increase in the 1820s was likely to have greater implications than in the previous two decades, while the decrease in the 1830s actually only met with greater activism. After 1820 intemperance was more of a threat to a settled society, and the settled society was more capable of discouraging it; and as Rorabaugh notes, temperance crusading also "satisfied many patriotic longings."[16] The most settled members of Jefferson County and thus the most opposed to intemperance were the members of the First Presbyterian Church of Watertown. And by the 1830s, First Presbyterian had apparently so thoroughly imbued the society with its concern with temperance that "sinners" were indeed reforming and asking to reunite with the church with the new converts from the conference meetings.

The First Presbyterian Church of Watertown, the paradigm of formalist efforts, differs from other local churches in the extent to which it carried out its formalist enterprises. The First Presbyterian Church of LeRay reacted more slowly in developing formalist interests and in counteracting intemperance. As the church had not reached stability until Finney arrived in 1824 as a settled minister, and since it was not the most socially elevated institution in the realm of James LeRay, it did not express a desire to supervise the rest of the community and did not form reform societies to assail moral desolation. Nonetheless it did contribute to the Commissioner's Fund, the Missionary Fund, and the Education Fund, to which all churches in the Presbytery contributed.[17] The level of benevolent reform activity varied in other local churches. The First Presbyterian Church of Theresa also in the northern section of the county, like the church in LeRay, did not form a temperance society or any other reform society, but did give to the Commissioner's Fund, the Missionary Fund, and the Education Fund.[18]

The First Presbyterian Church of Ellisburg, without the LeRay-imposed orderliness of the north, did form a temperance society on 26 December 1830 one month before Jedediah Burchard became its stated supply. However, Ellisburg was generally more interested in antiformalist reform. For example, Ellisburg, home of the earliest antiformal excitement in the Presbyterian churches of Jefferson County and site of Female Society missionaries' accusations of immorality, consistently manifested a staggering financial interest in antiformal benevolent movements such as the Bible Society,[19] but there are no indications that the temperance society in Ellisburg maintained a separate identity from the church in Ellisburg by holding regular meetings or by consistently prosecuting temperance violations.[20]

Similarly, the First Presbyterian Church of Adams never formed a temperance society and never prosecuted intemperance as vigorously as did the First Presbyterian Church of Watertown. But it did form a generic benevolent society in 1829 on the recommendation of the Presbytery of Watertown that churches form such societies. No further indications of the actions of this society appear in the records of the church, and no other church from the Presbytery of Watertown, whose records are extant, mentions this presbyterial action in 1829.[21]

Essentially, aside from the records of the First Presbyterian Church of Watertown, there are few indications from the churches themselves of their benevolent concerns. But P. H. Fowler's *Historical Sketch of Presbyterianism in the Synod of Central New York* suggests that the benevolent concerns of the church in Watertown, as well as its disciplinary concerns and antiformalization in the 1830s, were typical of the formalist denominations in other stable areas. Fowler's discussion of the history of benevolence in the synod indicates that sabbatarianism and temperance were the paramount benevolent concerns of the Presbyterians. While all churches disciplined those who violated the sabbath only some found themselves in a position to actively oppose the flagrant violation of the sabbath. Fowler thus asserts that the General Assembly first opposed the delivery of the mail on Sunday in 1812. And, he says that in the early 1820s, the furor over the profanation of the sabbath reached its apex along the future route of the Erie Canal when opposition arose to the transportation of the mail from Albany to Buffalo. Fowler does not allude to any sabbatarian activity in the Presbyteries of St. Lawrence, Watertown, or Ogdensburgh, and other extant primary and secondary sources do not indicate remarkable sabbatarian activity in Jefferson County.[22] Accordingly, although the concern with the sabbath, corresponds with the Presbyterian desire for "order and orthodoxy" and "law and order," it did not apparently develop as a significant preoccupation in northern New York where its desecration was not as egregious and where only the most formalist church in Jefferson County, First Presbyterian Church of Watertown, upheld the strictest reform and benevolence standards of the Presbyterians.[23]

Intemperance more easily generated interest in forming benevolent societies to counteract its effects in Jefferson County than did sabbatarianism. Both the presbyteries of Watertown and Ogdensburgh favored "total abstinence" from "ardent spirits." Moreover, Fowler notes that the decision to make a pledge of total abstinence a condition of church membership was advised by the Presbytery of Watertown in 1828 with the caveat that each church should individually make the decision to enforce that condition.[24] While other churches in Jefferson County formed temperance societies, evidently only the Watertown church opted to enforce the condition.

The only other benevolent reform that Fowler discusses is abolitionism. However, he does not describe Presbyterian interest in abolition primarily from the perspective of the sinfulness of slaveholding; instead, writing in 1877, he describes it with the intention of affirming the patriotism of New School Presbyterianism in the Civil War. Within his section on benevolence, Fowler follows his outlines of sabbatarianism and temperance reform with a subsection on "Patriotism of the Ministers and the Churches," in which he asserted that

> the *patriotism* of such Christians would be a matter of course. The revolution signally manifested it, as already remarked, and on the breaking out of hostilities against the Union, the men and women, whose denunciations of slavery was so largely the provocation of them, stood by their utterances, and as soldiers and the supporters and succorers of soldiers, fought and gave and worked in the maintenance of them.[25]

Presumably Fowler's reason for placing a description of Presbyterian patriotism among histories of Presbyterian reform was that patriotism and benevolent reform are equal indications of Presbyterian orderliness, orthodoxy, and lawfulness. In fact, Fowler's assertions regarding the position of New School Presbyterians during the Civil War would be a tenable description of Presbyterian efforts in general:

> Presbyterianism here prayed and preached, and upheld and encouraged the government by word and deed. Mr. Lincoln acknowledged the service of the church of the country at large and especially the cheer he got from it, and no church in any section of the country sent forth more encouragement and aid than did ours. It was no blind and headlong zeal that fired and impelled it, but a zeal according to knowledge.[26]

Fowler's declarations of Presbyterian patriotism as demonstrated through opposition to the evils of the slaveholding south require him to cite antislavery agitation among Presbyterians before the Civil War. But abolition clearly was not a widespread concern among law and order formalists, and apparently not a concern at all of Presbyterians in Jefferson County before 1840. Fowler's desire to maintain the impression of Presbyterian orderliness appears early in his description of antislavery efforts among Presbyterians: "Few of the resolutions and papers of the different Judicatories appear excessive in their tone and exceptionable in their sentiments."[27] Nowhere does Fowler assert that Presbyterian opposition was predicated on a disapproval of slavery or a concern for the slaves; for him it was entirely a political issue:

> Denunciations of the abrogation of the Missouri compromise, of the Kansas outrage, of the fugitive slave law, and of the assault on Mr. Charles Sumner;

> petitions for emancipation in the District of Columbia, and for emancipation throughout the country, and congratulations upon them, and tender sympathy is expressed for involuntary slaveholders and withering rebukes of reckless abolitionists.[28]

All of the issues Fowler considers essential to the antislavery effort are in some way politically based, while his final renunciation of "reckless abolitionists" manifests his objection to benevolent efforts that violated orderliness, orthodoxy, and the law. He notes further that these "reckless abolitionists" threatened the welfare of the Presbyterian church:

> The ultraists, it must be confessed, were violent and intolerant. They permitted no bounds to hostility to slavery, and no differences from them in opinions about suppressing it, and scarcely any sharing of interest between its abolition and any other good cause, and they held back from the destruction of nothing that they thought a hindrance to it. The welfare of a church, the prosperity of religion, the teaching of the Scriptures, the Bible itself were made sacrifices to it.[29]

Ultraists, according to Fowler's use here, represented the second definition, or the archetypically antiformalist group.[30] Fowler concludes his discussion of "ultraists" by noting that most of them ultimately left the Presbyterian church and that, although he "shrunk from their false fire," he considered them holy and "sincere Christian people."[31] Meanwhile, James H. Hotchkin, writing the history of Presbyterianism in western New York in 1848, does not consider Presbyterian antislavery efforts worthy of reference in his history of benevolence.[32] These sources indicate that abolitionism did not generally appeal to formalists, who sought orderliness rather than the overthrow of a corrupt though otherwise legal system.[33]

This position explains the difficulties Rhoda Bement faced when she "challeng[ed] the authority of her minister for his refusal to announce abolitionist lectures from his pulpit."[34] Glenn C. Altschuler and Jan M. Salzgaber describe her resulting trial in 1843 at the First Presbyterian Church in Seneca Falls as an indication of the "perfectionist" impulse bred by Second Great Awakening ardor. They contend, as do many other historians, that the Arminianism inherent in revivalism encouraged a belief in the freedom to act and a desire to eradicate all sins. More probably though, Rhoda Bement's efforts were not a result of revivalism, since revivalism did not lead to a widespread appearance of abolitionism in post-1830, revival-influenced Presbyterianism. Her efforts were the result of the fact that she was de jure a member of the Presbyterian church, but de facto a member of the antiformalist Wesleyan Methodist church in Seneca Falls. Essentially, the Presbyterian church brought her to trial and excommunicated her because she espoused the values of an antiformalist denomination.[35]

As a woman in a formalist denomination, she had much less capacity to express herself than did women in antiformalist denominations who followed the less stringent and more charismatic laws of their denominations that openly sought the influence and openness of the Holy Spirit.[36] And despite the apparent liberality of the Presbyterians in encouraging the revivals of the 1830s, Presbyterians remained concerned with only those moral issues that threatened law, order, and orthodoxy. While they could understand a concern over the propriety of slavery, they had greater concerns for women speaking in assemblies and for the deleterious effects of enthusiasm, whether in revivals or reform movements, that could disturb their relative stability. Thus, the difficulties Rhoda Bement experienced say less about the effects of revivalism than they do about the failure of revivalism to affect the Presbyterians, who maintained their formalist concerns even after the antiformalist revivals. The trial of Rhoda Bement is significant because of its distinctiveness. Most other Presbyterians did not approve of her actions, and she was excommunicated. If revivalism in and around Seneca Falls had led to widespread concern among Presbyterians about abolition and the right of women to speak publicly, the Presbyterians of Seneca Falls would not have rescinded their connection with Rhoda Bement. As I will suggest when I discuss antiformalist reform, Bement's concern and actions were the logical result of antiformalist practices and beliefs.

Finney, whose most outspoken reform interest was abolitionism (and even then reform was never one of his overriding interests), and his abolitionist convert, Theodore Dwight Weld, were actually not at all typical of antebellum Presbyterians, as Finney's defection from Presbyterianism suggests. Furthermore, Finney's revivals and meetings, in which he allowed women to speak in public, resembled antiformal assemblies. Thus, it is misleading to conclude that "Finney-ite" Arminian revivalism produced the reform impulse. The reform impulse for orderliness and orthodoxy, even for what some historians refer to as "perfectionism," was inherent in Presbyterian churches before Finney's revivals. In fact, the First Presbyterian Church of Watertown, which encouraged formalist reforms and disregarded the Finney revivals in northern Jefferson County in the mid-1820s, sought moral "perfection" in its members through discipline beginning in the mid-1820s. Three years before the antiformalization of the church in Watertown in the 1830s, the church instituted the temperance pledge for its members. In the meantime, the most revivalistically fervid churches in Jefferson County, the churches in Ellisburg, LeRay, and Adams, did not encourage moral probity to the same extent as did the nonrevivalistic Watertown church, and the towns outside of Watertown did not institute the temperance pledge at all. In fact, this reflects the pattern of formation of temperance societies after 1826; the American Temperance Society, for example, was organized not on the revivalistically fervid and allegedly perfectionist frontier but in staid Boston in 1826. And it was the moralistic Lyman Beecher, skeptical of Finney's earliest and most antiformal methods and intentions, who furthered the cause of temperance.[37]

In the meantime antimasonry was not a significant concern among Presbyterians. Following William Morgan's abduction and murder in Batavia, New York, before he could publish an expose of the Freemasons, two camps developed in the northeast and in New York state in particular: those who believed that a corrupt cabal, which was attempting to control the government, had had Morgan killed and had prevented his murderers from going to trial; and those who believed that the Masons were patriotic, upstanding citizens.[38] Presbyterians, who as a rule represented the highest class in northeastern communities, did not show a strong inclination to support antimasonry. The model of formalism, the First Presbyterian Church of Watertown, in fact condemned antimasonry as "ignorant" after some church members stated that they could not come to the communion table because other members of the church were Masons. The offended antimasons were allowed to leave the church in Watertown for the church in Rutland:

> Whereas these bretheren represent that they have acted conscientiously in absenting themselves from the Lords Supper & that they cannot now see it to be their duty to commune with this church whilst it retains in its communion members of the Masonic institution, although we consider that by such conduct they have violated their covenant with the Lord & his church, & have acted contrary to his word, yet as they reside in the vicinity of Rutland; as we desire their benefit; as we are bound, if it is possible to live peacibly with all men; & are persuaded that they have done this thing ignorantly, we do grant them permission to connect themselves with the church in Rutland.[39]

Four men and two women were dismissed from the church following this decree. It is significant that they did not live in the village of Watertown but in the vicinity of Rutland. They were then probably marginal members of the commercially oriented, relatively urban Watertown church. The only other significant Presbyterian discussion of antimasonry took place at the First Presbyterian Church of Adams, which in 1826 decided that all members of the session including the pastor, John Sessions, who were Masons should relinquish their Masonic membership. They renounced their membership on 1 January 1829.[40]

Extant newspapers indicate that antimasonic fervor achieved great strength in Jefferson County, and that in 1834, Masons in Watertown, including members of the session of the church in Watertown, renounced their Masonic membership. This change does not indicate a revolution in the values of the Presbyterians, merely a capitulation to societal pressure; the former Masons asserted in an article that they were leaving the Masons not because they agreed with the political denunciations of Masonry, but because they believed the social upheaval in opposition to it had negated the "benevolent" influence of Freemasonry. They further maintained that Masons were "patriotic," "virtuous and pure men," who could "never divest themselves of self-respect, nor consent that others should deprive them of civil rights by reason of their having been such." Thus, they asserted that they were renouncing their Masonic membership in favor of other more "expedient" benevolence.[41] If antimasonry is connected with revivalism among Presbyterians, it is probably less a result of an actual connection between a perfectionist theology resulting from the prevalence of revivals than it is the coincident result of antiformalism becoming so extensive in the culture, adapting to a small extent to the culture and thus appearing more palatable to Presbyterians in toned-down revivals, and in the predominant demand for the downfall of Masonry. Finney not surprisingly distinguished himself from the formalist stronghold by denouncing Masonry himself before the general formalist Presbyterian acquiescence in the 1830s. Nevertheless, his 1824 departure from the Masons in Adams was probably more a result of the fact that he was leaving Adams than of premature antimasonic sentiment.

These manifestations of the Presbyterian inclination in reform are an indication of the significance of Paul Johnson's description of Rochester's Presbyterian society in the midst of the Finney revivals of 1831. Johnson remarks that the wealthiest classes in Rochester sought to reform the community through the revivals. Since by the 1830s revivals had become a tool for temperance and sabbatarian reform among Presbyterians, Rochester's moralistic Presbyterians probably did hope to improve moral adherence in the community by inviting Finney to the Third Presbyterian Church. Johnson's discussion of the Rochester revivals reveals that neither abolitionism nor antimasonry was a concern of the reform-minded Presbyterians of Rochester.[42] After all, neither promised to improve Rochester's moral quality, and in fact could have threatened the orderliness of Rochester. Hence, Finney was merely the antiformalist vehicle for Presbyterian reform goals in a year when antiformalizing, reform-oriented revivals were unusually successful among Presbyterians. For as William McLoughlin has noted, Finney held the antiformalist view that reform would follow from widespread conversions of the unregenerate and not from political or social action to reform society.[43] However, the few reform interests Finney advocated, such as abolitionism, were not the interests of those who invited him to Third Presbyterian.

Baptists

Until formalization in the 1830s the records of the Black River Baptist Association are overwhelmingly concerned with the number of admissions to their churches. Just as the circular letters did not encourage discipline until formalization, they did not propound moralistic benevolent reform movements until formalization either. Still, while the Presbyterians maintained their formalist concern with moral probity despite the antiformalist influence of revivals, the Baptists maintained their overriding concern with salvation over morality, despite the formalist influence of reform concerns. And while Presbyterian reform reflected on a wider scale Presbyterian disciplinary concerns with orderliness and orthodoxy, Baptist reform reflected Baptist concerns with difficulties between people, as well as with the necessity of salvation. In the same way that Presbyterian reform began with an antiformalist inclination, which was dominant until the 1820s when Presbyterian congregations became settled enough to express their innate formalism, Baptists expressed their antiformalist impulse soon after their establishment of churches. Not until after formalization in the 1830s, however, did reform grow more appealing to antiformalists.

As with Presbyterians, missionary work was the preeminent mode of accomplishing the earliest Baptist reforms. Moreover, Baptist missionary conventions were the sole means of uniting Baptists beyond their local associations. While Presbygationalists established missionary societies soon after the settlement of a region in order to evangelize Presbygationalists without organized churches along the frontier, Baptists did not establish missionary societies in order to evangelize other Baptists. For Presbyterians, missionary societies represented the earliest stage in formalization. However, for Baptists the appearance of missionary societies signified emerging stability. Domestic missionary societies were not necessary among Baptists who did not need outside ministers to organize churches among them, since Baptists could call an uneducated farmer-minister from among potential or actual congregants. Thus, when Presbyterian missionary and Bible societies were losing their strength and prestige in the 1820s, Baptist missionary societies were forming. And not until the formalization of the Baptists in the 1830s were Baptists interested in forwarding essentially formalist reforms such as temperance and sabbatarianism. Rather than attempting to control the morality of a region, Baptist reformers sought to improve the condition of the oppressed.

Hence, the missionary impulse among Baptists satisfied the Baptist reformers' interest in succoring the downtrodden, usually in foreign countries such as Burma, where without native Baptists no Baptist churches could be formed without outside help. Unlike the Presbyterians who, in their missionary reports, usually depict areas without ministers and churches as morally desolate, Baptists depict those areas as suffering and pitiable:

> Thus reflecting on the multitude of benefits by which we are surrounded, our minds are excited to impart a portion of our substance, as a mean[s] of enlightening the poor Heathen, who grope in darkness, and the shadow of death. Our hearts bleed for these wretched beings, who are ignorant of the God that made them—of Christ who died for them—of their duty both towards God and man, and having no one to teach them—involved in the most dismal state of darkness, superstition and idolatry.[44]

The overwhelmingly pious and fervid residents—the women in particular—of Henderson and Ellisburg, who led in the formation of the Baptist Association for Foreign Missions of the Black River Association in 1817, also consistently led other towns in the financial support of the Foreign Missions.[45] These residents were the same people whose religious enthusiasm Presbygationalist ministers from the Female Missionary Society of the Western District described as characteristic of moral desolation.

However, the Baptist understanding of moral righteousness, as evidenced in the primacy of benevolent work through missionary societies, demonstrates the significance of the formalist misreading of the Baptist mentality. Since fervor was for the Baptists merely sincere public prayer, blessed by an outpouring of grace, and prayer was for the Baptists the chief means of achieving moral righteousness, the Baptists considered prayer the most efficient means of removing moral evil.

Furthermore, they concluded that concentration on a population's moral condition was misplaced benevolence and a misunderstanding of the root cause:

> In this day of abounding wickedness and alarming judgments, while our neighbors of another denomination, are forming what they call moral societies, professedly to check the raised progress of vice and promote morality: Let us who have been solemnly buried with Christ in baptism into death, feel the obligation we are under to walk in newness of life; and that we may obtain so desirable an object, let us reflect with due solemnity on our high profession. Our neighbors sprinkle their infant offspring, in the name of the sacred Trinity, while they are incapable of subscribing to articles of faith or of understanding what a profession of the Christian religion means, and the bonds they are laid under on this account, to watch as becometh the gospel, are not voluntary in them, but imposed on them by their parents or overseers—while we profess that we understandingly, believingly and heartily receive the Lord Jesus Christ as our Lord and law giver, and receive the ordinance of baptism in obedience to his command. We see that we have made an higher profession of religion than the greater part of those before mentioned, who are esteemed and dedicated visible members of the gospel church . . . that if after our publicly renouncing the wages of sin and service of satan, we turn back to our former course of living after the flesh, and pursue the empty shadows of the vain world, our sin must be doubly aggravating in the sight of God and men. . . . If the grace of God which bringeth salvation, doth not influence us to deny ungodliness and worldly lusts, and to live soberly, righteously and godly in this present world, we have not reason to fear that our profession is but a vain pretence.[46]

Although not argued precisely, the continued gist of this circular letter is that Baptists do not need to form moral reform societies because they have chosen their membership in a Christian church as adults, and because they have been baptized in the only legitimate way. Thus, they have received special grace that prevents the need for additional moral coercion. Moreover, those whom they encourage to join their churches will also receive this grace, a far more powerful force than a moral reform society. However, if any of them strays from the correct path, it will be that much more damning for them.

The circular letter also intimates that the moral reform to which the other denomination—apparently Presbyterians—were directing themselves was directed chiefly toward other Presbyterians. This follows logically to the extent that Presbygationalist missionaries did work primarily among other Presbygationalists, to form churches. Many of the missionaries disdained Baptists and Methodists, and did not urgently exhort them to join Presbygationalist churches. Furthermore, despite suggestions that Presbyterian moral reform was intended for the general population as much as it was for Presbyterians, all indications are that the movements acted dominantly among other Presbyterians through the disciplinary power of the churches and through demands that members recognize the sanctity of the sabbath and sign temperance pledges. The circular letter's assertion that the Baptists' means of receiving grace precluded the necessity of their forming moral reform societies also followed from this understanding of the function of moral reform.

Baptists in Jefferson County did, however, join with Presbyterians apparently as lesser members in the organization of the Jefferson County Bible Society in 1817. The society's range went beyond the churches to find those "destitute" of the Bible and then to provide them with the Scriptures. For the Presbyterians, this served foremost as a means of improving the morality of the nonchurchgoing population by encouraging them to join any church; while for the few Baptist members, this served chiefly as a method of bringing unfortunate "heathens" into churches. However, for Baptists in 1817, benevolent organizations outside of their churches, dominated by ministers from another denomination, were not the most appealing, and organizations whose subtly expressed principal aim was the improvement of morality did not satisfy Baptists interests. This changed after the 1830s, when the antiformalist Bible Society did not allay Presbyterian anxieties over specific moral ills, and when it began to appeal to Baptists who were formalizing but still essentially antiformalist.

Typical of the Baptists who worked for the success of the Bible Society in the 1830s was Jacob Knapp, whose success solidified formalist influence among the Baptists. In fact, Knapp's career reflects the evolution of Baptist interest in benevolence from the antiformalism of the Bible

Society to the formalism of temperance reform connected with revivalism. While enthusiasm had long been a staple among the Baptists, and while antiformalism usually characterized Baptist reform movements, Knapp institutionalized and formalized revivalism in the 1830s, and he initiated concern with institutionalized reform, beginning with Bible and missionary societies and ultimately leading to moralistic reform.

The transformation began in 1817 with the creation of the missionary society within the Black River Baptist Association. It satisfied the desire for an outside means of encouraging evangelization to the Baptist church, the prevailing concern of the revivalistically inclined members of the church. The missionary association also provided a sought-after means of expressing piety in addition to prayer. Circular letters after the organization of the association regularly encouraged Baptists to maintain a "consistent Christian character." This meant that merely praying in public or in "secret" was not enough to constitute a Christian life; one had also to demonstrate one's interest in the salvation of others. Additionally, the letters urged that merely giving to the missionary association was not enough, if one did not also pray in public and in private. The earliest complaint in 1828 was against those who attended church and prayed regularly but who did not support benevolence: "We are aware that many who are otherwise conspicuous christians, contribute but little or nothing to the fund of benevolence, to whom God hath given abundance."[47] And seven years later, when accessions were diminishing while discipline and benevolence were thriving, the circular letter expressed a conservative tone in its urging that "to work on the out-side while the in-side is neglected, is mere hypocrisy," and furthermore that charity did not involve only the "carnal" methods but that charity was also "simple holy affection—pure love to God and man."[48] These statements represented first an attempt to bring formalist reform ideas more fully into the Baptist churches in the years preceding formalization, and second, in the 1830s, efforts to check the success of these movements, which appeared to the still-antiformalist Baptists a false expression of piety, when they usurped the supremacy of prayer.

As missionary societies became an integral part of Baptist identity, the pious wishes of those working in foreign missions, such as Burma, began to appear as a further expression of Baptist piety. The Black River Baptist Association throughout its history had championed the support of the lower classes as well as the oppressed and had complained that wealth destroyed piety. However, it was not until the formalization, or maturation of the Missionary Society that the Black River Association explicitly and urgently advised simpler values, espoused by missionaries. The most obvious case was in 1832 when the association urged the acceptance of the "Rev. Mr. [Adoniram] Judson's Letter to the Female Members of Christian Churches in the United States of America." As a result of this, the association condemned in 1832 with Judson the vanity of dressing well, and in particular of wearing mourning apparel.[49] As with most Baptist reforms, this one had little to do with maintaining moral orderliness but noted that the suffering "infidels" in Burma were prevented from joining the Baptist church because they found that its members, who had traveled with missionaries to Burma, dressed too fashionably. Additionally, Judson found that the practice of dressing well led to the diminution of "Christian" feeling in the wearer:

> In raising up a Church of Christ in this heathen land, and in laboring to elevate the minds of the female converts to the standards of the gospel, we have always found one chief obstacle in that principle of vanity, that love of dress and display . . . which has, in every age and in all countries, been a ruling passion of the fair sex, as the love of riches, power, and fame has characterized the other. That obstacle lately became more formidable, through the admission of two or three fashionable females into the church, and the arrival of several missionary sisters, dressed and adorned in that manner, which is too prevalent in our beloved native land. On my meeting the church, after a year's absence, I beheld an appalling profusion of ornaments, and saw that the demon of vanity was laying waste the female department.[50]

After recognizing this "demon," Judson visited a native people, the Karens, who, he said, had begun to treasure wearing fine clothes and jewelry as a result of their contact with female missionaries. He began to urge female missionaries in Burma that they not wear ornaments because it represented an attachment to worldly values and because many Burmese were opting for ornaments over baptism, when given the choice. Consequently, Judson urged the formation of Plain Dress Societies among all denominations in the United States to end the problem of vanity at the source. However, there are no indications that the Presbyterians, Congregationalists, or Methodists responded favorably to Judson's exhortation.

Antimasonry surfaced in the Baptist churches in the 1820s and 1830s as a primarily antiformalist concern and paralleled Judson's concern with excessive ornamentation. In great contrast to the Presbyterian reaction to antimasonry, antimasonry for the Baptists was an all-consuming concern.

Baptist churches in Jefferson County commonly demanded that their membership renounce association with Freemasonry, and the Black River Baptist Association condemned antimasonry long before it did disorderly immorality. Since antimasonry was concerned with the apparent oppressive and corrupt use of power, the Baptists' description of Masonry embodied Judson's depiction of the male counterpart to lavish ornamentation: "riches, power, and fame."

Baptist churches expressed their opposition to antimasonry with the same certainty and virulence with which Presbyterians condemned intemperance. In 1832 the churches of the Black River Association met outside of the annual meeting to discuss whether the churches in the association should accept as members congregants of the Watertown church who had been excluded because they were Masons. They concluded that

> whereas the resolutions on the subject of Speculative Freemasonry, passed in the Convention at Whitesboroh [sic] have been & still are differently explained & differently understood, by . . . different Churches, & individuals, & beleiving [sic] that a deffinite [sic] & an explicit expression is required.—We are therefore of opinion that the Institution of Speculative Freemasonry, is a wicked institution, & ought to be disfelllowshiped [sic] & abandoned by every professed follower of the Lord Jesus.[51]

Three years before this resolution, the committee appointed by the association to determine the policy regarding Freemasonry had determined that the association as a body should not judge those who are Masons. However, the members of the committee opted to express their personal opinions in the publication of the association's "Minutes":

> *Resolved,* That we view with regret the existence of any attachment to that institution, and deem it the duty of all who have been connected with it, to do what is in their power to remove the grievance; and do recommend it to them to take such measures as may relieve the Association from any concern in the matter. We think that the difficulty should for the present, be referred to *themselves,* and be removed to a conference of *themselves,* and the result presented to the churches: and that the Association with this resolution dismiss the subject, thinking that advice to the churches should be deferred for the present.[52]

The consistency and strength of Baptist opposition to antimasonry, as well as the association's disinclination to involve itself in the dispute is more clearly apparent in the circular letter that urged Baptists to look beyond antimasonry:

> Are there not many in this and other Associations to be found, who seem to treat masonry as though it was the only thing to be feared or resisted in the camp? Surely, it is not the business of this circular to arrest or counteract a bible zeal for this or any other evil. But, brethren, a word to those who have from year to year, little or no concern for the Church of God, except when masonry is agitated, leaving it to serve alone on most other occasions. . . . Let it be sincerely inquired, whether pride, worldly mindedness, intemperance and covetousness are to be overlooked, and we to remain inactive, and perfectly unalarmed, until we find a brother who has masonic oaths upon him.[53]

Not surprisingly, both antimasonry and Second Great Awakening revivalism are associated with Jacksonian democracy. The enthusiastic revivalism associated with this era's fervency, even among formalists, was derived originally from antiformalist denominations, which advocated above all else the exaltation of the common person. In missionary work that meant bringing to the "heathen" the benefits—chiefly salvation—of knowledge of the Bible and of church membership. It meant allowing women to participate in the decisions and in the disciplinary proceedings of the church. For Judson's female followers this meant renouncing the attire of the powerful, while for male Baptists it meant renouncing the secret society of the powerful—Masonry.

Baptists expressed the same concern in their denunciation of slavery. Unlike the Presbyterians, the Baptist denunciation, which came approximately ten years sooner, was much less concerned with the politics of slavery and much more concerned with the immorality of holding human beings in bondage. In fact, those whom Fowler refers to as "ultraists" among the Presbyterian abolitionists are apparently most closely related to the Baptists, who manifested as much fervor in their opposition to slavery as in their revivals.

Among the churches in the Black River Association, the first and most strident denunciation of slavery appeared in the records of the First Baptist Church of Adams in 1837:

> 1st Resolved—That we consider the holding of human beings as property, to be a practice forbidden by the law of God; at variance with the Gospel of

> Jesus Christ; a practice, which no legislation can make morrally [sic] right. Which no wourldly [sic] consideration can justify—
>
> 2d Resolved—That our Brethren at the South in supporting American Slavery are guilty of Violating the Law of Christ—Which requires us "to love our Neighbour as ourselves"—"to do unto others as we would they should do unto us"—and of a violation of his great commission to teach all Nations—
>
> 3d Resolved—That as we stand in connection with them as members of Christs Church (and as silence upon this subject would bid them Gods speed;)—we feel it our duty to enter our solemn protest against Slavery as a highhanded sin against Heaven—and that while our Brethren continue to practice of this System of oppression and brutalising human beings made in the image of God; We cannot sanction this most fruitful source of vice by communing with them at the Lords Table.[54]

As is typical with Baptist moral concerns, orderliness and orthodoxy are not prominent issues. The primary issue the church raises reflects the Baptist disciplinary concern with personal disputes; the Church in Adams considered it wrong to mistreat people, and it saw in the slave system a replica of the evil oppressiveness of antimasonry. Moreover, the holding of slaves resembled the carnal ornamentation that Judson had seen in some women.

The first reference to the problem of slavery appeared in the "Minutes of the Black River Baptist Association" in 1838 in connection with all of the benevolent objects that Baptists upheld. In both 1838 and 1839 the association's condemnations of slavery asserted that slavery constituted a wrong done by one human being against another, and that, in contradistinction to the Presbyterian position, such "oppression" should be opposed regardless of the political consequences. The listing of the other Baptist-supported moral causes reflected post-1830 formalization within the basically antiformalist denomination.[55]

As a reflection of the post-1830 membership in the Jefferson County Bible Society, the Black River Association for the first time in its history in 1838 advocated the support of the "Bible cause [which] holds first place among the Benevolent Institutions of the age; and should receive the cordial support of every Christian."[56] Domestic and foreign missions also remained prominent Baptist reform concerns. However, domestic missions did not parallel Presbygationalist domestic missions that sought to form Presbygationalists into churches. Domestic missions resembled foreign missions in that the aim was to evangelize "heathens" such as Native Americans.[57]

Sabbath Schools and the "Tract Cause" were new interests for Baptists, but ones which represented well Baptists concerns with evangelization. The new-found interest with ministerial education in the 1830s, though, manifests the influence of formalization. It was no longer sufficient for farmer-ministers to labor among their neighbors. Many ministers needed training in order to succeed as missionaries, and many uneducated ministers caused the association embarrassment:

> The manner of examining and setting apart candidates to the work of the gospel ministry, in time past, has been attended with some embarrassment: And . . . it is important that an opportunity should be afforded for a more thorough examination than what can generally be had, where the examination and ordination take place on the same day.[58]

Thus, the association urged greater bureaucratization in the "setting apart" of ministers and greater formalization in the choosing of ministers. This development would snowball; more educated ministers after 1830 would eventually be less open to enthusiastic revivals, but more interested in orderliness.

"Moral reform societies," which the association had opposed in 1814, and temperance reform became acceptable interests by 1838. Nonetheless, the association appended a note to its 1838 minutes indicating that "a resolution on Temperance was adopted in connexion with the above [African emancipation]; but on account of having been mislaid, is omitted in the Minutes."[59] Finally, in 1838 the Baptists reacted to intemperance in the same way that the Presbyterians had in 1827: "In the judgment of this Association, the hand of fellowship should be withheld from all those who *make, sell,* or, as a beverage, *use* ardent spirits."[60] They did not, however, urge the formation of temperance societies.

The Baptists' advocacy of moral reform evidences the continued influence of antiformalism despite formalization, as they opposed "licentiousness" but did not exhort other Baptists to defeat it. Instead they asserted cryptically "that the prevalency of Licentiousness should awaken the attention and call forth the philanthropick efforts of every christian, to promote virtue and moral purity."[61]

Thus, into the 1830s Baptists consistently demonstrated an antiformalist interest in evangelization over the maintenance of doctrinal purity, and evinced a greater concern with maintaining moral purity through baptisms than through efforts to control society. After formalization, the antiformalist tinge remained; Baptist moral concerns never identified entirely with Presbyterian concerns, even though the Baptists eventually took an interest in temperance. And even when the Presbyterians demonstrated an interest in a Baptist reform such as abolition, the Presbyterians remained more interested in the political and patriotic implications of the reform than with the morality of slavery. Probably to the Presbyterians slavery appeared less immoral than to the Baptists, because antislavery agitation resulted in disorder, while slavery itself caused no disorder in the lives of northern Presbyterians.

Methodist reform interests, on the other hand, are not as easily gauged. No church records remain. However, changes in the *Methodist Magazine* and the *Methodist Quarterly Review* indicate that Methodist reform closely resembled Baptist reform. In 1829 the first article in opposition to intemperance appeared, and with the arrival of Bangs and the transformation of the *Magazine* into the *Quarterly Review*, reform interests such as temperance, colonization of the slaves, sabbatarianism, the American Bible Society, and theological education became common. Additionally, in 1840, the Jefferson County Bible Society remarked favorably that, for the first time, Methodists were actively participating in the society's efforts.[62] Nevertheless, the Methodists also maintained their antiformalism, as they continued to extol the values of extemporaneous preaching and to applaud "Old Methodism" as "Christianity in earnest."[63]

Although Nancy Hewitt's division of nineteenth-century female benevolence in Rochester into ultraist, perfectionist, and benevolent well describes the class stratification of moral reform concerns, it does not work for Jefferson County. Perfectionist reform does not appear to have developed there.[64]

The Presbyterians of Jefferson County represent Hewitt's benevolent class in Rochester. They sought to improve conditions and to "order and control society," but they did not want to become overly involved with working among the impoverished. Hewitt posits that this interest in "order and control" resulted from the influence of "a more rationalistic religious tone, most forcefully articulated by Asahel Nettleton, Lyman Beecher, and Nathaniel Taylor." New Haven theology, however, was an eastern phenomenon that most fully expressed the formalist perspective. It is unlikely that benevolent reformers in Jefferson County were responding to New Haven theology as much as they were characterizing themselves as formalists.

She argues that perfectionist women were married to upwardly mobile husbands in the commercial economy. These women, she says, responded best to Finney's revivals. Such a group of men or women simply does not appear in the primarily agrarian communities of Jefferson County. On the other hand, the women, whom she refers to as "ultraists," appeared as both men and women among the Baptists. Hewitt contends that in Rochester, ultraists were generally Hicksite Quakers from agricultural regions who had no stake in the governing order. The Baptists in Jefferson County, though, resemble these Hicksite women. They too lived in agricultural regions, and did not demonstrate an interest in maintaining the governing order.

While Fowler often appended to his descriptions of Presbyterian actions the reassurance that the Presbyterians had acted patriotically, the Baptists never demonstrate such a concern. The Baptists' interest in overturning the powerful cabal of Masons, their allowing of women to participate in the churches' decisions and disciplinary actions, and their distress over the oppression of slaves all denote that Baptists in Jefferson County were, like the Hicksite Quakers in Rochester, radical, nonhierarchical, and agrarian. Furthermore, given the early influence of the Henderson and Adams Baptists on Finney's theology, it is likely that this reform philosophy influenced him. The perfectionist impulse Hewitt identifies in Rochester may have been a later Finneyite convergence of benevolence and ultraism. Nevertheless, the phenomenon was foreign to Finney's home in Jefferson County.

John Corrigan's description of the Businessman's Revival in 1858 Boston bears some resemblance to revival and reform during the Second Great Awakening in Jefferson County. Just as in Jefferson County where religious expression mirrored the social order, Corrigan asserts that the revival among the middle classes of Boston was "an enactment of the social order in Boston."[65] Although those who participated in the revival expressed themselves emotionally, Corrigan notes that they "frequently made the point that there were no 'excesses' or 'religious fanaticism' in the revival. Prayer meetings were viewed as controlled expressions of religious piety."[66] In effect, the revival of the middle classes in Boston was a formalist affair. Also just as in Jefferson County, the revival did not necessarily create an interest in reform. Instead, abolitionism and temperance (as well as spiritualism) were "alternative thrills" to revivalism. Rather than finding that the revival led to increased interest in reform, Corrigan contends that reform movements provided "emotional engagement" for those who may not have been interested in the revivals. The temperance movement, for example, afforded "emotional meetings, exuberant marches, tear-jerking testimonies, and heartfelt pleas."[67] Still, despite this (controlled) emotional expression, those involved in the temperance movement seem to have favored the formalist social order as they rejected radicals who favored women's rights, or the "hyperemotional" abolition movement.[68] On the other hand, abolitionists and Methodists disparaged the "machinery" of the formalist revival.[69]

These findings of a similar social order in 1858 Boston suggest that the structure of revival and reform in 1820s and 1830s Jefferson County typified revival and reform throughout the Northeast. They also suggest that future studies of Second Great Awakening revivalism may want to delineate more clearly the realms of the revivalists and the reformers.

6
Conclusion

Few historians have sought to understand the social environment in which Charles Finney experienced his conversion and in which he first formulated his beliefs. Because of the easier availability of records from urban areas, and because of a greater geographical and historical familiarity with cities such as Rochester and Utica than with Watertown and Evans Mills, historians have overlooked the significance of an obscure rural region. Moreover, because of the greater concern among Presbyterians for maintaining records, historians have ignored the encouragement of fervor coming from the Baptists and Methodists, whose records are meager. As a result of the oversight, historians have often mistaken a normal nineteenth-century expression of fervor for a response to disorder, and they have misidentified the fervor as a Presbyterian phenomenon. Fervor was for Jefferson County's Baptists and Methodists, and probably for most rural Baptists and Methodists, until 1830 normal and expected.

Until the 1830s, most Presbyterians in the north frowned on ecstatic revivalism as unseemly and impious. Instead they advocated strict moralism. Although socioeconomic factors, such as the different structures of communities in the northern, southern, and central sections of Jefferson County, did provide different environments for the expression of piety, it was less through the outside effect of disastrous social changes and more through the effect of decades of interaction that the formalist Presbyterians and antiformalist Baptists and Methodists grew more similar. Finney's interaction with the groups sped, but did not cause, mutual assimilation. In both the northern and southern sections, the nonelites were willing to engage in fervid religious expression.

After 1830, Presbyterians partially through Finney's influence began to consider planned, orderly revivals a sign of piety as long as the revivals engendered interest in improving the moral quality of the community. Thus, Presbyterians who had long viewed themselves as the bastion of moral rectitude did not develop an interest in moral reform as a result of a perfectionist impulse inherent in revivalism; they adopted revivalism as a new means of maintaining moral order. In the meantime, even the antiformalists could not maintain the excitements that drove genuinely intense revivalism. So by the 1830s, revivalism became for them an expected and planned practice, much like the form the Presbyterians appropriated. However, the antiformalists maintained their interest in evangelism rather than moralism; they channeled their interests into missionary work and into efforts to uplift the oppressed rather than into societal moral improvement.

Finney labored in Jefferson County from 1824 to 1825 in small, unconventionally structured communities, such as Evans Mills, Leraysville, and Antwerp. He brought to the Presbyterians of these communities, who had no settled ministers since the time of their establishments as communities, the expression of spontaneous piety common to Baptists and Methodists. Later when he traveled to Utica, New York, and Rochester, his attempts to formulate and codify the best means for encouraging the expression of piety created in his own theology the same routinization of the formerly spontaneous Baptist and Methodist expression of faith that northern Presbyterians in general experienced after 1831. However, like the Baptists and Methodists, he continued to support evangelical reform rather than moral reform.

Eventually Baptists and Methodists did evolve to the point that they joined the Presbyterians as formalist faiths, but antiformalism did not disappear. The antiformalist and formalist interaction that catalyzed the Second Great Awakening has continued into the twentieth century, while antiformalism continues to thrive without the impetus of disastrous outside forces. Since the formalization of revivals in the 1830s, revivalism has not defined antiformalism. In the twentieth century, the same disorder and enthusiasm deriving from "Baptism by the Spirit" appears among Pentecostalists, who like nineteenth-century Baptists and Methodists, maintain more of an interest in evangelical reform than in moral reform. New Age groups are also antiformalist in their belief in an ill-defined cosmic force whose function resembles that of the Holy Spirit. Meanwhile, mainline Protestants—including Methodists and American Baptists, as well as Fundamentalists, chiefly Southern Baptists—are formalists in their maintenance of orderliness in their services and, especially among the Fundamentalists, in their easily apparent moral agendas.

Turner, Bergson, and Durkheim provide useful terms for understanding modern religion, as they do for understanding nineteenth-century frontier religion. Antiformalists tend toward antistructure, and formalists tend toward structure. As in the nineteenth-century, antistructural religions do not represent a condition dependent on structure; in the twentieth century these too are open religions. The formalist or structured religions are closed religions. Furthermore, the level of structure in the denominations suggests the level of structure in the secular lives of the adherents. There are some indications that Pentecostalists have begun to formalize and that with this formalization has come an elevation in their social status.[1] However, part of its appeal traditionally has been its ability to respond to its followers' sense of dislocation and alienation.[2] In the same way that antiformalists represented their marginality through their fervor in the nineteenth century, modern Pentecostalists respond to their estrangement with fervor in the twentieth century. Although Fundamentalism seems to attract a following similar to that of Pentecostalism, Fundamentalism actually tends to attract a less-alienated following, one that would aspire to a closed religion. George Marsden has noted, for example, that a large number of Fundamentalists are engineers who seek the same level of exactness and certitude in their religion that they do in their work.[3] They have joined the ranks of the middle class more than have Pentecostalists.

Mainline Protestants share characteristics with the formalists of the nineteenth century. They attract the middle to upper middle class and are likely to work in commercial and political fields that encourage the formalism that reappears in their denominations. New Age followers are less easily evaluated according to this pattern, as their antiformalism has discouraged formal membership lists. However, it appears that it attracts those who perceive that they should correctly align themselves with the "dominant social and economic system," in the same way that they need to align themselves with cosmic forces.[4]

In all of these examples, antistructure or antiformalism is not an aberrant condition in reaction against structure or formalism. The antiformalists or open religions can be defined against structure and formalism in the same way that structure and formalism are defined against antistructure and antiformalism. Open religion and antistructure is as permanent a condition as is closed religion, although both groups are subject to formalization and antiformalization. Pentecostalists are in some cases institutionalizing their fervor, while nonevangelical formalists such as the Episcopalians and Catholics are developing Pentecostal or charismatic branches. Similarly, formalist mainline churches are incorporating New Age interests, such as concern for the environment, while the New Age may find its concern for the environment turning into a legalistic, formalist value.

Here too David Brooks's example of sixties radicals is helpful.[5] Sixties radicals were largely students who were not participating in the business world. They sought a world of free expression and honest emotions, as they rebelled against the stilted, formal social order of the fifties. They expressed themselves in revivals such as Woodstock, smoked pot, and used LSD, all of which

> appeared to be little more than senseless clamor and cacophony. Rock music and folk songs expressed the various moods of the new-light movement but could give it no direction. Like a Pentecostal meeting, the Spirit gripped different people in different ways, and each was left to express it in the form which spoke to him or her.[6]

According to William McLoughlin, these radicals participated in the Fourth Great Awakening, which in 1978, McLoughlin anticipated would last until approximately 1990. In the nineties, David Brooks returned to the United States from Europe. Upon his return, he noticed that "suddenly massive corporations like Microsoft and the Gap were on the scene, citing Gandhi and Jack Kerouac in advertisements. And the status rules seemed to be turned upside down. Hip lawyers were wearing those teeny tiny steel-framed glasses because now it was apparently more prestigious to look like Franz Kafka than Paul Newman."[7] Brooks observed that he could no longer easily distinguish between the bohemian counterculture and the business world; the antiformalist sixties generation and the formalist business class had become one: "Defying expectations and maybe logic, people seemed to have combined the countercultural sixties and the achieving eighties into one social ethos."[8] It may not be as illogical as Brooks suggests. It seems that the antiformalist and formalist dialectic may be historical destiny, constantly leading to new syntheses.[9]

NOTES

Chapter 1. Introduction

1. "Genuine" here refers to revivals among nonelites prior to 1830.

2. Twain, 112.

3. Ibid., 118–19.

4. Jon Butler, "Enthusiasm Described and Decried: The Great Awakening as Interpretive Fiction," *Journal of American History* 69 (1982): 305–25; idem, *Awash in a Sea of Faith: Christianizing the American People* (Cambridge: Harvard University Press, 1990), 164–65.

5. Whitney Cross was the first to use the term in *The Burned-Over District: The Social and Intellectual History of Enthusiastic Religion in Western New York, 1800–1850* (Ithaca: Cornell University Press, 1950).

6. The terms "elite" and "nonelite" in this chapter refer narrowly to certain groups. "Elite" here refers to those who have access to commercial and political authority, as would be the case most obviously in the county seat, and among those with exceptional wealth. "Nonelite" or "marginal" refers to those who do not have access to such authority. Later in this book, "elite" will be equivalent to "formalist," and "nonelite" to "antiformalist."

The relationship that elites and nonelites form between themselves is less important than are the structures of their separate societies. An organization or a society with elites is here understood to have a bureaucracy and a hierarchy. Nonelites have more equitable social relationships that are carried on without the imposition of a bureaucracy.

7. David Brooks, *Bobos in Paradise: The New Upper Class and How They Got There* (New York: Simon & Schuster, 2000).

8. Ibid., 33, 35.

9. Ibid. 138–39.

10. William McLoughlin in *Revivals, Awakenings, and Reform* (Chicago: University of Chicago Press, 1978), 206, argues that the Fourth Great Awakening, was marked not by revivalistic preaching but by a nonrational, "impulsive" counterculture, which began in the sixties when "our norms" no longer "match[ed] our daily experience."

11. Peter W. Williams, *Popular Religion in America: Symbolic Change and the Modernization Process in Historical Perspective* (Urbana and Chicago: University of Illinois Press, 1989), 242, 231; and Victor Turner, *The Ritual Process: Structure and Anti-structure* (Ithaca: Cornell University Press, 1979).

12. Williams, 4–5.

13. Examples of those who have treated popular religion as the unofficial practice of religion within denominations are Robert Anthony Orsi, *Madonna of 115th Street: Faith and Community in Italian Harlem, 1880–1950* (New Haven: Yale University Press, 1985); Ann Taves, *The Household of Faith: Roman Catholic Devotions in Mid-Nineteenth-Century America* (Notre Dame, Ind.: University of Notre Dame Press, 1986); Patricia U. Bonomi, *Under the Cope of Heaven: Religion, Society, and Politics in Colonial America* (New York: Oxford University Press, 1986); Gerald Strauss, "The Reformation and Its Public in an Age of Orthodoxy," in R. Po-Chia Hsia, ed., *The German People and the Reformation* (Ithaca: Cornell University Press, 1988), 192–214.

Some of those who have treated the civil and cultural religious aspects of popular religion are Catherine Albanese, *Nature Religion in America: From the Algonkian Indians to the New Age* (Chicago: University of Chicago Press, 1990), and *America: Religions and Religion* (Belmont, California: Wadsworth, 1992); Robert Bellah, *The Broken Covenant: American Civil Religion in Time of Trial* (New York: Seabury, 1975).

14. Williams, 18.

15. Ibid., 17–18.

16. Ibid., 17.

17. Ibid., 106–107.

18. Ibid., 108.

19. Later I will exchange the terms antistructure and structure for antiformal and formal.

20. Williams summarizes Turner's definition of *communitas* as "The condition or experience of total participation by individuals in a group so that individual identity is absorbed in the group" (232). Turner distinguishes between its forms in three ways. "Existential" or "spontaneous" *communitas* is a momentary experience. "Normative" *communitas* develops when existential *communitas* becomes institutionalized. And "ideological" *communitas* represents "utopian models of society based on existential *communitas* (Turner, 131–32). Fervor in Jefferson County before 1830 was not momentary, institutionalized, or utopian.

21. Henri Bergson, *The Two Sources of Morality and Religion* (Notre Dame, Ind.: University of Notre Dame Press, 1977).

22. John Macquarrie, *Twentieth-Century Religious Thought: The Frontiers of*

Philosophy and Theology, 1900–1980, rev. ed. (New York: Charles Scribner's Sons, 1981), 172–73.

23. Normative *communitas* most closely approximated the condition that existed in the fervent churches of Jefferson County. However, the fervent in Jefferson County were not reacting against a structure; they were depicting the lack of structure in their lives. Furthermore, when the structured community in Jefferson County did adapt revivalism for its own purposes, it was less to seek an accommodation to a changing social structure and more to retrench from a level of structure that no longer responded to their needs. The congregations, nonetheless, remained "closed."

The fervor of the antistructural communities also did develop a structure as Turner predicts, but these communities continued to consider fervor the correct form of religious expression. Their antistructure never defined itself in relation to a structure. Bergson's understanding of open religion works best here as it does not assume that open religion is an abnormal condition, and it does allow for the bureaucratizing of this form of religion.

24. Emile Durkheim, *The Elementary Forms of Religious Life,* trans. Joseph Ward Swain (New York: Collier, 1961).

25. George M. Thomas, *Revivalism and Cultural Change: Christianity, Nation Building, and the Market in the Nineteenth-Century United States* (Chicago: University of Chicago Press, 1989), 37–38, 41, 203n.6.

26. Curtis Johnson, *Islands of Holiness: Rural Religion in Upstate New York, 1790–1860* (Ithaca: Cornell University Press, 1989), 67n.1 and 68; and David L. Rowe, *Thunder and Trumpets: Millerites and Dissenting Religion in Upstate New York, 1800–1850* (Chico, Calif.: Scholars Press, 1985), 71–93.

Chapter 2. Jefferson County

1. See David L. Rowe, *Thunder and Trumpets: Millerites and Dissenting Religion in Upstate New York, 1800–1850* (Chico, Calif.: Scholars Press, 1985), 72–93; Perry Miller, *The Life of the Mind in America from the Revolution to the Civil War* (New York: Harcourt Brace Jovanovich, 1965),11; and Nathan O. Hatch, *The Democratization of American Christianity* (New Haven: Yale University Press, 1989), 52.

2. See, e.g., Carol Sheriff, *The Artificial River: The Erie Canal and the Paradox of Progress, 1817–1862* (New York: Hill & Wang, 1996), 150. Curtis Johnson in *Islands of Holiness: Rural Religion in Upstate New York, 1790–1860* (Ithaca: Cornell University Press, 1989) rejects this tendency to overemphasize urban areas and provides a thorough bibliography of works on urban areas (3n.3). Randolph

Roth in *The Democratic Dilemma: Religion, Reform, and the Social Order in the Connecticut River Valley of Vermont, 1791–1850* (New York: Cambridge University Press, 1987) and Judith Wellman in "The Burned-Over District Revisited: Benevolent Reform and Abolitionism in Mexico, Paris, and Ithaca, New York, 1825–1842" (Ph.D. dissertation, University of Virginia, 1974) also treat rural areas.

3. Whitney R. Cross, *The Burned-Over District: The Social and Intellectual History of Enthusiastic Religion in Western New York, 1800–1850* (Ithaca: Cornell University Press, 1950), 76.

4. George M. Thomas, *Revivalism and Cultural Change: Christianity, Nation Building, and the Market in the Nineteenth-Century United States* (Chicago: University of Chicago Press, 1989), 14, 17. While I fully accept Thomas's description of isomorphism, I examine revivalism from a much different perspective. He is chiefly interested in post-1830 revivalism as "practical rationalization," while I am concerned with the "substantive rationality" of pre-1830 revivalism, as well as with the practical rationalization of post-1830 revivalism. Thomas draws the distinction between forms of rationality on 203n.4, but he does not connect substantive rationality with revivalism.

5. "Stability" throughout the rest of this work will refer to areas that are not obviously undergoing extreme change. Thus, areas that have passed the initial stages of development and are not, for example, experiencing the disruption of the opening of the Erie Canal will fit the definition of stability.

6. Among the prominent merchants in Brownville was Peleg Burchard, the revivalist Jedediah Burchard's brother. Though he later "failed," he was catapulted to the position of customs officer or "collector" in Cape Vincent, town of Lyme. Other notable merchants in Watertown who as a result improved themselves were Jabez Foster, Orville Hungerford, Marianus W. Gilbert, and Joseph Hawkins (who defeated Perley Keyes in his bid for Congress in 1828). Hough, 428, 430, 431, 435.

7. Thomas F. Gordon, *Gazetteer of the State of New York* (Philadelphia: Printed for the Author, 1836), 485.

8. Surveys of Macomb's Purchase done by James Constable are in the Constable Papers, Cornell University Department of Manuscripts and Archives, accession no. 608; and James Constable's diary at the New York State Archives, Albany. The Chassanis Tract was surveyed by "Simon Desjardines, chamberlain of King Louis XVI, and Pierre Pharoux, a Parisian engineer and architect" (Sister Mary Christine Taylor, S.S.J., *A History of the Foundations of Catholicism in Northern New York: United States Catholic Historical Society Monograph Series 32* [New York: United States Catholic Historical Society, 1976], 21–22.)

9. Franklin B. Hough, *A History of Jefferson County in the State of New York, from the Earliest Period to the Present Time* (Watertown: Sterling & Riddell, 1854), 15, 39–41, 44; Thomas F. Powell, *Penet's Square: An Episode in the Early History of Northern New York* (Lakemont, N.Y.: North Country Books, 1976), 116. I have depended chiefly on Hough for my understanding of the history of Jefferson County. Many of the histories of the county written in the nineteenth century are little more than inaccurate copies of Hough. Hough, a physician, at the time he wrote this history, was the New York State Census Commissioner in Albany. Permission from the New York State Legislature for him to take time from his census duties to write the histories of Jefferson, St. Lawrence, and Franklin Counties is in the New York State Archives, Albany.

10. Powell, 14–19.

11. Taylor, 23n.22.

12. The Town of Gouverneur, one of the sites of Finney's early work was named for Morris. Roger G. Kennedy in *Orders from France: The Americans and the French in a Revolutionary World* (New York: Knopf, 1989) indicates that LeRay's sister, Madame Foucault, was Morris's mistress (38n).

13. Quoted in Taylor, 22 from *Journal de Castorland, Relation du voyage at des etablissements des Emigres dans L'Amerique Septentrionale (1793–1796)* trans. F. B. Hough, at the New York State Library, Albany.

14. Ibid., 116–19, 134; and Amy Friedlander et al., "Fort Drum Cultural Resources Project, Report No. 2, 1986: Re-evaluation of the Rural Historic Contexts for the Fort Drum, N.Y. Vicinity. Prepared for the U.S. National Park Service, Middle Atlantic Region, Philadelphia, Pa. and the 10th Mountain Division, Fort Drum, N.Y.," (East Orange, N.J.: Louis Berger, 1986), 2–2.

15. David M. Ludlum, *Social Ferment in Vermont, 1791–1850* (New York: Columbia University Press, 1939), 13.

16. Lewis D. Stilwell, "Migration from Vermont (1776–1860)," *Proceedings of the Vermont Historical Society* 5 (June 1937): 118–19, 139, 165; Whitney R. Cross, *The Burned-Over District: The Social and Intellectual History of Enthusiastic Religion in Western New York, 1800–1850* (Ithaca: Cornell University Press, 1950), 6; David Maldwyn Ellis, "The Yankee Invasion of New York," *New York History* 32 (1951): 7–8; Wilmond W. Parker, "The Migration from Vermont to Northern New York," *Proceedings of the New York State Historical Association* 33 (1934): 398–406; Powell, 145–46.

17. Roth, 26.

18. George Washington Gale, *The Autobiography (to 1834) of George Washington Gale (1789–1861) Founder of Galesburg, Illinois, and Knox College* (New York City, 1964), 100–101.

19. Hough, 25.

20. Charles Hambrick-Stowe in *Charles G. Finney and the Spirit of American Evangelicalism* (Grand Rapids, Mich.: Eerdmans, 1996), 41 states that Finney describes Brownville "perhaps tongue-in-cheek as 'a village of considerable size'" Given Brownville's stature as a commercial center within the county, this was probably not a tongue-in-cheek comment. Compared to the agricultural villages of Evans Mills, Antwerp, and Adams, Brownville was a fairly substantial community.

21. Friedlander et al., 2–25, 2–47; and Dorothy Kendall Cleaveland, "The Trade and Trade Routes of Northern New York from the Beginning of Settlement to the Coming of the Railroad," *The Quarterly Journal of the New York State Historical Association* 4 (October 1923): 205–31.

22. Sheriff discusses the pre-canal trade route along Lake Ontario and the St. Lawrence River, 19–20.

23. The route across Lake Ontario commonly served as access to Jefferson County for travelers as well as traders. Francis Asbury traversed the lake from Kingston, Ontario to Sackets Harbor in 1811 and 1813, and Brigham Young traveled across the lake in 1835. Francis Asbury, *Journal* (New York: N. Bangs and T. Mason, 1821), 313, 348; and Richard E. Bennett, "'Plucking Not Planting': Mormonism in Eastern Canada," in *The Mormon Presence in Canada,* Brigham Y. Card, et al. eds., (Logan: The University of Utah Press, 1990).

24. Hough, 283.

25. Ibid., 277.

26. Hough, 420–28. Patrick Wilder, formerly at the Sackets Harbor Battlefield Site, questions Brown's alleged military prowess and believes that Brown's later achievements derived partially from Brown's capacity for self-aggrandizement.

27. The Finney Papers contain a letter from a recent Finney convert S. C. Kanady, a lawyer in the Town of LeRay, to Finney, in which Kanaday advises Finney that LeRay would be at Finney's meeting the next day. As LeRay was a Catholic, as well as a friend of Kanady, and as LeRay was aware that Kanady and Finney were also close, Kanady hoped that Finney would avoid making any statements that would offend LeRay's religion. Microfilm, Roll 1, Leraysville, 31 July 1824. See also Dupuis and Rosell, 113 and 113n.21.

28. Quoted in Kennedy, 36. In *Emigres in the Wilderness* (Port Washington, Long Island, N.Y.: Ira J. Friedman, 1941; repr., 1967), T. Wood Clarke indicates that the LeRays could engage in trade as they were not part of the hereditary aristocracy (9). Clarke's book is the most extensive of all the histories of the French presence in northern New York, but it is also, as Donald Stewart asserts in the "Introduction," more entertaining than scholarly ([viii]).

29. Hough, 442–43. The LeRay Papers, at the Cornell University Department of Manuscripts and Archives (accession no. 2186), contain land records as well as records of LeRay's Caribbean trade. Jacques Milbert visited the North Country and James LeRay in 1815. The snow impressed him as much as it had George Washington Gale, and convinced him that the resulting isolation would prevent the area from being heavily populated. Jacques Milbert, *Picturesque Itinerary of the Hudson River and the Peripheral Parts of North America,* trans. Constance D. Sherman (Ridgewood, N.J.: Gregg Press, 1968), 155, 158.

30. Friedlander, 2–7.

31. Milbert, 154. The mansion now serves as the residence of the commanding officer of the 10th Mountain Division at Fort Drum. See Kennedy, 23–25.

32. Kennedy, 41–42.

33. Kennedy indicates that Bonaparte " 'forgot' to abdicate the crown of the Indies" (354).

34. Ibid., 353–57.

35. Kennedy, 221–28; 259–64.

36. *The Memoirs of Charles G. Finney: The Complete Restored Text,* Richard A. G. Dupuis and Garth M. Rosell, eds. (Grand Rapids: Academie Books, 1989), 98. Finney also mentions that "the land in the township belonged to Mr. Parish, a rich landholder residing in Ogdensburgh. To encourage the settlement of the township, he had built them a brick meeting house. But the people had no mind to keep up public worship; and therefore the meeting house was locked up" (97). Rosell and Dupuis indicate that the Mr. Parish in Ogdensburgh was George Parish. David Parish committed suicide in 1826 after his financial condition had continued to decline (97n.5).

37. Kennedy, 264. Hough notes that the church was built in 1816, three years before the organization of a Presbyterian congregation in Antwerp, and that in 1849 the church was sold to Roman Catholics for $600 (94).

38. Kennedy, 44–45, 26; Hough, 446. Kennedy asserts that Plessis was named for a friend and that "there is even a town named for his dog." The village of Plessis is actually that town.

As for the disastrous arrival of the canal, LeRay, not realizing the potential negative consequences of the opening of the Erie Canal, had attempted in 1812 to garner European financing for it. He failed. Powell, 141.

39. Powell, 169–82; Kennedy, 44; Taylor, 25–26, 126–31. See also chapter 3.

Taylor also mentions the following as refugees from France after Napoleon's defeat: "Count Pierre Real, chief of police; Captain Louis Peugnet, officer of the *corps d'elite;* Louis Augustin de Caulaincourt, Duke of Vincenza; General Desfourneaux; General Roland; and Count Grouchy, whose failure to arrive with reinforcements had insured Napoleon's defeat at Waterloo" (24).

40. Hough, 436.

41. "Memoirs of William D. Ford," in the William D. Ford Papers, New-York Historical Society.

42. Hough, 447.

43. Roth asserts that Vermonters, who sought to establish a standing order similar to that found in southern New England, favored "strong government and state-supported churches, which would uphold order and restrain the passions and the selfishness that lay in the human heart. They all spoke out in favor of a standing order, calling for government action to preserve religion, morality, and order on the Vermont frontier" (32).

44. LeRay's papers are at the Cornell University Department of Manuscripts and Archives, accession no. 1678; and at the Jefferson County Historical Society. Parish's papers are in the Saint Lawrence University Archives.

45. See map of Jefferson County, at the end of this chaper. The crosshatching representing lots in the northern sections of the county, where the European nobility settled, indicates the lack of localized town structure. The southern section and the midsection, where the local nobility did not as noticeably overshadow other elites, show clear outlines of towns.

46. Hough indicates that "on the arrival of Mr. Parish, he visited every family, and assured them that they might depend upon any indulgence that might be reasonably asked. The sincerity of this promise they never found reason to distrust" (88).

Given Parish's concern to provide "any indulgence that might be reasonably asked," it is also likely that he—as well as his counterpart, LeRay—responded charitably to those who could not meet their land payments. On the other hand, Elisha Camp, the land agent in Sackets Harbor, Town of Hounsfield, representing rapacious New York investors, often received rigid instructions to enforce all debts owed them. Thus, he also encountered more insolvencies. See Elisha Camp Papers, Box 1, including frequent correspondence with the investors and, in particular, letters from the investors' representative to Camp, dated 15 September 1820, and 22 December 1820, in the Cornell University Department of Manuscripts and Archives, accession no. 696.

47. See chapter 3 for Methodist and Baptist geographical predominance, as well as for names of church members and position of commercial or political importance in the county.

48. Curtis Johnson, *Islands of Holiness: Rural Religion in Upstate New York, 1790–1860* (Ithaca: Cornell University Press, 1989), 38, 146. Johnson also sees the

increased success of the Universalists in the mid-1830s as an indication of the loss of the evangelicals' prominence. As I will relate in chapter 4, the Universalists in Jefferson County reached the height of their prominence in 1824 and 1825 after Hosea Ballou visited Watertown, and in apparent response to the success of revivalism.

49. Hough, 395–96; 399.

50. Ibid., 397. Additionally, the Sons of Temperance organized in 1851; the Jefferson County Industrial Association formed in 1843; and the Watertown Mechanics' Association was created in 1844.

51. Ibid., 398.

52. Finney belonged to the Rising Sun Lodge in Adams. His honorable discharge dated 6 May 1824 and sent to him in Evans Mills by George Andrus is in the Finney papers, microfilm, roll 1.

53. Most of the lodges in Jefferson County were disbanded during the antimasonic crisis. Ibid., 409–12.

54. Ibid., 406. I will consider in greater detail benevolent associations and reform movements in chapter 5.

55. J. Le Ray de Chaumont, *An Address, Delivered to the Meeting of the Agricultural Society of Jefferson County, December 29, 1817* (Watertown: John H. Ford., Jr., 1818), 4.

56. From the program of the First Fair of the Jefferson County Agricultural Society, 1818, at the Jefferson County Historical Society.

57. In his discussion of secularization in Cortland County, Johnson does not consider William Clebsch's argument in *From Sacred to Profane America: The Role of Religion in American History* (New York: Harper & Row, 1968) that one result of the success of American Protestantism is that its "achievements [were] profane in fruition" (ix). Hence, churches lost some of their local power because that power had become institutionalized in the community outside of the churches. This is consonant with Don Harrison Doyle's representation of the small town in *The Social Order of a Frontier Community: Jacksonville, Illinois, 1825–70* (Urbana and Chicago: University of Illinois Press, 1983).

Johnson argues that the evangelicals were a small portion of the population to begin with. However, I find it difficult to make such an argument, given the commonness of errors in church membership records and the lack of Methodist membership rolls. Additionally, developing on the belief that most people were not evangelicals, Johnson's argument depends on the view that the churches considered themselves "islands of holiness" in the midst of a nonevangelical world. An adversarial perspective does appear in church records in which churches seem to believe that they are a small bastion of holiness in the midst of moral collapse.

However, this does not mean that the churches actually were "islands" or that the world was in the throes of moral collapse. This was their perspective, which gave them purpose.

58. The population of Jefferson County in 1820 was 32,952; in 1830, 48,493; and in 1840, 60,984. U.S. Census figures. See Friedlander, 2–23, Table 2.1.

59. Cross, 56.

60. Taylor, 27, 108, 120; Hough, 395.

61. See chapter 5.

62. See in the "Records of the First Presbyterian Church of Watertown" any one of numerous church trials beginning in 1822.

63. Roth, 44–45.

64. *New York State Census* (1835).

65. Whitney R. Cross, *The Burned-Over District: The Social and Intellectual History of Enthusiastic Religion in Western New York, 1800–1850* (Ithaca: Cornell University Press, 1950), 84, 85–86.

66. *New York State Census* (1845). Merchants, manufacturers, and professionals includes merchants, mechanics, manufacturers, attorneys, and physicians and surgeons.

67. *New York State Census* (1845). The following are included in the calculation of agricultural production: barley, peas, beans, buckwheat, turnips, potatoes, flax, wheat, corn, rye, oats, butter, cheese.

68. *New York State Census* (1845). For consistency the numbers for home-manufactured cloth also come from the 1845 census. The 1845 census contains much more information than the census of 1835. Thus, most of the information contained in these tables has come from the later census. I took the numbers for table 1 from the census of 1835 because they were available then and because, as Cross predicted, the numbers had noticeably evened out by 1845.

Chapter 3. The Foundations of Fervor

1. The Benjamin Wright under whom Finney studied should not be confused with Benjamin Wright, the surveyor of the future site of the Erie Canal and of the lots that later became towns in Jefferson County (Garth Rosell and Richard A. G. Dupuis, *The Memoirs of Charles G. Finney: The Complete Restored Text* [Grand Rapids: Academie Books, 1989], 22n.29). Finney notes in his *Memoirs* and Gale concurs in his autobiography that Wright followed Finney into the church (Rosell and Dupuis 37–38; George W. Gale, *The Autobiography (to 1834) of George Washington Gale (1789–1861), Founder of Galesburg, Illinois, and Knox College* [New York: privately printed, 1964], 180–81). The records of the First Presbyterian

Church of Adams indicate that Wright joined the church less than a month after Finney on 10 January 1822 and that Wright became a member of the Session on 27 March 1827. See also Rosell and Dupuis, 38n.40.

A letter from Finney, the lawyer, to Elisha Camp, land agent at Sackets Harbor, New York, dated January 22, 1821, is in the Elisha Camp papers in the Cornell University Department of Manuscripts and Archives, accession number, 696, box 2. This may be the only extant archive from Finney's time as a lawyer:

> Sir:
> It not being convenient for Mr. Wright to attend to your cause at Rodman, he handed me your letter, & desired me to attend to it. The objection you mentioned is not tenable, as there is a *Subsequent Statute* in effect repealing the claim which you referred to. I succeeded however in quashing the suit, on account of the summons being made returnable *at my office at S.* Harbor it being a public house, I took exception to the Jurisdiction of the court (and whether the objection was tenable or untenable is immaterial). I prevailed as the court decided he had no Jurisdiction. I could not draw much from the plaintiff in conversation but his counsel informed me that he was prepared to prove that you employed Miles—they also expected Waldo from the Harbor as a witness, you will probably be able to learn from *him* what they can prove by him—They have a letter which they probably *think* to make use of on trial, (which by the by is *no evidence*) purporting to be from the Trustees of the corporation of the Village which shows that they considered you responsible to Miles for his labors—What they *can* in reality *prove* I know not. but [sic] his counsel *seemed* to have much confidence in the action and that he had all the necessary proof. The action will probably be commenced de nove immediately. I give you the information that you may be prepared to meet them and give them "change in their own coin."
> Yours respectfully,
> C.G. Finney

Camp was facing suit from numerous people for a variety of reasons. It is difficult to discern what this case involved.

2. Rosell and Dupuis, 6, 6n.31; and George F. Wright, *Charles Grandison Finney* (Boston and New York: Houghton Mifflin, 1891; repr. Ann Arbor: University Microfilms, 1979), 3.

3. Rosell and Dupuis, 21.

4. December 31, 1821, session records of the First Presbyterian Church of Adams, N.Y., microfilmed at the Presbyterian Historical Society, Philadelphia, by the Genealogical Society of the Church of Jesus Christ of Latter-day Saints.

5. Gale, 185.

6. David L. Weddle's understanding of the law and revivals belongs to this post-1830 era. "The Law and the Revival: A New 'Divinity' for the Settlements," 47 *Church History* (June 1978): 196–214. Beecher's benevolence was his means to counteract the disestablishment of Congregationalism in Connecticut in 1818. See William G. McLoughlin, "Introduction," in Charles G. Finney, *Lectures on Revivals of Religion* (Cambridge: Harvard University Press, 1960), xviii.

7. In New York State, the relatively populated centers within towns are villages. Frequently, but not always, the village has the same name as the town. Evans Mills and Leraysville were villages in the Town of LeRay. Leraysville no longer exists; it was subsumed by the expansion of the United States Army facility, Fort Drum.

8. The *Eighth Annual Report* (at the Oneida County Historical Society, Utica, N.Y.) lists branches in Watertown, Adams, Cape Vincent, Ellisburg, Henderson, Little Sandy Creek, and Alexandria (19).

9. *Eighth Annual Report,* 18.

10. Rosell and Dupuis, 66.

11. *Sixth Annual Report,* 10.

12. Rosell and Dupuis, 133–34.

13. Rosell and Dupuis, 115. The records of the First Presbyterian Church of LeRay from 1 August 1824 to 24 April 1825 contain references to Finney's work. In addition to more regular meetings of the church, a large increase in the numbers of people seeking admittance into the church is apparent. However, it happens frequently that the name of new admittants is not included. Furthermore, the names given in the records fall far short of two hundred.

The church shifted to Dutch Reformed from Presbyterianism on 19 August 1824, possibly as a result of the large number of converts Finney made among the German immigrants outside Evans Mills. The church reverted to Presbyterianism on 12 February 1825, and the examination of the records by the presbytery on 24 February indicates that all was in order in Evans Mills, despite concerns about Finney's fanaticism. After Finney's departure, the church meetings again become infrequent. The records are kept at the church. David Maldwyn Ellis discusses the preference for Presbyterian churches along the New York frontier in "The Yankee Invasion of New York," *New York History* 32 (1951): 14.

14. Gale, 96–98.

15. Rosell and Dupuis, 90.

16. Charles Hambrick-Stowe, *Charles G. Finney and the Spirit of American Evangelicalism* (Grand Rapids, Mich.: Eerdmans, 1996), 123.

17. See Rosell and Dupuis, 1–139; and Gale, 176–88.

18. Rosell and Dupuis, 105.

19. Henri Bergson, *The Two Sources of Morality and Religion* (Notre Dame, Ind.: University of Notre Dame Press, 1977); Victor Turner, *The Ritual Process: Structure and Antistructure* (Ithaca: Cornell University Press, 1979); Ernst Troeltsch, *The Social Teaching of the Christian Churches* (New York; Harper & Row, 1949); David L. Rowe's discussion of Troeltsch, in *Thunder and Trumpets: Millerites and Dissenting Religion in Upstate New York, 1800–1850* (Chico, Calif.: Scholars Press, 1981), 71–72; and Howard Clark Kee et al., *Christianity: A Social and Cultural History* (New York: Macmillan, 1991), 572–73; Whitney R. Cross, *The Burned-Over District: The Social and Intellectual History of Enthusiastic Religion in Western New York, 1800–1850* (Ithaca: Cornell University Press, 1950), 166.

20. On Finney's formalization, see Garth Rosell, "Charles Grandison Finney," in Reid et al., 439–40; and Hambrick-Stowe, 208. And compare Cross, 162, 165, and Keith J. Hardman, *Charles Grandison Finney, 1792–1875: Revivalist and Reformer* (Syracuse: Syracuse University Press, 1987), 82.

21. *The Second Annual Report* (1818) of the Female Missionary Society of the Western District describes Gale's work in Ellisburg, Henderson, and Adams.

22. Gale indicates that "Whiskey and its concomitants, gambling, dancing, litigating, prevailed," in the Town of Ellisburg in 1817 (99–100, 133).

23. Paul Brent Hensley, "An Eighteenth-Century World Not Quite Lost: The Social and Economic Structure of a Northern New York Town, 1810–1880," Ph.D. dissertation, College of William and Mary, 1979. Hensley studies Canton in northern St. Lawrence County.

24. Connecticut disestablished Congregationalism in 1818 and Massachusetts disestablished Congregationalism in 1833.

25. The records of the First Presbyterian Church of Adams note that Gale joined the church as a licentiate of the Presbytery of Hudson in 1819. He was ordained three months later. No specific dates are given at this point in the records.

Like many churches of this era in the western sections of New York, in 1821 the church in Adams changed from Congregational to Presbyterian in accordance with the Plan of Union of 1801, in which it was agreed by the Presbyterians and the Congregationalists that they would share congregations. Churches abided by the decision of the majority in determining which denomination they preferred. Frequently, frontier areas preferred Presbyterianism as it provided a sense of cooperation in the wilderness. Overwhelmingly, in Jefferson County the churches ultimately opted for Presbyterianism.

26. Selden Family Papers, Cornell University Department of Manuscripts and Archives, accession no. 1655.

27. However, before formally establishing the Manual Labor Institute, Gale visited the University of Virginia and Monticello. Neither impressed him:

> I told her [Miss Cars] that externally, and as far as I could see the arrangements, they were splendid, but it would not prosper on its present plan [because it did not offer religious instruction]. She said she hoped it would while Mr. Jefferson lived. He had spent so much time, and taken such a deep interest in it; but it did not prosper long. Insubordination, riots, and other evils attending such a system ensued. . . .
> . . . [Monticello] was a kind of museum. We had but little time to examine the grounds, but so far as I could judge, there was nothing very attractive. Gale, 247, 248.

Although the plan of the University of Virginia did not influence Gale's plan for his institute, the plan of the Baptist Hamilton Institute, established outside of Utica in 1817 probably did. See *Autobiography of Elder Jacob Knapp with an Introductory Essay by R. Jeffrey* (New York: Sheldon, 1868), 24.

28. Gale, 7–16, 96–103, 176–88; Hambrick-Stowe, 47.

29. P. H. Fowler, *Historical Sketch of Presbyterianism within the Bounds of the Synod of Central New York* (Utica: Curtis & Childs, 1877), 279; "J. Burchard" appears as a subscriber to support the United Presbyterian Church of Sackets Harbor in 1824, even though Burchard and the pastor of the Sackets church, Samuel Snowden, were polar opposites. Records are at the church.

30. Gale, 165.

31. Ibid., 166.

32. As a result of this complaint, the synod did ultimately assert that it would not recognize Black River Association candidates until the Presbytery of Watertown had approved them (Fowler, 136). Thus, the association agreed that in the future they would

> require of candidates for a license to preach the gospel a good knowledge of English language, and also of Geography, Astronomy, Natural Philosophy, Logic, Rhetoric, Church History, a knowledge of Biblical History, and a systematic acquaintance of Theology. We must also have a good evidence of an irreproachable moral and religious character.

(Centennial History of the Black River and St. Lawrence Association of Congregational Ministers and Churches" (n.p., n.d.), 8, kept with the records of the First Congregational Church, Copenhagen, Lewis County, New York.)

33. He supplied the First Presbyterian Church of Brownville in 1825, First Presbyterian Church of Ellisburg in 1829 and 1832, Second Presbyterian Church of Watertown (now Stone Presbyterian Church) in 1832. F. C. O'Brien, "History and

Directory of the First Presbyterian Church, Brownville, New York" (Watertown, N.Y.: n.p.,n.d.); "History of Stone Street Presbyterian Church" (n.p., n.d.); and records of Stone Presbyterian Church, 1832. The preceding secondary sources are in the churches box in the Jefferson County Historical Society, Watertown, New York. Records of the Ellisburg church are at the Presbytery of Northern New York in Potsdam, New York. Records of Stone Presbyterian Church are at the church in Watertown. Cross indicates that Burchard was also in the village of Cape Vincent with the American Home Missionary Society support (188).

34. Paul Johnson, *A Shopkeeper's Millennium: Society and Revivals in Rochester, New York, 1815–1837* (New York: Hill & Wang, 1978), 119.

35. Fowler, 279–80.

36. Wright, 256, 318–19.

37. Russell Streeter, *Mirror of Calvinistic Fanatical Revivals, or Jedediah Burchard & Co. During a Protracted Meeting of Twenty-Six Days in Woodstock, Vt.* (Woodstock, Vt.: published by the author, 1835); C. G. Eastman, *Sermons, Addresses & Exhortations, by Rev. Jedediah Burchard with an Appendix Containing Some Account of the Proceedings, Held under His Direction, in Burlington, Williston, and Hinesburgh, Vt., December, 1835 and January, 1836* (Burlington: Chauncey Goodrich, 1836).

38. James Hotchkin, *History of the Purchase and Settlement of Western New York and of the Rise, Progress, and Present State of the Presbyterian Church in That Section* (New York: M. W. Dodd, Brick Church Chapel, 1848), 170.

39. According to Fowler, Myrick, who was ordained by the Presbytery of Oneida, worked in a church in the Town of Litchfield for a short time. He was excommunicated in 1833 for "denying the Saints' Perseverance and inculcating Perfectionism, with disorganizing churches and encouraging confusion and disorder in religious meetings, with defaming the Presbyterian Church and using improper language in preaching and praying. . . ." Fowler summed up Myrick's habits in much less positive language than what he used to describe Burchard: "He was an enthusiast, probably sincere, but wrought up to the point of derangement, and while gathering large assemblies and exciting them, his proper place was the asylum rather than the pulpit" (278). Myrick discussed the reasons for his excommunication in a letter to Finney 10 January 1833 (photostat from the Finney Papers in Whitney R. Cross Papers, Cornell University Department of Manuscripts and Archives, accession no. 1678.) Myrick was not admitted to the Black River Association, probably as a result of the synod's ruling against the association's lax admissions.

He wrote to Finney expressing concern about Burchard's methods in 1832 (photostat in Cross Papers). He also indicated that residents of Jefferson County were urging him to work there—since all of Jefferson County's revivalists had departed for larger fields. Myrick, however, could not find time to appear in Jefferson County.

Eventually, the synod also condemned the itinerancy of Burchard and Myrick in particular, and urged that each church receive the special care of its own pastor. This resulted in disciplinary proceedings against an itinerant in Chenango Presbytery (Fowler, 137).

40. Cross, 188.

41. Ibid., 161.

42. In his report, as an indication of his intense prayer, Nash urges the Board of Directors to "pray much; pray fervently." *Eighth Annual Report,* 16. Carthage and Wilna produced thirty hopeful converts as a result of Nash's labors, despite the lack of an established Presbyterian church, and despite a large Roman Catholic population in these areas (Fowler, 199).

43. Quoted in Rosell and Dupuis, 72n.43.

44. Hambrick-Stowe, 123.

45. The Cross Papers contain photostats from the Finney Papers of letters from Nash and Myrick, which are representative of their concern for the changes then taking place in Finney. The Nash letter is dated November 26, 1831; and the Myrick letters are dated Jan. 30, 1832 and Jan. 10, 1833.

46. Knapp, xiii–xiv.

47. Ibid., xi, xii.

48. Ibid., xvi. Finney's name appears rarely in the records of the Bible Society of Rutland (later the Jefferson County Bible Society) while he was working in Jefferson County, but Knapp's name appears frequently during his time in Jefferson County. The names of other Presbyterian ministers appear regularly in these records. As a rule, only Finney is missing. Records of the Bible Society are at the Jefferson County Historical Society.

49. Ibid., 27.

50. Ibid., 11–27; Franklin B. Hough, *A History of Jefferson County in the State of New York* (Albany: Joel Munsell; Watertown: Sterling & Riddell, 1854), 393.

51. Rev. P. Douglass Gorrie, *The Black River Conference Memorial: Containing Sketches of the Life and Character of the Deceased Members of the Black River Conference of the M.E. Church* (New York: Carlton & Phillips, 1852).

52. Letter from William Case to Nathan Bangs, March 30, 1818, Nathan Bangs Papers, United Methodist Archives, Drew University; Hatch, 201–205.

53. "Journal of the Rev. John Taylor, on a mission through the Mohawk and Black River Country, in the Year 1802," in *Documentary History of the State of New York: Volume 3* Christopher Morgan and E. B. O'Callaghan, M.D., eds. (Albany:

Weed, Parsons, Public Printers, 1850), 1106. See also P. H. Fowler, *Historical Sketch of Presbyterianism within the Bounds of the Synod of Central New York* (Utica: Curtiss & Childs, 1877), 93–96.

54. Taylor, 1114. Some historians have noted that frontier Methodists may have borrowed some of their enthusiasm from Scots-Irish Presbyterians. This cannot have been the case in northern New York, where the Presbyterians were not Scots-Irish but New England Congregationalists who, after the Plan of Union of 1801, opted for Presbyterianism along the frontier in order to maintain intercongregational cohesiveness.

55. Ibid., 1120.

56. Ibid.

57. Ibid., 1123.

58. Ibid., 1120–123.

59. Nathaniel Dutton Papers, Jefferson County Historical Society, Watertown.

60. Denmark is in Lewis County.

61. Joshua Bradley, A.M., *Accounts of Religious Revivals in Many Parts of the United States from 1815 to 1818 Collected from Numerous Publications, and Letters from Persons of Piety and Correct Information* (Albany: G. J. Loomis, 1819; repr., Wheaton, Ill.: Richard Owen Roberts, 1980), 213–26.

62. The minutes of the Black River Baptist Association for 1816 note that the church in Henderson had sixty-six baptisms, while the church in Ellisburg had sixty-three. Other churches during the same year had anywhere from zero to three baptisms. The one exception was Brownville, which had sixteen (at the American Baptist Historical Society, Colgate Rochester Divinity School, Rochester, New York).

63. Records of the First Presbyterian Church of Adams, N.Y., microfilmed by the Genealogical Society of the Church of Jesus Christ of Latter-day Saints at the Presbyterian Historical Society, Philadelphia. See also Hough, 77.

64. Records of the First Presbyterian Church of Adams, 1819; and Fowler, 185.

65. In addition to the occasional existence of benevolent society records (usually the Sabbath School), Presbyterian churches maintain two sets of records: those of the society, and the session. Through the society, the trustees, in accord with New York State law, represent the legal and financial interests of the church, while the members of the session consult with each other in making the purely religious decisions of the church. For example, those seeking admission to the church must first describe their "experiential and doctrinal knowledge of the Gospel" to the session. And all disciplinary cases go before the session.

66. Rev. E. Lazell was the first minister to preach at the Presbyterian church in Watertown. However, as he was a missionary and as he had an outside business (operating a distillery), he did not preach at the church regularly. See Frederick H. Kimball, *Years of Truth: A History of the First Presbyterian Church of Watertown, New York, 1803–1953* (Watertown: Hungerford & Holbrook, 1953), 26–27; and the 1803 session records of the First Presbyterian Church of Watertown at the church.

The records of the Watertown Ecclesiastical Society indicate that on 30 December 1820 the trustees voted to request members of the church to pay their subscriptions for Banks's salary in advance in order to relieve him from his financial embarassment. Ethel Bronson of Rutland, writing to his brother Isaac on October 17, 1818, mentioned that Banks's brother Moses had gotten himself into financial difficulties and that Banks was taking over his brother's farm (Bronson Papers, New York Public Library Manuscripts Room). It is possible that Banks's efforts to salvage his brother's business led to Banks's own demise. In any case, the First Presbyterian Church of Watertown paid George S. Boardman eight hundred dollars per annum, while it had paid Banks originally four hundred dollars and subsequently three hundred dollars (records of the Watertown Ecclesiastical Society, 27 July 1815, 12 October 1818, 31 May 1821).

67. The society was originally known as the Watertown Religious Society. In 1814, it changed to the Watertown Ecclesiastical Society (records of the Watertown Ecclesiastical Society at the First Presbyterian Church of Watertown). John Corrigan in *Business of the Heart: Religion and Emotion in the Nineteenth Century* (Berkeley: University of California Press, 2002) describes an analogous phenomenon in Boston during the Businessman's Revival. According to Corrigan, the promoters of the revival in Boston contended that the revival "joined persons of different religious backgrounds in a concerted embrace of God" (231, 248). He notes that this union of different persons referred only to middle-class Protestants.

68. Not surprisingly the one exception was in the other commercially oriented town, Brownville. The residents of the village of Perch River formed the Moral and Religious Society of Perch River. However, the society was not connected with one denomination, as it financed the building of a union church in 1851.

69. Presbyterian record keeping is a strong indication of the formality of the denomination. The regulations of the presbytery strictly required that every meeting begin by prayer; that the minutes of the meeting include the names of all those attending; that a stated clerk be appointed to record regularly the actions of the session and the names of all those admitted to the church by the session; that, except in those cases when no minister is available, the pastor act as moderator; and that the meeting be closed by prayer.

Every February when the Presbytery of St. Lawrence (later the Presbytery of Watertown), met, the moderator of the meeting (one of the local ministers) examined the records and indicated any shortcomings in following these rules. For example, when Finney was the pastor of the church in LeRay, Boardman, the moderator of presbytery, on 24 February 1825 approved the records with two exceptions:

> 1st In two cases the session met & no record is made of the presence of any member of session excepting the moderator
>
> 2nd adjourned once without prayer

70. The records of the First Presbyterian Church of Watertown of 16 February 1832 note that a member of the church was suspended without citation as a result of the accusations of two elders.

71. Records of the First Presbyterian Church of Adams, 19 June 1823, 14 December 1823, 28 December 1828, and 1 May 1829.

72. Ibid., 9 September 1825.

73. Ibid., 4 February 1828.

74. Fowler, 468.

75. In February 1822, Boardman's church reported the addition of fifty-nine people on examination in 1821. Fowler indicates, however, that ninety-three people joined the church (190). Garth Rosell and Richard Dupuis quote several sources on the origins of the revivals of 1821 in Jefferson County. Most sources indicate that the revival (not surprisingly) began in the southern county towns of Adams and Henderson. The report from the *Boston Recorder,* 2 January 1822, asserts that the revival began in Watertown. This is also the only report that contends that "Perhaps only in Rodman can the work be said to be powerful." Emory Osgood's report of 18 February 1822 affirms that although early signs of a revival appeared first in Watertown and Sackets Harbor, the work in those places was not "general." In fact, this reference indicates that the more successful work was in Adams, after Burchard had worked at the Presbyterian Church there. It is unlikely that Boardman personally had anything to do with encouraging the revival (Rosell and Dupuis, 35–36nn.30–31).

Among the Baptists, Osgood's assessment makes the most sense. The records of the Black River Baptist Association for 1822 reveal that the greatest number of additions were in Ellisburg with ninety-two, Henderson with fifty-eight, Adams with thirty-four, and Rodman with thirty-two. LeRay reported no additions and Watertown does not appear in the report.

76. Kimball, 55. In *Protestants and Pioneers: Individualism and Conformity on the American Frontier* (Chicago: University of Chicago Press, 1964), T. Scott Miyakawa similarly depicts Presbyterian discipline (22). See also Curtis Johnson, 117.

77. Session records of the First Presbyterian Church of Watertown, 22 February 1828.

78. Ibid., 6 March 1835.

79. Ibid., 13 October 1829.

80. Ibid., 2 May 1829.

81. Ibid., 11 June 1829.

82. Rev. John Ingersoll was a Presbygationalist minister from Lisbon, St. Lawrence County. He became pastor of the First Presbyterian Church of Ellisburg in 1838 (Col. Robert G. Ingersoll file, morgue of the *Watertown Daily Times*).

83. Session records of the First Presbyterian Church of Watertown, notes from the meeting at which Fuller and Ripley's excommunications were announced, 31 October 1829.

84. Ripley and his wife had in fact been found guilty of "ante-nuptial fornication" on 11 March 1829. They confessed on 27 March.

85. Second Presbyterian later became Stone Street Presbyterian Church, and since the church on Stone Street burned down, is now Stone Presbyterian Church. The records survived the fire and are kept at the church.

86. Ibid.

87. Ibid., 31 October 1829.

88. Ibid., 9 September 1829.

89. Ibid., 10 November 1829.

90. Ibid., 24 April 1830.

91. Ibid., 31 July 1830.

92. Quoted from a letter from Nash to Finney 6 August 1830 in Finney Papers, microfilm, roll 2, in Rosell and Dupuis, 111n.12.

93. Records of the First Presbyterian Church of LeRay, kept at the church; and records of the First Presbyterian Church of Ellisburg, kept at the Presbytery of Northern New York, Potsdam, New York.

94. Hough, 106–107; Fowler quotes the records of the Presbytery of St. Lawrence, which note that in Brownville "hostility to the work was strong and untiring" (199). See also Rosell and Dupuis, 111n.13.

95. In his autobiography, George W. Gale indicates that of all the ministers in Jefferson County, he and Wells exchanged pulpits the most frequently, as his congregation would not allow him to exchange with anyone else (223).

96. F. C. O'Brien, "History and Directory of the First Presbyterian Church, Brownville, New York" (Watertown, New York: n.p., n.d.), in the churches box at the Jefferson County Historical Society, Watertown.

97. Hough, 231. Lazelle also formed Congregational churches in Burr Mills, Adams (separate from the one formed by Taylor), and Lorraine. The records from these churches are not extant. See "Centennial History of the Black River and St. Lawrence Association of Congregational Ministers and Churches" (n.p.,n.d.), 4, kept with the records of the First Congregational Church of Copenhagen, Lewis County, New York.

98. Records of the First Presbyterian Church of LeRay at the church, Evans Mills, New York.

99. Hough states that several ministers preceded Finney in Antwerp (570–71). However, Finney notes that Universalist antagonism had prevented regular Presbyterian services before he arrived (Rosell and Dupuis, 98).

100. Gale could have made a similar assessment of Boardman, but he chose instead to make no assessment of Boardman and to indicate only that Mrs. Boardman was "Mrs. Gales' most intimate associate before her marriage" (Gale, 223–24).

101. Fowler, 648.

102. "Mr. Snowden's Journal," *Eighth Annual Report* (1824) of the Female Missionary Society of the Western District (8–10).

103. Ibid., 8.

104. Ibid., *Ninth Annual Report* (1825), 9.

105. Hough, 169–70.

106. Cross,173. Rowe notes that the "pietist dynamic," or the effects of antiformalism (in other words a lack of excessive stability, the chief ingredient of revivals) resulted in schisms from the Baptists such as the Free Will Baptists, Universalists, and Shakers (80). This accords with Cross's belief that a period following intense religious fervor will result in "heterodox" movements.

107. Hough, 77–78; 169–70.

108. *First Annual Report* of the Female Western Missionary Society of the Western District (1817), 4–5.

109. *Second Annual Report* (1818), 4.

110. Ibid.

111. Bradley, 214; and the *Third Annual Report* (1819), 17.

112. Ibid., 18–19.

113. Ibid., 20.

114. "The Rev. Adams W. Platt's Report," *The Sixth Annual Report* (1820), 3; and "The Rev. Jonas Coburn's Report," *Fifth Annual Report* (1821), 15.

115. "Rev. Oliver Ayer's Report," *Fourth Report* (1820), 9. The tone missionaries gave to their reports may have derived in part from their interest in encouraging increased financial support from their readers, although this is questionable since the missionaries would have received no benefit from increased donations. Increased donations would have provided for the hiring of more missionaries, not for increased salaries. However, even if the missionaries had an ulterior motive, this would still not diminish the interpretive value of these reports. First, the tone of the reports falls into the regional pattern. Second, the manner in which missionaries go about drumming up this support tells us something about what they value. Formalist missionaries decry a lack of orderliness, while antiformalist missionaries bewail inequality and oppression.

116. Ibid., 10.

117. "Rev. Oliver Ayer's Report," *Sixth Annual Report* (1821): 4.

118. Fowler refers to the clergy of the Synod of Utica as "orthodox and orderly," and he contends that excitements never endured in the Synod of Utica. This seems to contradict partially his positive depictions of Finney and Burchard. However, Fowler's goal in describing both Burchard and Finney is to indicate that neither was as extravagant as they had been described. Thus, he maintained the impression that the clergy of the Synod were always "orthodox and orderly."

The difference in Fowler's and Hotchkin's perspective in this matter is telling; while Fowler, writing from the vicinity of the source of the revivalism, attempts to demonstrate Finney's, Burchard's, and the other revivalists' orderliness and orthodoxy, Hotchkin, writing from the allegedly fervid western portion of the state, decries their heresy.

119. I am making an artificial distinction between a "settled" ministry and an "established" ministry. I have argued that most areas did not experience a revival until they had a "settled" minister. Henderson and Ellisburg had a series of "settled" but not "established" ministers, in the form of a constant flow of missionaries from the Female Missionary Society.

120. The records of the Presbytery of Watertown were destroyed in a fire, but Fowler who depends on them in his history of the synod and quotes from them at length, does not mention Henderson even once as a site of fervor. However, the reports from the missionaries of the Society, Emory Osgood's letters (quoted in Rosell and Dupuis) and the records of the Black River Baptist Association indicate very strongly that overwhelmingly the towns in the southern section of the county were the most enthusiastic in the county.

121. Hotchkin, 170, 172.

122. Ibid., 174–75.

123. Taylor, 1120.

124. Records of the First Baptist Church of Adams, kept at the home of the clerk, Noreen MacIntosh, village of Honeyville, Town of Adams; and "Historical Sketch of the Black River Baptist Association," in the "Minutes of the Fortieth Anniversary of the Black River Baptist Association" (1849), 7. Hough indicates that although Emory Osgood originally created a separate church in Henderson, the scattered members of the Smithville and Henderson churches later united in Smithville under Osgood (169).

125. Hough, 162, 169, 199, 242, 297. By definition antiformalist churches do not keep records as formally (or as clearly) as do formalists. Thus, some of the dates of formation of the Baptist churches are hard to verify. For example, the chronology of church formation in the "Historical Sketch of the Black River Baptist Association," differs from Hough's chronology:

> In 1803 the churches of Turin [Lewis County] and Rutland were formed. In 1804 the church in Ellisburgh. In 1805 the church of Adams. In 1806 the church in Boonville [Lewis County]. In 1808 the churches previously formed were associated together in the capacity of an Association. . . .
>
> At their first anniversary, in 1809 the Watertown and Ellisburgh churches were added.

Except in the case of the Rutland church, whose records do not begin until 1811, but which appears to have been formed in 1808, Hough's chronology agrees with the extant church records indicating that the church in Adams was formed in 1802. Hough's later assertion that the Watertown church was formed in 1823 refers to the church in the village of Watertown, as opposed to the church in the Town of Watertown, which was formed earlier. See records of the First Baptist Church of Rutland, Jefferson County Historical Society, Watertown, New York; records of the First Baptist Church of Adams, September 1802; Hon. Albert D. Shaw, *Historic Reminiscences of the Baptist Church and Society, of Watertown, N.Y.* (Watertown, N.Y.: *Daily Times* Printing and Publishing House, 1890); and "Historical Sketch, 11. Jacob Knapp was associated with the church in the village.

126. See also T. Scott Miyakawa, 36–41.

127. "Records of the First Baptist Church of Rutland," 15 August 1812.

128. Records of the First Baptist Church of Marion, microfilm in the Cornell University Department of Manuscripts and Archives, accession no. 6063. As these records are restricted I am prevented from using the names of any of the members of the church.

129. "Records of the First Presbyterian Church of Watertown," 1 June to 5 July 1825.

130. Fowler, 136.

131. Nash's letters are chiefly devoted to discussions of prayer, as Nash was known for his ability to pray fervently. See for example, Nash to Finney 26 November 1831, photostat from Finney Papers in Cross Papers, Cornell University Department of Manuscripts and Archives, accession no. 1678.

132. "Minutes of the Black River Baptist Association," (1826), 7.

133. "Minutes of the Black River Baptist Association" (1825), 2. Notably, the New Haven church is not in Jefferson County. There are four points to consider with regard to the church in New Haven in particular, and the value of considering exclusion rates in general. First, such an extraordinary number of exclusions at the church in New Haven suggests the possibility that something unusual, possibly a schism, took place there. The New Haven church's rate of exclusion is not matched by any other church in its association, and it is remarkable when compared with the Jefferson County churches.

Second, Curtis Johnson does point out that the Baptists in Cortland County excluded proportionally many more members than did the Presbyterians and Congregationalists in Cortland County (91, 190). It is possible that this was also the case in Jefferson County. Whether it was, is irrelevant to my argument. I am refraining from making a similar comparison in this study for a number of reasons, chief among them the uneven regional and chronological availability of records from individual churches, and the differences among same denomination churches across Jefferson County's geographical regions. For example, the narrative accounts of the Presbyterian churches in Watertown show that they took much stronger stances against wrongdoing than did the Presbyterian churches in LeRay and Ellisburg. On the other hand, the First Baptist Church in Watertown demonstrated greater formalism in its narrative accounts than did the Baptist church in Adams. Compiling the exclusion figures for all of the churches of a certain denomination in Jefferson County would not advance or hinder my argument that Presbyterians were generally formalist and that formalists favored a strict environment, or that Baptists were usually antiformalist and that Baptists favored an informal environment. Such a compilation of exclusion rates would cloud the understanding of these concerns by lumping together all churches of one denomination across regions. I do contend that the church in Watertown represented the formalist ideal (and some other Presbyterian churches did not), and I do find that my interpretation of ideal Presbyterian formalist morality is supported by Fowler's and Hotchkin's accounts of Presbyterianism in central and western New York.

The issue is that formalist churches in their narrative accounts in their church records allow issues of morality and propriety to dominate their meetings, even if they do not ultimately excommunicate members as a result of these discussions. By and large, these formalist churches were Presbyterian. Nonetheless, churches such as First Baptist in Watertown did display greater formalism than some other Baptist churches, while the Presbyterian church in Ellisburg displayed less formalism than many other Presbyterian churches.

Third, my concern is not whether the Baptists as a whole or the Presbyterians as a whole excluded more members in Jefferson County or anywhere else, but how they interpreted their moral priorities. Exclusion rates tell us nothing about a church's level of moral concern. A church may devote much of its time to deploring moral lapses, but it may only exclude for the most serious breaches. Also the manner of discussing morality is important. Unlike Presbyterians in general, Baptists in general did not seek to maintain orderliness and orthodoxy; they sought to maintain pleasant relationships among members. Moreover, the most valuable statistical study here would be among causes for excommunication. But the Baptists too often neglect to mention causes.

Fourth, if exclusion rates could be seen to dispute my assertion of the greater concern with morality among Presbyterians than among Baptists, Johnson's table of compared exclusion rates still does not prove that Baptists excluded more heavily than did Presbyterians. Johnson makes no comparisons between Presbyterians and Baptists from 1801 to 1825. He does compare Baptist and Congregational levels of exclusion, but Congregationalists, because of their looser structure, tended to allow for much more antiformalism than did Presbyterians. Jefferson County's Congregationalists under the Plan of Union overwhelmingly preferred to become Presbyterians, because Presbyterianism allowed frontier churches the opportunity for cohesiveness with other churches within the presbytery. Clearly, different social dynamics led Cortland's residents to greatly favor Congregationalism over Presbyterianism, while Jefferson County residents favored Presbyterianism over Congregationalism.

134. "Minutes of the Black River Baptist Association" (1826), 1.

135. Ibid.

136. A similar relation holds for Presbyterianism; during periods of unusually heavy admissions to churches, discipline is light or nonexistent. The character of the society has as much to do with this facet of revivalism as does the character of the church, as Fowler decries the moral state of the people in northern New York following the War of 1812 but notes that the people, suffering he believes from a shortage of ministers and consequently immorality, managed to experience a great outpouring of the Holy Spirit in 1815. Predictably, Fowler mentions Ellisburg as one of the churches suffering from ministerial destitution and thus

moral decay. Nonetheless, Ellisburg along with Henderson was considered one of the earliest sites of the 1815 fervor in Jefferson County. See Fowler, 180, and Bradley, 214.

137. This is evinced, for example, in the "Minutes of the Black River Baptist Association" (1816), 11; (1821), 14–15; and "The Historical Sketch of the Black River Baptist Association," 8.

138. Quoted in Frederick A. Norwood, *The Story of American Methodism: A History of the United Methodists and Their Relations* (Nashville: Abingdon, 1974), 163 from Jesse Lee, *Short History* (1810), 50.

139. Norwood, 163 quoting from Charles Johnson, *Frontier Camp Meeting* (1955), 211.

140. Fowler, 176–77.

141. Hough, 392.

142. Ibid., 298, 194, 135, 77, 108.

143. Ibid., 170, 165.

144. *Methodist Magazine* (1818): 75–76.

145. Ibid. (1827): 323. Isaac Puffer's biography is contained within P. Douglas Gorrie, *Black River and Northern New York Conference Memorial. Second Series Containing Sketches of the Life and Character of the Deceased Members of the Above Conference Not Included in the Former Work Brought down to the Present Time* (Watertown, N.Y.: Charles E. Holbrook, 1881). As is the case with most biographies contained in this volume and the first (*The Black River Conference Memorial: Containing Sketches of the Life and Character of the Deceased Members of the Black River Conference of the M.E. Church* [New York: Carlton & Phillips, 1852]) the sketches are hagiographical, and give no indication of the success of the Methodists in the region. Understandably, Gorrie complains in the first volume about the dearth of material on the Methodists in northern New York [5].

146. Joseph Haroutunian, *Piety versus Moralism* (New York: Henry Holt, 1932) notes in a discussion of Jonathan Edwards that Edwards would "not permit himself to lose sight of the fact that to be religious and to be moral are two different things. Morality is natural, religion is supernatural" (45).

David L. Rowe makes a similar argument by describing the sectarian impulse of the antiformalists as a stage closest to that of the mystic in Ernst Troeltsch's continuum ranging from the mystic to the church:

> Traditionally pietists have answered these questions in one of two ways. One group, the formal pietists, emphasizes the word—the law, authority, and structure, as revealed in the Bible and incorporated in Christian institutions. Churches, tract societies, Sunday schools, all have the quadruple

> functions of interpreting scripture, evangelizing the world, converting sinners to righteousness, and enforcing obedience to the rule of divine law. Institutions assume authority to specify behavior by elucidating law and then persuading others to live by those laws. We have already encountered a similar temperament in postmillennialism which looks to human agencies to perfect the world in preparation for the inauguration of the Millennium. This argument is also present in orthodox Calvinism of the Old School. The second group, the antiformal pietists, emphasizes the spirit over the word. They believe individuals must be absolutely free to interpret the Bible in the special light God gives them, implying a more direct relationship with God. Antiformalists believe human agencies are inadequate to reform sin—only God has the power to do that by working on sinners. Human authority inevitably absorbs human depravity and holds the potential for setting itself up in opposition to God's authority. Those who hold this are closely akin to premillennialists and Perfectionists (71).

Curtis Johnson recognizes the validity of this argument in *Islands of Holiness: Rural Religion in Upstate, New York, 1790–1860* (Ithaca: Cornell University Press, 1989), but finds that "discipline proceedings varied little among denominations," and that the antiformalists attempted to maintain more vigorous standards than did the Congregationalists, the "dominant formalist group between 1801 and 1819" (68, 89–93).

In Jefferson County, Congregationalist churches predominated before the widespread opting among these churches for Presbyterianism. Congregationalist churches, thus, experienced their strength in Jefferson County during the period of the least structure. And Congregationalists, although also formalist, were not as structured as the Presbyterians who were troubled by the Congregationalists' laxness in admitting ministerial candidates. Discipline in the formalist denominations requires a settled minister and structure. Baptist discipline is less structured to begin with, and thus can function informally without structure.

Johnson argues that in the decades following 1801–1819, and in particular the period from 1826–1842, secularization caused people to begin to question the authority of the churches over them in disciplinary proceedings as a result of the acceptance of Arminianism inherent in "Finney's" New Measures, introduced by Jedediah Burchard. Arminianism, he argues, provided the congregations with the authorized belief that they could act on their own: "The New Measures men had taken American individualism, baptized it with Arminian and perfectionist doctrine, and set it loose to wreak havoc with the church" (109). As I will indicate below, changes did take place in the 1830s, but they were not a result of Finney's Arminianism.

147. Rowe refers to those who became involved in nineteenth-century moral reform as evangelists and those who were involved in revivalism as pietists. He agrees that pietists are concerned with morality, but asserts that sometimes that concern means separating oneself from the world, as have the Amish, rather than contending with immoral forces in the world (70n.3). He does not elaborate on this. I will take up the distinction and connection between revivalism and reform in the next chapter.

148. Hough's list of historically significant men from this era is comprised of county officials who lived in Watertown, the county seat; businessman, also living in Watertown; and the northern nobility.

149. I agree with Cross's assertion that Rochester and Utica were more fervid than were Syracuse and Buffalo, because Rochester and Utica had manufacturing economies that led them to maintain contact with the surrounding rural areas, while Syracuse and Buffalo had commercial economies that separated them from their rural neighbors (Cross, 65). When I refer to commercial economies in the towns of Jefferson County, I am not distinguishing the towns' economies from those of manufacturing towns. I am, however, referring to economies that were not based primarily on farming.

Chapter 4. The Maturation of the Churches

1. David L. Rowe, *Thunder and Trumpets: Millerites and Dissenting Religion in Upstate New York, 1800–1850* (Chico, Calif.: Scholars Press, 1985), 73.

2. Ernst Troeltsch, *The Social Teachings of the Christian Church* (New York: Harper & Row 1949); Rowe, 71–72; Howard Clark Kee et al., *Christianity: A Social and Cultural History* (New York: Macmillan, 1991), 572–73.

3. Rowe, 81.

4. Ibid, 81–89. Rowe also quotes Elder John Peck who was delighted with the formalization both inside of and outside of his denomination. He noted the changes in "widely extended fields—the populous towns, villages and cities—the turnpikes, canals, and railroads—the churches and houses for worship—the Bible, tract and missionary societies, domestic schools and Bible classes—the extensive revivals of religion—and the literary and theological seminaries" (87–88).

5. Frederick A. Norwood, *The Story of American Methodism: A History of United Methodists and Their Relations* (Nashville: Abingdon, 1974), 163.

6. Nathan O. Hatch, *The Democratization of American Christianity* (New Haven: Yale University Press, 1989), 204.

7. Hatch, 193. "Antiformalization" is my term.

8. Ibid., 199.

9. It is possible that Finney incorporated his experience with Methodists into his early preaching, since the Presbyterian Church in Adams was shared by Methodists for a few years, and since Finney used the anxious bench in Evans Mills. But the Baptist influence on Finney is more clearly evident than the Methodist influence. Essentially, Finney's methods in the earliest years were a combination of a pragmatic understanding of the best way in which to reach the mass of people, and apparently an adoption of the Baptist methods to which he had grown accustomed in his youth. After all, Finney, despite his similarities in preaching, considered the Methodist revivals in Evans Mills "spurious." And aside from his short-lived disagreement with the Baptist minister in Gouverneur, Finney displayed a greater affinity for the Baptists in northern New York than he did for the Methodists (Garth Rosell and Richard A. G. Dupuis, eds., *The Memoirs of Charles Grandison Finney: The Complete Restored Text* [Ann Arbor, Michigan: Academie Books, 1989]). It was after Finney moved to Oberlin in 1835 that clearly Methodist ideas, such as perfectionism and sanctification, became part of his theology (Charles Cole, *The Social Ideas of the Northern Evangelists, 1826–1860* [New York: Columbia University Press, 1954], 63. Even the fact that Finney was willing by 1835 to be a professor indicates that he too had evolved to the extent that he had lost his initial concerns that education completely destroyed ministerial candidates.

10. Finney contends that until he moved to Adams, he "had never lived in a praying community" (Rosell and Dupuis, 8). This seems an odd statement, given Henderson's fervor. Finney may have internalized the prevailing formalist (Presbyterian) point of view regarding Henderson as immoral because of its fervor.

Finney, however, is apparently correct in asserting that his family had joined no church (Rosell and Dupuis, 33); for although he and his family attended Osgood's church, their names do not appear in the records of the First Baptist Church of Adams, which united with Osgood's church to form one church. The records are kept at the home of the clerk, Noreen MacIntosh, Honeyville, New York.

11. Rosell and Dupuis, 34–35.

12. Ibid., 8–9.

13. Ibid., 10–13.

14. Charles Hambrick-Stowe, *Charles G. Finney and the Spirit of Evangelicalism* (Grand Rapids, Mich.: Eerdmans, 1996), 24.

15. Ibid., 174.

16. P. H. Fowler, *Historical Sketch of Presbyterianism within the Bounds of the Synod of Central New York* (Utica: Curtis & Childs, 1877), 266.

17. James Hotchkin, *History of the Purchase and Settlement of Western New York and of the Rise, Progress, and Present State of the Presbyterian Church in That Section* (New York: M. W. Dodd, 1848), 140.

18. Ibid., 161, quoted from the report of the General Assembly.

19. The Homer Congregational Church also sought outside help, when after enjoying five protracted meetings in 1831 it brought in Jedediah Burchard to continue the work (Curtis Johnson, *Islands of Holiness: Rural Religion in Upstate New York, 1790–1860* [Ithaca: Cornell University Press, 1989], 48).

The most notable exceptions to the revivals of 1831 were, as Whitney Cross noted in 1950, the churches in Buffalo and Syracuse, apparently because their commercial economies did not encourage contact with antiformalist, agricultural areas; while Rochester's manufacturing economy resulted in frequent contact with farmers who brought their wheat to the mills. Whitney R. Cross, *The Burned-Over District: The Social and Intellectual History of Enthusiastic Religion in Western New York, 1800–1850* (Ithaca: Cornell University Press, 1950), 75. The agricultural areas surrounding Rochester and Syracuse did report large additions in 1831. See Hotchkin, 326–27, 488–91, 519–20; and Fowler, 231–32.

20. Paul Johnson, *A Shopkeeper's Millennium: Society and Revivals in Rochester, New York, 1815–1837* (New York: Hill & Wang, 1978).

21. Fowler, 229.

22. Ibid; and the records of the First Presbyterian Church of Ellisburg, 1831, at the Presbytery of Northern New York, Potsdam, New York. Adams remains a center for enthusiasm, or more accurately in the era of formalization and antiformalization "interest." Adams's position as the most stable of the southern communities made it more capable of accepting the changes in revivalism.

23. Fowler, 230. Fowler notes that the "wordly portion of the community" in Jefferson County was disturbed by the protracted meetings, and that it thus called a convention at the court house (229). This dissension was very likely from the Universalists who were a powerful presence in Jefferson County, and the only group likely capable or interested in organizing a meeting to oppose the protracted meetings.

24. "Interest" in religion more accurately describes the perspective of the participants after 1830 than does "enthusiasm."

25. Records of the First Presbyterian Church of Watertown, 12 March 1833 to 19 July 1833.

26. Records of Stone Presbyterian Church, Watertown New York, kept at the church.

27. Records of the First Presbyterian Church of Watertown 14 February 1832, kept at the church; records of the First Presbyterian Church of Adams, 10 February 1831, microfilmed by the Genealogical Society of the Church of Jesus Christ of Latter-day Saints at the Presbyterian Historical Society, Philadelphia; records of the First Presbyterian Church of LeRay, 1831, kept at the church.

28. Records of the First Presbyterian Church of Theresa, kept at the church; and Fowler, 235. The fact that it took Second Presbyterian in Watertown and First

Presbyterian in Theresa two years after the arrival of their ministers to experience a revival does not call into question my assertion in chapter 3 that the revivals in the mid-1810s and mid-1820s in Jefferson County were primarily the result of the arrival of a settled pastor after years of instability. Since Second Presbyterian separated from First Presbyterian in Watertown, most of its earliest members were admitted on recommendation; and the church in Theresa had a pastor in 1828.

Nathan M. Flower, a member of the session at the church in Theresa named his son after Roswell Pettibone. Roswell Pettibone Flower was the thirty-third governor of New York State from 1892–1894.

29. Myrick to Finney 10 January 1832, photostat in the Whitney R. Cross Papers, Cornell University Department of Manuscripts and Archives, accession no. 1678.

30. Fowler, 236n.

31. Records of the First Presbyterian Church of LeRay; and Franklin B. Hough, *A History of Jefferson County in the State of New York from the Earliest Period to the Present Time* (Albany: Joel Munsell; Watertown: Sterling & Riddell, 1854), 194.

32. "Historical Sketch of the Black River Baptist Association" (Adams, N.Y.: E. J. Clark, 1849).

33. "Associational Statistics" of the Black River Baptist Association from 1822 to 1883, at the American Baptist Historical Society, Colgate-Rochester Divinity School, Rochester, New York.

34. Ibid.

35. Records of the Adams Village Baptist Church, 29 March 1808 and 7 May 1808.

36. "Minutes of the Black River Baptist Association," from 1810 to 1830.

37. Ibid., 1831, pp. 9–10.

38. Ibid., 1832, p. 5; 1833, pp. 5–6.

39. Ibid., 1836, 7.

40. "Minutes of the Jefferson Baptist Association" (1836), 7–12. The Jefferson Baptist Association was formed in 1835 by some of the Baptist churches in Jefferson County because their ministers found traveling to the distant meetings within the wide geographical bounds of the Black River Association difficult. Without explanation, the churches of the Jefferson Association reunited with the Black River Association in 1838.

41. Ibid., 12.

42. "Minutes of the Black River Baptist Association," 1838, 11–12. It is unlikely that statements such as these in the Baptist Association records indicate a jeremiad against perceived declension, simply because concern with morality was not present among Baptists prior to the 1830s.

43. Ibid., 14.

44. Ibid., 15.

45. Records of the First Baptist Church of Adams, 7 February 1835.

46. Ibid., 9 May 1835.

47. "Minutes of the Jefferson Baptist Association" 1836, 14–15.

48. In addition to the Mormons and the Universalists, the formation of the Millerites, Antimission Baptists, and the Methodist Protestant Church indicate a tendency toward schism that can be viewed as a form of "ultraism." Much historiographical confusion has developed around the terms "perfectionist" and "ultraist." In general, the terms are treated as if they had identical meanings. However, I use "perfectionist" to refer only to those who believed in the possibility of leading lives of sinless perfection. Thus, I do not find the term an appropriate description of Finney's theology before 1835.

For the numerous uses to which these terms have been subjected in twentieth-century historiography, see Nancy Hewitt, *Women's Activism and Social Change: Rochester, New York, 1822–1872* (Ithaca: Cornell University Press, 1984); Glenn C. Altschuler and Jan M. Saltzgaber, *Revivalism, Social Conscience, and Community in the Burned-Over District: The Trial of Rhoda Bement* (Ithaca: Cornell University Press, 1983), 144; and Whitney R. Cross, *The Burned-Over District: The Social and Intellectual History of Enthusiastic Religion in Western New York, 1800–1850* (Ithaca: Cornell University Press, 1950), 238. I am basing my understanding of the nineteenth-century use of "ultraist" on Fowler, 159–60.

49. Hough asserts that the Swedenborgians first established a church in Henderson in 1825 (170). At the bottom of the pages of the 1832 "Minutes of the Black River Baptists Association," at the American Baptist Historical Society, Reverend N. G. Chase writing from Henderson pencilled a draft of a letter in which noted that the "Swedenburghs" added to the diversity of Henderson, but that he did not expect them to last long. In the 1832 "Minutes" Reverend Chase is identified as a minister from Otsego Association; he is not officially designated as a minister from Henderson.

50. Ibid., 84.

51. Ibid., 72.

52. The records of the First Presbyterian Church of Adams indicate that Ezra Griswell preferred to attend the meetings of the "sect called Christians" rather than the meetings of the Presbyterian church "tho it did not appear that he had embraced the more obnoxious sentiments of that sect" (12 April 1821).

53. Cross, 330, Map 24. Letters from the phalanx in Watertown are kept at the Jefferson County Historical Society, Watertown, New York: Esther H. Schenck to Eliza F. Schenck, 27 July 1844; and an anonymous letter dated 29 November

1843. The letters indicate that members of the phalanx had traveled to Watertown from outside Jefferson County.

54. Persijs Kolberg, former director of the Jefferson County Historical Society has informed me of the Zoarite presence. The Society of the Separatists of Zoar was a communitarian organization formed by Joseph Michael Bimeler (or Bäumler) in Germany. Most Zoarites settled in Ohio in 1817 (W. M. Ashcraft, "Joseph Michael Bimeler [Bäumler]," *Dictionary of Christianity in America,* Daniel G. Reid, et al., eds. [Downers Grove, Ill.: InterVarsity Press, 1990], 153–54).

55. Cross notes that the southeast corner in the vicinity of Ellisburg demonstrated "sustained Adventist enthusiasm" (289, Map 23; 294). Rowe indicates that Millerites were persecuted in Jefferson County. When the Millerite Samuel Rhodes traveled through Ellisburg, a mob attacked him (110). And A. P. Weaver of Sackets Harbor received a letter from his neighbors parodying his Adventist beliefs (108).

56. William T. Field and Lovina R. Hayes, "History of All Souls Church: The Story of the Universalist Church and the Unitarian Universalist Church in Watertown, New York," pamphlet at All Souls Church, Watertown, New York.

57. "A Partial Sketch of Rev. Pitt Morse's Life," handwritten essay at All Souls Church; and "Honor Memory of Rev. Pitt Morse: Universalists Lay Wreath on Grave of Early Preacher," *Watertown Daily Times* 14 June 1920; and "Two Pioneer Preachers," *Times* 9 May 1934, in the Pitt Morse file of the morgue of the Watertown Daily Times, Watertown, New York.

58. Hosea Ballou to Pitt Morse, 29 July 1824, in the archives of Harvard University Divinity School. "Partial Sketch" notes that Ballou and Morse agreed in their opposition to the restorationists, who believed that the soul must go through a period of cleansing after death. Ballou and Morse believed in immediate salvation.

59. In the case of John Gotham who was charged by the First Presbyterian Church in Watertown with buying a parcel of land for less than its worth and of believing in the tenets of the Universalists, testimony that he had attended Ballou's dedication proved damning (records of the First Presbyterian Church of Watertown, 6 June 1825).

60. Hatch, 126.

61. Records of the First Presbyterian Church of Watertown, 18 April 1823.

62. Ibid., 13 February 1824.

63. *Herald of Salvation* (17 May 1832): 101.

64. *Herald of Salvation* (15 January 1824): 61.

65. Ibid., 61–62.

66. See records of the First Baptist Church of Rutland, 18 May 1822, at the Jefferson County Historical Society, Watertown; and records of the First Baptist

Church of Adams, 12 July 1834, at the home of the clerk, Noreen MacIntosh, Honeyville, New York.

67. Rowe, 80; Curtis Johnson, 68n.4.

68. See any one of several references to the Universalists in Hatch in which he groups the Universalists with Baptists, Methodists, Free Will Baptists, and Disciples of Christ (21, 40, 56, 66, 127, 134, 170).

69. Russell E. Miller, *The Larger Hope: The First Century of the Universalist Church in America, 1770–1870* (Boston: Unitarian Universalist Association, 1979), 26.

70. Ibid., 243–44.

71. Ibid., 169. Miller cites Robert Baird, *Religion in America; or, An Account of the Origin, Progress, Relation to the State, and Present Condition of the Evangelical Churches in the United States, with Notices of the Unevangelical Denominations.* (New York: Harper, 1844), 269, 276, 277, 282.

72. See, for example, *A Sermon on the Doctrine of Election, Delivered in Watertown on Sunday Nov. 10th, 1822. By the Rev. Pitt Morse* (Watertown: Seth A. Abbey, 1823); *Answer to Rev. H. S. Johnsons' Two Sermons against Universalism: Delivered in Canton, N.Y. in 1831 and Published in 1833 by Pitt Morse, Pastor of the First Universalist Church and Society in Watertown, N.Y. Dedicated to All Candid Christians, but More Particularly to the Readers of Mr. Johnson's Sermons* (Watertown: Printed at the [American] Eagle Office, 1834); *Sermons in Vindication of Universalism, by Pitt Morse, Pastor of the First Universalian Church and Society in Watertown, N.Y. "Omnia Explorate: bonum tenete." In reply to "Lectures on Universalism; by Joel Parker, Pastor of the 3d Presbyterian Church, Rochester"* (Watertown: Printed by Woodward & Calhoun, 1831).

73. *Herald of Salvation* (3 May 1823): 93.

74. "Address on Education," November 1840, p. 11, in the archives of Harvard University Divinity School.

75. Ibid., 13. See also "On the Education of Children," in the archives of Harvard University Divinity School.

76. *Herald of Salvation* (28 August 1824): 102.

77. Ibid.

78. Ibid., 102–103.

79. In a collection of Morse's sermons at Harvard University Divinity School, p. 17.

80. Quoted from an unidentified article by Hough in John A. Haddock, *The Growth of a Century as Illustrated in the History of Jefferson County, New York from 1793 to 1894* (Philadelphia: Sherman, 1894), 732.

81. *Herald of Salvation* (9 October 1824): 127.

82. "Historical Sketch," 5; Field and Hayes, 15.

83. Rowe, 72.

84. Hatch, 58.

85. Joseph Smith, *History of the Church of Jesus Christ of Latter-day Saints: Volume 2,* B. H. Roberts, ed. (Salt Lake City: Deseret, 1978), 225–26.

86. Hatch, 208.

87. Smith, 225.

88. Richard L. Bushman, *Joseph Smith and the Beginnings of Mormonism* (Urbana and Chicago: University of Illinois Press, 1984), 26–29.

89. Evidently Theresa does not appear in the High Council's report since some of the Theresa converts had already begun the trek west.

90. Personal communication with Asael LaFave, Historian of the Town of Theresa, and Clerk of the Session of the First Presbyterian Church of Theresa, 13 August 1991; Harry F. Landon, *The North Country: A History Embracing Jefferson, St. Lawrence, Oswego, Lewis, and Franklin Counties, New York* (Indianapolis, Ind.: Historical Publishing, 1932), 299–300; Richard E. Bennett, "'Plucking Not Planting': Mormonism in Eastern Canada, 1830–1850," *The Mormon Presence in Canada* (Logan: Utah State University Press, 1990), 29.

91. Personal communication with Asael LaFave, 13 August 1991; and records of the First Presbyterian Church of Theresa, 1 December 1835; and 2 June 1838.

92. Andrew Jensen, "William Huntington," *Latter-day Saint Biographical Encyclopedia: A Compilation of Biographical Sketches of Prominent Men and Women in the Church of Jesus Christ of Latter-day Saints: Volume 1* (Salt Lake City: Andrew Jensen History Company and Deseret News, 1901), 368. The Records of the First Presbyterian Church of Adams do not accurately list the names of members prior to Gale's arrival in 1819. Thus, although Huntington's name does not appear in the records there is no reason to believe that he did not in fact join the church.

93. The records of the First Presbyterian Church of Adams end in 1834. Hence it is impossible to know what the reaction was to Huntington's departure. Huntington and his family may have been the five baptisms mentioned in the report of the High Council from Pillar Point in 1835.

94. Jensen, 368–70. The records of the First Presbyterian Church of Watertown contain a reference to Mr. and Mrs. William Huntington, who had been members of the church at least since 1831. The records state:

> The committee to visit Mr. and Mrs. Huntington reported that they had respectedly [sic] seen them that *both avowed* belief in Mormonism but fellowshipped the church & had not changed their belief in Evangelical doctrines excepting that they believed immersion to be the true mode of

> baptism—Mr. Huntington recently appeared to be wavering in his belief as to the truth of Mormonism & that Mrs. Huntington now believed it to be wrong & regretted what she had done.

This appeared in the records on 3 November 1836, after the Huntingtons are believed to have left for Nauvoo. It is unclear whether this is the same Huntington family.

95. Stanley B. Kimball, *Heber C. Kimball: Mormon Patriarch and Pioneer* (Urbana and Chicago: University of Illinois, 1981), 310.

96. Richard S. Van Wagoner and Steven C. Walker, "Zina D. H. Young," in *A Book of Mormons* (Salt Lake City: Signature Books, 1982), 415–18; and Joan Iverson, "The Mormon-Suffrage Relationship: Personal and Political Quandaries," *Frontiers* 11 (1990): 11. Iverson asserts that Zina Young's interest in suffrage exacerbated the differences between the National Women's Suffrage Association (Susan B. Anthony and Elizabeth Cady Stanton) and the American Women's Suffrage Association (Lucy Stone and Henry Blackwell), because the NWSA allowed polygamous women to participate in its efforts, while the AWSA decried polygamy as "barbarism" (8–16).

97. See Huntington file, morgue of the *Watertown Daily Times.*

Chapter 5. The Progress of Reform

1. William G. McLoughlin, "Introduction," in Charles Grandison Finney, *Lectures on Revivals of Religion* (Cambridge: Harvard University Press, 1960), xliv; and Finney, "Hindrances to Revivals," ibid., 286–87.

2. Curtis Johnson, *Islands of Holiness: Rural Religion in Upstate New York, 1790–1860* (Ithaca: Cornell University Press, 1989), 118.

3. T. Scott Miyakawa, *Protestants and Pioneers: Individualism and Conformity on the American Frontier* (Chicago: University of Chicago Press, 1964), 22.

4. Miyakawa, 22.

5. "Mr. Finney's Journal," *Eighth Report of the Female Missionary Society of the Western District* (1824): 17.

6. "Mr. Adam W. Platt's Report," *Sixth Report* (1822): 8–9.

7. "Rev. Henry Smith's Report," ibid., 18.

8. James H. Hotchkin's history of missionary efforts in western New York leads to the same conclusion. With one exception none of the several missionary societies he describes in western New York lasted beyond the period of initial formation. The one exception was the American Home Missionary Society, which as a national organization was constantly meeting a need to reformalize on the

frontier (*A History of the Purchase and Settlement of Western New York and of the Rise, Progress, and Present State of the Presbyterian Church in That Section* [New York: M. W Dodd, 1848], 176–202).

9. Hotchkin asserts that in the Bible Societies of western New York

> the members . . . were mostly connected with Presbyterian or Congregational congregations. The Episcopalians and the Methodists generally preferred not to unite with other denominations, in any organization of a religious character; and the Baptists, for a season, mostly stood aloof from the Societies. (257)

10. Records of the Bible Society of Rutland, 28 January 1824, p. 25, at the Jefferson County Historical Society, Watertown, New York.

11. Ibid., 29 January 1823, p. 19.

12. Ibid., "Address of the Board of Directors of the Jefferson County Bible Society, to the friends of the Bible cause in said County," 17 July 1832, p. 44.

13. Records of the First Presbyterian Church of Watertown, 12 August 1828.

14. Ibid., 11 March 1829.

15. Ibid., 31 January 1831.

16. Rorabaugh, *The Alcoholic Republic: An American Tradition* (New York: Oxford University Press, 1979), 8–9, 187, 194.

17. Records of the First Presbyterian Church of LeRay, kept at the church in Evans Mills.

18. Records of the First Presbyterian Church of Theresa, kept at the church in Theresa.

19. The annual reports of the Jefferson County Bible Society unfailingly report that Ellisburg gave at least twice as much as other towns, including much wealthier and much more populated towns such as Watertown and Brownville.

20. Records of the First Presbyterian Church of Belleville in Ellisburg, kept at the Presbytery of Northern New York in Potsdam, New York.

21. Records of the First Presbyterian Church of Adams, microfilmed at the Presbyterian Historical Society, Philadelphia, by the Genealogical Society of the Church of Jesus Christ of Latter-day Saints.

22. P. H. Fowler, *Historical Sketch of Presbyterianism within the Bounds of the Synod of Central New York* (Utica: Curtiss & Childs, 1877), 141–44.

23. Intemperance and sabbath breaking are the classic moral concerns of the Puritans and their descendants. See David D. Hall, *Worlds of Wonder, Days of Judgment* (New York: Alfred Knopf, 1989), 91. Richard R. John does find that sabbatarianism reform was dominated by the Presbyterians and Congregationalists

and in some cases opposed by Baptists; and Ann Douglas also notes that Baptists opposed the move to end Sunday delivery of the mail. See John, "Taking Sabbatarianism Seriously: The Postal System, the Sabbath, and the Transformation of American Political Culture," *Journal of the Early Republic* 10 (Winter 1990): 217–67; and Douglas, *The Feminization of American Culture* (New York: Doubleday, 1977), 33.

24. Fowler, 144–45.

25. Ibid., 145–46.

26. Ibid., 146.

27. Ibid., 154.

28. Ibid., 155.

29. Ibid., 159–60.

30. See chapter 4.

31. Fowler, 160.

32. Hotchkin's discussions of benevolence are limited to missionary labors, Bible Societies, Education Societies, and Sunday schools (176–202; 253–63).

33. Curtis Johnson's assertion that abolitionism in Cortland County appealed primarily to Presbyterians and Congregationalists seems to indicate that Cortland County was not typical in its benevolence (120). As a rule, abolition seems to have appealed most strongly to antiformalists and to Scotch-Irish Presbyterians, who did not make up the mass of Presbyterians in northern New York. See M. S. Shanaberger, " Abolition and the Churches," in *Dictionary of Christianity in American,* Daniel G. Reid et al., eds. (Downers Grove, Ill.: InterVarsity Press, 1990), 23–24. John R. McKivigan in *The War against Proslavery Religion: Abolitionism and the Northern Churches, 1830–1865* (Ithaca: Cornell University Press, 1984) indicates that many Presbyterians involved themselves in the antislavery movement, but he also notes that the General Assembly never passed resolutions condemning slavery. Many Presbyterians did personally oppose slavery, but active reform in opposition to slavery ran counter to official Presbyterian interest in orderliness. For example, the General Assembly stated in 1836 that a condemnation of slaveholders "would tend to distract and divide the denomination" (45). Presbyterians were generally more interested in reforms of such disorderly activities as "promiscuous dancing" and horse racing than they were in abolition (167–69).

34. Glenn C. Altschuler and Jan M. Salzgaber, *Revivalism, Social Conscience, and Community in the Burned-Over District: The Trial of Rhoda Bement* (Ithaca: Cornell University Press, 1983), 9.

35. Glenn C. Altschuler, "Varieties of Religious Activity: Conflict and Community in the Churches of the Burned-Over District," in Altschuler and Salzgaber, 143.

36. See Jan M. Salzgaber, "For the Salvation of the World! Revivalism and Reform in Seneca Falls, New York," in Altschuler and Salzgaber, 58n.67.

37. D. W. Carlson, "Temperance Movement (1820s-1860)," in Reid et al., 1163.

38. Steven C. Bullock argues that antimasonry was a result of a reinterpretation of patriotism. Originally Masons were regarded as principled and upright Jeffersonians. However, in the 1820s, Jacksonians began to consider the values of the Jeffersonians unethical and thus assailed them, as in the antimasonic crisis ("A Pure and Sublime System: The Appeal of Post-Revolutionary Freemasonry," *Journal of the Early Republic* 9 [Fall 1989]: 359–73). Bullock's article includes a photocopy of a membership certificate from the Masonic lodge to which Finney belonged in Adams (365).

39. Records of the First Presbyterian Church of Watertown, 12 December 1829, 9 January 1830.

40. The session announced this renunciation in the records of the church on 6 January 1829.

41. Reprint of an article from the *Watertown Register* dated 7 October 1834 in *The Courier* (Sackets Harbor) 16 April 1836, kept in the basement of the *Watertown Daily Times.*

42. Paul Johnson, *A Shopkeeper's Millennium: Society and Revivals in Rochester, New York, 1815–1837* (New York: Hill & Wang, 1978).

43. McLoughlin, xliv. Despite McLoughlin's recognition of Finney's antiformalism, although McLoughlin does not use the term "antiformalist," he nonetheless considers it ironic that Finney, like his opponent Samuel Hopkins, advocated "disinterested benevolence" (xlii). The benevolence that Finney and Hopkins advocated differed in that Finney promoted antiformalist interests, while Hopkins championed orderly and orthodox, formalist reforms.

44. "A Letter from the United Female Society in Henderson, Dated May 29, 1816," in the "Minutes of the Black River Baptists Association" (1816): 6, at the American Baptist Historical Association, Colgate-Rochester Divinity School, Rochester, New York.

45. From 1817 to 1840 donations to missionaries were the highest and the most frequent from Henderson and Ellisburg, as was also the case with the Jefferson County Bible Society.

46. "Minutes of the Black River Baptist Association" (1814): 9–10.

47. Ibid. (1828): 7.

48. Ibid. (1835): 9–11.

49. Ibid. (1832): 6. Adoniram Judson was a Congregationalist founder of the American Foreign Missionary Society. On his way to India, he began to believe

in the necessity of baptism by immersion. He then formed the Baptist Foreign Mission Society and moved to Burma, initiating the Baptists' fascination with the Burmese missions.

50. *Rev. Mr. Judson's Letter to the Female Members of the Christian Churches, in the United States of America* (Providence: H. H. Brown, 1832), 3–4.

51. Records of the First Baptist Church of Adams, 4 September 1832, kept at the home of the clerk, Noreen Macintosh, Honeyville, New York.

52. "Minutes of the Black River Baptist Association" (1829): 4–5.

53. Ibid. (1830): 7.

54. Records of the First Baptist Church of Adams, 16 September 1837. McKivigan indicates that northern Baptists failed to oppose slavery unifiedly, but his argument does not necessarily contradict this one. He identifies the greatest opposition to abolitionism among Baptists who had immigrated from the South to the Northwest, and among antimission Baptists (47). Jefferson County's Baptists did not immigrate from the south, did not live in the northwest, and were not antimission Baptists.

55. "Minutes of the Black River Baptist Association" (1838): 10; (1839): 8.

56. Ibid. (1838): 9; (1839): 7.

57. Ibid.

58. Ibid. (1838): 7.

59. Ibid., 10.

60. Ibid. (1839): 8.

61. Ibid.

62. Records of the Jefferson County Bible Society, 28 January 1840.

63. *Methodist Quarterly Review* (1837): 212.

64. Like "ultraist," the term "perfectionist" has been subject to numerous interpretations. As I use it, perfectionist refers only to the primarily Methodist belief in the possibility of attaining sinless perfection through a second blessing. Such a definition of perfectionism is incompatible with a term such as "perfectionist reform." As Hewitt uses it, "perfectionist" refers to a certain class of women.

Hewitt followed Paul Johnson's research on Rochester with *Women's Activism and Social Change: Rochester, New York 1822–1872* (Ithaca: Cornell University Press, 1984), a study of reform-minded women in Rochester. She breaks into three groups the reform organizations in Rochester: ultraists, perfectionists, and benevolent women (40). She asserts that perfectionists were wives of upwardly mobile husbands, who began their benevolent work in the 1830s as a result of the "Finneyite" revivals, and she argues that they attempted "to eradicate rather than ameliorate social ills." This assertion is premised on the perfectionist impulse latent in Finney's theology, which did not become evident until 1835 when he was at Oberlin.

She contends that "ultraists" were primarily agrarian women who had moved to the city. Because they were not products of the cult of true womanhood, they had a less hierarchical view of society and no stake in the standing order. Generally, she considers ultraists and Hicksite Quakers identical. And it is these same women whom she identifies as the force behind women's rights in the nineteenth century: especially Lucretia Mott and Elizabeth Cady Stanton. (See also Hewitt, "Feminist Friends: Agrarian Quakers and the Emergence of Woman's Rights in America," *Feminist Studies* 12 [Spring 1986]: 27–49.)

Benevolent women most closely resemble the class whom Paul Johnson recognized at the Finney revivals. Their concern was to ameliorate rather than to eradicate social ill, in order to create order and to maintain control.

Hewitt's presentation of benevolence is perceptive but would not work in Jefferson County, which had a less-stratified class structure and which evidenced no distinctions between ultraist women and perfectionist women. Like Paul Johnson, Hewitt presents evidence of a society responding to the imported revivals, and she demonstrates the repercussions of the formalization of revivals.

65. John Corrigan, *Business of the Heart: Religion and Emotion in the Nineteenth Century* (Berkeley: University of California Press, 2002), 248.

66. Ibid., 249.

67. Ibid., 120, 122–23.

68. Ibid., 123.

69. Ibid., 249.

Chapter 6. Conclusion

1. Jeffrey K. Hadden and Anson Shupe, *Televangelism: Power and Politics on God's Frontier* (New York: Henry Holt, 1988), 82–83.

2. Peter W. Williams, *Popular Religion in America: Symbolic Change and the Modernization Process in Historical Perspective* (Urbana and Chicago: University of Illinois Press, 1989), 43.

3. George Marsden, *Understanding Fundamentalism and Evangelicalism* (Grand Rapids, Mich.: Eerdmans, 1991), 166.

4. Williams, *America's Religions: Traditions and Cultures* (New York: Macmillan, 1990), 319.

5. David Brooks, *Bobos in Paradise: The New Upper Class and How They Got There* (New York: Simon & Schuster, 2000).

6. William G. McLoughlin in *Revivalism, Awakenings, and Reform* (Chicago: University of Chicago Press, 1978), 209.

7. Brooks, 9.

8. Ibid., 10.

9. Georg Wilhelm Freidrich Hegel, *The Phenomenology of Spirit* (1807) and *The Philosophy of History* (1822). See also Karl Marx and Friedrich Engels, *The Communist Manifesto,* although the dialectic between antiformalists and formalists seems to lead to the revitalization of capitalism rather than its destruction.

BIBLIOGRAPHY

Primary Sources

Church and Association Records

All Souls Church, Watertown, at the church.

Bible Society of Rutland (later the Jefferson Bible Society), Jefferson County Historical Society, Watertown, New York.

Black River Baptist Association, at the American Baptist Historical Society, Colgate-Rochester Divinity School, Rochester, New York.

Female Bethel Society of Sackets Harbor, New York, Pickering-Beach Museum, Sackets Harbor.

Female Moral Reform Society of Sackets Harbor, Pickering-Beach Museum.

Female Western Missionary Society, Oneida County Historical Society, Utica.

First Baptist Church of Adams, at the home of the clerk, Noreen MacIntosh, Honeyville, New York.

First Baptist Church of Marion, Wayne County, at the Center for the Study of Early Religious Life in Western New York, Cornell University, Department of Manuscripts and Archives, accession no. 6063 (Restricted).

First Baptist Church of Rutland, at the Jefferson County Historical Society.

First Baptist Church of Watertown, at the church.

First Presbyterian Church of Adams, microfilmed by the Genealogical Society of the Church of Jesus Christ of Latter-day Saints at the Presbyterian Historical Society, Philadelphia.

First Presbyterian Church of Ellisburg, at the Presbytery of Northern New York, Potsdam, New York.

First Presbyterian Church of LeRay, at the church.

First Presbyterian Church of Theresa, at the church.

First Presbyterian Church of Watertown, at the church.

Friends Quarterly Meeting, LeRay, microfilmed by the Genealogical Society of the Church of Jesus Christ of Latter-day Saints at the Haviland Records Room of the Friends Historical Society, New York.

Jefferson Baptist Association, American Baptist Historical Society.

Jefferson County Agricultural Society, at the Jefferson County Historical Society.
Jefferson County Board of Supervisors, in the Supervisor's Office, Jefferson County Office Building, Watertown.
Stone Presbyterian Church, Watertown, at the church.
United Presbyterian Church of Sackets Harbor, New York, at the church.
Watertown Ecclesiastical Society (later the Watertown Religious Society), at the First Presbyterian Church of Watertown.

General Sources

Asbury, Francis. *Journal.* New York: N. Bangs and T. Mason, 1821.
Bangs, Nathan. Papers. United Methodist Archives, Drew University.
Bronson, Ethel. Papers. New York Public Library.
Camp, Elisha. Papers. Cornell University, Department of Manuscripts and Archives, accession no. 696.
Constable, James. Papers. Cornell University, Department of Manuscripts and Archives, accession no. 608.
The Courier (Sackets Harbor), kept in the basement of the *Watertown Daily Times.*
Cross, Whitney R. Papers. Cornell University, Department of Manuscripts and Archives, accession no. 1678.
Dutton, Nathaniel. Papers. Jefferson County Historical Society.
Eastman, C. G. *Sermons, Addresses & Exhortations, by Rev. Jedediah Burchard with an Appendix Containing Some Account of the Proceedings, Held under His Direction, in Burlington, Williston, and Hinesburgh, Vt., December, 1835 and January, 1836.* Burlington: Chauncey Goodrich, 1836.
Finney, Charles Grandison. Papers, microfilmed by University microfilms, Ann Arbor, Mich.
———. *Lectures on Revivals of Religion,* ed. William G. McLoughlin. Cambridge: Harvard University Press, 1960.
———. *Memoirs of Charles Grandison Finney: The Complete Restored Text,* ed. Garth M. Rosell and Richard A. G. Dupuis. Grand Rapids, Mich.: Academie Books, 1990.
Ford, William D. Papers. New-York Historical Society.
Gale, George W. *The Autobiography (to 1834) of George Washington Gale (1789–1861), Founder of Galesburg, Illinois, and Knox College.* New York: privately printed, 1964.
Herald of Salvation (Watertown, New York), at All Soul's Church, Watertown.
Hubbard, Noadiah. Papers. Jefferson County Historical Society.
Huntington Family. File, Morgue of the *Watertown Daily Times.*
Ingersoll, Col. Robert G. File, Morgue of the *Watertown Daily Times.*

[Judson, Adoniram]. *Rev. Mr. Judson's Letter to the Female Members of the Christian Churches in the United States of America.* Providence: H. H. Brown, 1832.

Knapp, Jacob. *Autobiography of Elder Jacob Knapp with an Introductory Essay by R. Jeffrey.* New York: Sheldon, 1868.

LeRay, James. Papers. Cornell University, Department of Manuscripts and Archives.

Methodist Magazine. 1818–1829.

Methodist Quarterly Review. 1830–1840.

Morse, Pitt. Papers and Sermons. Harvard University Divinity School Archives.

———. File, Morgue of the *Watertown Daily Times.*

———. *A Sermon on the Doctrine of Election, Delivered in Watertown on Sunday Nov. 10th, 1822 by the Rev. Pitt Morse.* Watertown: Seth A. Abbey, 1823.

———. *Answer to the Rev. H. S. Johnsons' Two Sermons against Universalism: Delivered in Canton, N.Y. in 1831 and Published in 1833 by Pitt Morse, Pastor of the First Universalist Church and Society in Watertown, N.Y. Dedicated to All Candid Christians, But More Particularly to the Readers of Mr. Johnson's Sermons.* Watertown: Printed at the [American] Eagle Office, 1834.

———. *Sermons in Vindication of Universalism, by Pitt Morse, Pastor of the First Universalist Church and Society in Watertown, N.Y. "Omnia Explorate: bonum tenete." In reply to "Lectures on Universalism; By Joel Parker, Pastor of the 3d Presbyterian Church, Rochester."* Watertown: Printed by Woodward & Calhoun, 1831.

Selden Family. Papers, Cornell University, Department of Manuscripts and Archives, accession no. 1655.

Smith, George W. Papers, in the vault of the *Watertown Daily Times,* Watertown, New York.

Streeter, Russell. *Mirror of Calvinistic Fanatical Revivals, or Jedediah Burchard & Co. during a Protracted Meeting of Twenty-Six Days in Woodstock, Vt.* Woodstock, Vt: published by the author, 1835.

Taylor, Rev. John. "Journal of the Rev. John Taylor, on a Mission through the Mohawk and Black River Country, in the Year 1802." In *Documentary History of the State of New York: Volume 3.* ed. Christopher Morgan and E. B. O'Callaghan, M.D. Albany: Weed, Parsons, Public Printers, 1850.

Selected Sources and Secondary Works

Ahlstrom, Sydney E. *A Religious History of the American People.* New Haven: Yale University Press, 1972.

Albanese, Catherine L. *America: Religions and Religion.* Belmont, Calif.: Wadsworth, 1992.

———. *Nature Religion in America: From the Algonkian Indians to the New Age.* Chicago: University of Chicago Press, 1990.

Altschuler, Glenn C., and Jan M. Saltzgaber. *Revivalism, Social Conscience, and Community in the Burned-Over District: The Trial of Rhoda Bement.* Ithaca: Cornell University Press, 1983.

Becker, Martin Joseph. *A History of Catholic Life in the Diocese of Albany, 1609–1864: United States Catholic Historical Society Monograph Series, 31.* New York: United States Catholic Historical Society, 1975.

Bellah, Robert. *The Broken Covenant: American Civil Religion in Time of Trial.* New York: Seabury, 1975.

Bennett, Richard E. "'Plucking Not Planting' Mormonism in Eastern Canada, 1830–1850." In *The Mormon Presence in Canada,* ed. Brigham Y. Card et al., 19–34. Logan: Utah State University Press, 1990.

Bergson, Henri. *The Two Sources of Morality and Religion.* Notre Dame, Ind.: University of Notre Dame Press, 1977.

Bonomi, Patricia U. *Under the Cope of Heaven: Religion, Society, and Politics in Colonial America.* New York: Oxford University Press, 1986.

Bradley, Joshua, A. M. *Accounts of Religious Revivals in Many Parts of the United States from 1815 to 1818 Collected from Numerous Publications and Letters from Persons of Piety and Correct Information.* Albany: G. J. Loomis, 1819; repr., Wheaton, Ill.: Richard Owen Roberts, 1980.

Brooks, David. *Bobos in Paradise: The New Upper Class and How They Got There.* New York: Simon & Schuster, 2000.

Bullock, Steven C. "A Pure and Sublime System: The Appeal of Post-Revolutionary Freemasonry." *Journal of the Early Republic* 9 (Fall 1989): 359–73.

Bushman, Richard L. *Joseph Smith and the Beginnings of Mormonism.* Urbana and Chicago: University of Illinois Press, 1984.

Butler, Jon. "Enthusiasm Described and Decried: The Great Awakening as Interpretive Fiction." *Journal of American History* 69 (1982): 305–25.

———. *Awash in a Sea of Faith: Christianizing the American People.* Cambridge: Harvard University Press, 1990.

Carwardine, Richard. *Transatlantic Revivalism: Popular Evangelicalism in Britain and America, 1790–1865.* Westport, Conn.: Greenwood Press, 1978.

"Centennial History of the Black River and St. Lawrence Association of Congregational Ministers and Churches." n.p., n.d., kept with the records of the First Congregational Church of Copenhagen, Lewis County, at the church.

Clarke, T. Wood. *Emigres in the Wilderness.* Port Washington, N.Y.: Ira J. Friedman, 1941; repr., 1967.

Cleaveland, Dorothy Kendall. "The Trade and Trade Routes of Northern New

York from the Beginning of Settlement to the Coming of the Railroad." *The Quarterly Journal of the New York State Historical Association* 4 (October 1923): 205–31.

Clebsch, William. *From Sacred to Profane America: The Role of Religion in American History.* New York: Harper & Row, 1968.

Cole, Charles. *The Social Ideas of the Northern Evangelists, 1826–1860.* New York: Columbia University Press, 1954.

Conkin, Paul K. *Cane Ridge: America's Pentecost.* Madison: University of Wisconsin Press, 1990.

Corrigan, John. *Business of the Heart: Religion and Emotion in the Nineteenth Century.* Berkeley: University of California Press, 2002.

Cross, Whitney R. *The Burned-Over District: The Social and Intellectual History of Enthusiastic Religion in Western New York, 1800–1850.* Ithaca: Cornell University Press, 1950.

Davis, David Brion. "The New England Origins of Mormonism." *New England Quarterly* 27 (June 1953): 147–68.

DePillis, Mario. "The Quest for Religious Authority." *Dialogue: A Journal of Mormon Thought* 1 (1966): 68–88.

———. "The Social Sources of Mormonism." 37 *Church History* (March 1968): 50–79.

Douglas, Ann. *The Feminization of American Culture.* New York: Doubleday, 1977.

Douglas, Mary. *Natural Symbols: Explorations in Cosmology.* New York: Random House, 1970.

Doyle, Don Harrison. *The Social Order of a Frontier Community: Jacksonville, Illinois, 1825–70.* Urbana and Chicago: University of Illinois Press, 1983.

Durkheim, Emile. *The Elementary Forms of Religious Life,* trans. Joseph Ward Swain. New York: Collier, 1961.

Elkins, Stanley, and Erick McKittrick. "A Meaning for Turner's Frontier." *Political Science Quarterly* 69 (1954): 321–53; 565–602.

Ellis, David Maldwyn. "The Yankee Invasion of New York," *New York History* 32 (1951): 3–17.

Field, William T., and Lovina R. Hays. "History of All Souls Church: The Story of the Universalist Church in Watertown, New York." Pamphlet at All Soul's Church, Watertown.

Fowler, P. H. *Historical Sketch of Presbyterianism within the Bounds of the Synod of Central New York.* Utica: Curtis & Childs, 1877.

Friedlander, Amy, et al. "Fort Drum Cultural Resources Project, Report No. 2, 1986: Re-evaluation of the Rural Historic Contexts for the Fort Drum, N.Y. Vicinity. Prepared for the U.S. National Park Service, Middle Atlantic

Region, Philadelphia, Pa. and the 10th Mountain Division, Fort Drum, N.Y." East Orange, N.J.: Louis Berger, 1986.

Giblin, R. Joseph. *Renaissance at St. James Parish Carthage, New York.* Carthage, N.Y.: R. Joseph Giblin, 1979.

Gordon, Thomas F. *Gazetteer of the State of New York.* Philadelphia: Printed for the author, 1836.

Gorrie, Rev. P. Douglas. *The Black River Conference Memorial: Containing Sketches of the Life and Character of the Deceased Members of the Black River Conference of the M.E. Church.* New York: Carlton & Phillips, 1852.

———. *Black River and Northern New York Conference Memorial. Second Series Containing Sketches of the Life and Character of the Deceased Members of the Above Conference Not Included in the Former Work Brought Down to the Present Time.* Watertown, N.Y.: Charles E. Holbrook, Printer, 1881

Hadden, Jeffrey K., and Anson Shupe. *Televangelism: Power and Politics on God's Frontier.* New York: Henry Holt, 1988.

Haddock, John A. *The Growth of a Century as Illustrated in the History of Jefferson County, New York from 1793 to 1894.* Philadelphia: Sherman, 1894.

Hall, David D. *Worlds of Wonder, Days of Judgment.* New York: Alfred Knopf, 1989.

Hambrick-Stowe, Charles E. *Charles G. Finney and the Spirit of American Evangelicalism.* Grand Rapids, Mich.: Eerdmans, 1996.

Hardman, Keith J. *Charles Grandison Finney, 1792–1875: Revivalist and Reformer.* Syracuse: Syracuse University Press, 1987.

Haroutunian, Joseph. *Piety versus Moralism.* New York: Henry Holt, 1932.

Hatch, Nathan O. *The Democratization of American Christianity.* New Haven: Yale University Press, 1989.

Hendricks, Tyler Owen. "Charles Finney and the Utica Revivals of 1826: The Social Effect of a New Religious Paradigm." Ph.D. dissertation, Vanderbilt University, 1983.

Hensley, Paul Brent. "An Eighteenth-Century World Not Quite Lost: The Social and Economic Structure of a Northern New York Town, 1810–1880." Ph.D. dissertation, College of William and Mary, 1979.

Hewitt, Nancy. *Women's Activism and Social Change: Rochester, New York, 1822–1872.* Ithaca: Cornell University Press, 1984.

———. "Feminist Friends: Agrarian Quakers and the Emergence of Women's Rights in America." *Feminist Studies* 12 (Spring 1986): 27–49.

Hill, Marvin S. "The Rise of Mormonism in the Burned-Over District: Another View." *New York History* 61 (October 1980): 411–30.

Hotchkin, James H. *A History of the Purchase and Settlement of Western New York and of the Rise, Progress, and Present State of the Presbyterian Church in That Section.* New York: M. W. Dodd, Brick Church Chapel, 1848.

Hough, Franklin B. *A History of Jefferson County in the State of New York from the Earliest Period to the Present Time.* Albany: Joel Munsell; Watertown: Sterling & Riddell, 1854.

Iverson, Joan. "The Mormon-Suffrage Relationship: Personal and Political Quandaries." *Frontiers* 11 (1990): 8–16.

Jensen, Andrew. *Latter-day Saint Biographical Encyclopedia: A Compilation of Biographical Sketches of Prominent Men and Women in the Church of Jesus Christ of Latter-day Saints: Volume 1.* Salt Lake City: Andrew Jensen History Company and Deseret News, 1901.

John, Richard R. "Taking Sabbatarianism Seriously: The Postal System, the Sabbath, and the Transformation of American Political Culture." *Journal of the Early Republic* 10 (Winter 1990): 217–67.

Johnson, Curtis. *Islands of Holiness: Rural Religion in Upstate New York, 1790–1860.* Ithaca: Cornell University Press, 1989.

Johnson, Paul. *A Shopkeeper's Millennium: Society and Revivals in Rochester, New York, 1815–1837.* New York: Hill & Wang, 1978.

Kee, Howard Clark, et al. *Christianity: A Social and Cultural History.* New York: Macmillan, 1991.

Kennedy, Roger G. *Orders from France: The Americans and the French in a Revolutionary World.* New York: Knopf, 1989.

Kimball, Frederick H. *Years of Truth: A History of the First Presbyterian Church of Watertown, New York, 1803–1953.* Watertown: Hungerford & Holbrook, 1953.

Kimball, Stanley B. *Heber C. Kimball: Mormon Patriarch and Pioneer.* Urbana and Chicago: University of Illinois, 1981.

Landon, Harry F. *The North Country: A History Embracing Jefferson, St. Lawrence, Oswego, Lewis, and Franklin Counties, New York.* Indianapolis, Ind.: Historical Publishing, 1932.

Ludlum, David M. *Social Ferment in Vermont, 1791–1850.* New York: Columbia University Press, 1939.

Macquarrie, John. *Twentieth-Century Religious Thought: The Frontiers of Philosophy and Theology, 1900–1980,* rev. ed. New York: Charles Scribner's Sons, 1981.

Marsden, George. *Understanding Fundamentalism and Evangelicalism.* Grand Rapids, Mich.: Eerdmans, 1991.

Mathews, Donald. "The Second Great Awakening as Organizing Process." *American Quarterly* 21(1969): 21–43.

McKivigan, John R. *The War against Proslavery Religion: Abolitionism and the Northern Churches, 1830–1865.* Ithaca: Cornell University Press, 1984.

McLoughlin, William G. *Modern Revivalism: Charles Grandison Finney to Billy Graham.* New York: Ronald Press, 1959.

———. *Revivals, Awakenings, and Reform: An Essay on Religion and Social Change in America, 1607–1977.* Chicago: University of Chicago Press, 1978.

Milbert, Jacques. *Picturesque Itinerary of the Hudson River and the Peripheral Parts of North America.* Constance D. Sherman, trans. Ridgewood, N.J.: Gregg Press, 1968.

Miller, Perry. *The Life of the Mind in America from the Revolution to the Civil War.* New York: Harcourt Brace Jovanovich, 1965.

Miller, Russell E. *The Larger Hope: The First Century of the Universalist Church in America, 1770–1870.* Boston: Unitarian Universalist Association, 1979.

Miyakawa, T. Scott. *Protestants and Pioneers: Individualism and Conformity on the American Frontier.* Chicago: University of Chicago Press,1964.

Morrison, Howard A. "The Finney Takeover of the Second Great Awakening during the Oneida Revivals of 1825–1827." *New York History* 59 (January 1978): 27–53.

Muller, H. N., III, and John J. Duffy. "Jedidiah Burchard and Vermont's 'New Measure' Revivals; Social Adjustment and the Quest for Unity." *Vermont History* 46 (1978): 5–20.

———. *An Anxious Democracy: Aspects of the 1830s.* Westport, Conn.: Greenwood Press, 1982.

Norwood, Frederick A. *The Story of American Methodism: A History of the United Methodists and Their Relations.* Nashville: Abingdon, 1974.

Orsi, Robert Anthony. *Madonna of 115th Street: Faith and Community in Italian Harlem, 1880– 1950.* New Haven: Yale University Press, 1985.

Parker, Wilmond W. "The Migration from Vermont to Northern New York." *Proceedings of the New York State Historical Association* 33 (1934): 398–406.

Powell, Thomas F. *Penet's Square: An Episode in the Early History of Northern New York.* Lakemont, N.Y.: North Country Books, 1976.

Pritchard, Linda. "The Burned-Over District Reconsidered." *Social Science History* 8 (Summer 1984): 243–65.

Reid, Daniel G. et al., eds. *Dictionary of Christianity in America.* Downers Grove, Ill.: InterVarsity Press, 1990.

Rorabaugh, W. J. *The Alcoholic Republic: An American Tradition.* New York: Oxford University Press, 1979.

Rosell, Garth, and Richard A. G. Dupuis, eds. *The Memoirs of Charles Grandison Finney: The Complete Restored Text.* Ann Arbor, Mich.: Academie Books, 1989.

Roth, Randolph A. *The Democratic Dilemma: Religion, Reform, and the Social Order in the Connecticut River Valley of Vermont, 1791–1850.* New York: Cambridge University Press, 1987.

Rowe, David L. *Thunder and Trumpets: Millerites and Dissenting Religion in Upstate New York, 1800–1850.* Chico, Calif.: Scholars Press, 1985.

Ryan, Mary. *Cradle of the Middle Class: The Family in Oneida County, New York, 1790–1865.* New York: Cambridge University Press, 1981.

Shaw, Hon. Albert D. *Historic Reminiscences of the Baptist Church and Society, of Watertown, N.Y.* Watertown, N.Y.: Daily Times Printing and Publishing House, 1890.

Sheriff, Carol. *The Artificial River: The Erie Canal and the Paradox of Progress, 1817–1862* New York: Hill & Wang, 1996.

Shipps, Jan. *Mormonism: The Story of a New Religious Tradition* Urbana and Chicago. University of Illinois Press, 1985.

Smith, Rev. John Talbot. *A History of the Diocese of Ogdensburgh.* New York: John W. Lovell, n.d.

Smith, Joseph. *History of the Church of Jesus Christ of Latter-day Saints: Volume 2.* ed. B. H. Roberts. Salt Lake City: Deseret, 1978.

Stilwell, Lewis D. "Migration from Vermont (1776–1860)." *Proceedings of the Vermont Historical Society* 5 (June 1937).

Strauss, Gerald. "The Reformation and Its Public in an Age of Orthodoxy." in R. Po-Chia Hsia, ed., *The German People and the Reformation.* Ithaca: Cornell University Press, 1988.

Taves, Ann. *The Household of Faith: Roman Catholic Devotions in Mid-Nineteenth-Century America* Notre Dame, Ind.: University of Notre Dame Press, 1986.

Taylor, Sister Mary Christine, S.S.J. *A History of the Foundations of Catholicism in Northern New York: United States Catholic Historical Society Monograph Series 32.* New York: United States Catholic Historical Society, 1976.

Thomas, George M. *Revivalism and Cultural Change: Christianity, Nation Building, and the Market in the Nineteenth-Century United States.* Chicago: University of Chicago Press, 1989.

Troeltsch, Ernst. *The Social Teachings of the Christian Churches.* New York: Harper & Row, 1949.

Turner, Victor. *The Ritual Process: Structure and Anti-structure.* Ithaca: Cornell University Press, 1979.

Twain, Mark. *The Adventures of Huckleberry Finn.* Philadelphia: Running Press, 1986.

Van Wagoner, Richard S., and Steven C. Walker. *A Book of Mormons.* Salt Lake City: Signature Books, 1982.

Walters, Ronald G. *American Reformers, 1815–1860.* New York: Hill & Wang, 1978.

Weddle, David L. "The Law and the Revival: A New 'Divinity' for the Settlements." 47 *Church History* (June 1978): 196–214.

Wellman, Judith. "The Burned-Over District Revisited: Benevolent Reform and Abolitionism in Mexico, Paris, and Ithaca, New York, 1825–1842." Ph.D. dissertation, University of Virginia, 1974.

———. "Crossing Over Cross: Whitney Cross's *Burned-Over District* as Social History." *Reviews in American History* 17 (March 1989): 159–74.

Williams, Peter W. *Popular Religion in America: Symbolic Change and the Modernization Process in Historical Perspective.* Urbana and Chicago: University of Illinois Press, 1989.

———. *America's Religions: Traditions and Cultures.* New York: Macmillan, 1990.

Wright, George F. *Charles Grandison Finney.* Boston and New York: Houghton, Mifflin, 1891; repr. Ann Arbor: University Microfilms, 1979.

INDEX

C

D